WONDER WOMAN

Dedicated to my parents, Joan and Karl Haussegger,
who taught me to have courage.
And in memory of Aaron—
who taught us all about living.

WONDER WOMAN

The myth of 'having it all'

VIRGINIA HAUSSEGGER

ALLEN&UNWIN

First published in 2005

Allen & Unwin
83 Alexander Street
Crows Nest NSW 2065
Australia
Phone: (61 2) 8425 0100
Fax: (61 2) 9906 2218
Email: info@allenandunwin.com
Web: www.allenandunwin.com

National Library of Australia
Cataloguing-in-Publication entry:

Haussegger, Virginia.
   Wonder woman : the myth of having it all.

   ISBN 1 74114 410 8.

   1. Feminism. 2. Work and family. 3. Childlessness. I.
   Title.

305.42

Set in 12/15 pt AGaramond by Bookhouse, Sydney
Printed by Griffin Press, South Australia

10 9 8 7 6 5 4 3 2 1

Contents

Author's Note

During the course of writing this book I've often hoped that no-one ever reads it. Well, no-one that knows me. Not because I don't think it's worth reading. I do. But because there is a lot of me in it. And despite my public profile as a journalist and TV news presenter, I hate this kind of exposure. I really hate it.

There, I've said it.

So why am I writing this at all? For two reasons. Firstly, I couldn't *not* write it. I had to get this monkey off my back. It was driving me crazy. And secondly, when I found myself struggling to climb up the sides of a murky pit of despair, during my mid to late thirties, I searched desperately for books by Australian women that would somehow reflect my own experience. I couldn't find any. Not one. Which got me wondering why the hell not? Why aren't we talking about the issues that are central to the lives of women in their twenties, thirties and forties? Issues of fertility and procrastination; of choice and chance; ambition and career; of finding love in seemingly loveless times; of weighing up the merits of motherhood against unencumbered freedom; of copping a gob full of patriarchy in the workplace and being forced to swallow it; of coming to terms with childlessness, while grappling with the divide between mothers and non-mothers; of questioning feminism and its unintended outcomes, and of contemplating our failure in the quest to 'have it all'.

When I first committed pen to paper and voiced some of my own pain and frustration, the public response was, well, considerable, as you will see in chapter 2. Clearly I wasn't the only woman trying to climb out of that pit. Opinionated, angry, lonely, frustrated women's voices began to shout from everywhere. It was as if suddenly something had been unleashed, and everyone had something to say about it. Not all of it was nice. But in the rush of noise, one thing became alarmingly clear: women's voices had been quiet for too long. We needed to talk, and were ready to listen.

While I remain uncomfortable about revealing some pretty raw stuff about my own life in the early chapters of this book, I knew it would be disingenuous and unacceptable not to. To try and make sense of the growing unease I have about the way we are living our lives, I have prevailed upon a number of women to tell me their stories; and in some cases to share their own pain. They have all done so with exceptional generosity— something I found deeply humbling, particularly in the knowledge that some of the women I interviewed do not agree with my take on what's going on. In fact a couple stand quite opposed to various aspects of what I have to say. Kate, who you'll meet in chapter 8, bellowed at me down the phone line a couple of years ago when she read the original article that kick-started this book. 'What the hell are you doing, Virginia?' was her incredulous cry. Nevertheless, in the spirit of furthering fulsome discourse, Kate agreed to talk and share her story here.

This book is my attempt to investigate, penetrate and unravel what I see as the key issues in the lives of many women around me right now, but it is by no means comprehensive. It is unashamedly selective. I am not an academic, and I do not purport to speak for, or about, women whose lives are vastly different from mine, and about which I have no real experience. My focus is the lives of women from a similar class, background and education to myself. To protect their privacy, and to avoid any career backlash, I have changed the names of some of the women. Others have been upfront and frank about who they are.

If I don't want those who know me to read this book, then who *do* I want to read it? That has always been clear to me. It's for the woman who finds herself up against it and wonders if she's alone. I wrote this book to tell you, 'No, you are not alone'.

Wonder

noun & verb: *n.* **1.** an emotion excited by what is unexpected, unfamiliar, or inexplicable, esp. surprise mingled with admiration or curiosity etc. **2.** a strange or remarkable person or thing. *v.* **1.** to be filled with wonder or great surprise etc. **2.** desire or be curious to know etc. **3.** ask oneself with puzzlement or doubt about; to question.

Woman

1949

For a long time I have hesitated to write a book on women. The subject is irritating, especially to women; and it is not new . . . the voluminous nonsense uttered during the last century seems to have done little to illuminate the problem. After all, is there a problem? And if so, what is it?

Simone de Beauvoir, *The Second Sex*

1963

The problem lay buried, unspoken, for many years . . . a problem that has no name.

Betty Friedan, *The Feminine Mystique*

1970

The time has come when some women are ready to listen, and their number is growing; it is time also for those women to speak, however uncertainly, however haltingly, and for the world to listen.

Germaine Greer, *The Female Eunuch*

1994

Did we pay a price? Most of us did . . . there is still so much unfinished business.

What will your issues be? You will have to decide, but I think it is likely that, as happened with us, you won't choose them—they will choose you.

Anne Summers, 'Letter to the Next Generation'

1999

The contradictions women face have never been more bruising than they are now. The career woman doesn't know if she is to do her job like a man or like herself . . . Is motherhood a privilege or a punishment? . . .

The rhetoric of equality is being used in the name of political correctness to mask the hammering that women are taking.

Germaine Greer, The Whole Woman

2003

In many cases, women wonder just what it is that was won.

Anne Summers, The End of Equality

Wondering what's so bloody wonderful

I t's not like I woke up one day and found myself childless. That was a progressive thing. But I did wake up one day to find myself angry. That was a sudden thing. I was angry about being childless. Angry that at the age of 38 I was suddenly 'too old', and my fertility bits were—in the carefully chosen words of my gynaecologist—'probably buggered'. I was angry that while I had a dream job—the job I had set my sights on a decade earlier—I felt unfulfilled. Angry that all I had to show for the past fifteen years, or more, were a few journalism awards and a household of expensive clutter. Angry that many around me believed I had a perfect life, and I knew I didn't. Angry that while I had always considered myself independent and unconventional, I was suddenly mourning my lack of convention and wishing I had a little weatherboard house with a garden and a picket fence. Most of all, I was angry that I seemed to be out of control of my emotions, and possibly out of my mind.

All in all—it was a rotten morning.

It's now been some time since that black awakening and there has been plenty of head banging in the interim. If this was a quaint tale, I'd add 'and a lot of water has passed under the bridge'. But there is nothing charming or quaint about what I have to say. However, it's true, rivers and torrents have gushed under the proverbial bridge.

My anger isn't over, although I'm managing it better. The journey of coming to terms with my own childlessness, though, has forced me to examine deeply my situation and how I came to be in it. It's not just an issue of being childless, it's also about being in a position that is not conducive to having a child—even if I could. It's about not being where I thought I would be in my late thirties. It's about owning up to the choices I've made—both knowingly and unknowingly. It's about being honest with myself about how much my childlessness is a result of 'chance', how much is conscious 'choice', and how much is due to the career woman's syndrome of 'creeping non-choice'. It's also about examining what role feminism has played in encouraging and supporting the paths I've taken.

But it's not all about me.

In my search for clarity, while I felt like a walking, talking contradiction, I've found myself picking the brains of women around me. Women I know well, some not so well, and some not at all. Some women I've deliberately sought out, driven by a vague hunch that I might learn something from them. In an unexpected but delightful way, others have sought me out. And some are dear friends, both old and new. Regardless of how I've come upon these women, whose stories, musings and private preoccupations have been included in this book, there has been one recurring and overwhelming theme in all our lives: the quest to 'have it all'; and none of us have nailed it.

Like an infuriating radio jingle that won't let up, the 'have it all' mantra has been sung with tedious repetition over the past couple of decades. But it's morphed from being a pesky gimmick, to take on the weight and significance of a precious holy grail. To 'have it all' has not only become a life quest, it has become a birthright promise to all women born post-1960, generation X, Y and beyond. Which is downright tragic, when you consider what a load of crap it really is.

The humourless feminist . . .

It was enough to make any woman want to throw rotten eggs, but we don't do that these days—certainly not in Parliament House. The occasion was International Women's Day, 2004. The National Party's Senator Julian McGauran strode into the senate chamber full of bonhomie for his fellow female colleagues. They probably weren't feeling the same for him. No sooner had one of the minority gender raised the issue of family planning and women's health, than Senator McGauran was throwing his eyes and his arms skyward. 'On International Women's Day,' he boomed with dramatic emphasis, 'you would think they would come into this parliament and celebrate the occasion with a bit more generosity. But, no . . .' And on he went.

No doubt, the few women in the chamber squirmed in their seats, as they so often are forced to do in Australia's patriarchal place of politics. One of them, Senator Natasha Stott Despoja, once the youngest woman in federal parliament, was bristling. For as long as she could stand it, she let Senator McGauran rave on about why women have tremendous cause to celebrate, and why they 'should not come in here with negative beat-ups just to take a political opportunity on such a day'. After ten minutes she could stand it no more—Senator Stott Despoja got to her feet. Yes, International Women's Day was indeed a day to celebrate, she told the chamber, but it was also a day to reflect. And from where she stood, along with all the other women in that place, and outside it, the view was pretty lousy. She told the chamber she was sick of it. 'Today, whether it annoys Senator McGauran or not, I feel like a humourless feminist.' And from there she detailed a litany of failed policy and government inaction that added to the already heavy burden in women's lives.[1]

No doubt the speech would have made Senator McGauran smirk at the predictability of the complaint, and he probably wished the pesky senator would learn to shut up. Thankfully she never has. The moment highlights, yet again, the 'Oliver Twist' syndrome women face. In theory, and on paper (not mine), the World for Women must be Wonderful. People like Senator McGauran can't understand why women continue to bleat. Which is how women are made to feel like Oliver—a puny, grubby little beggar—if we ask for more. 'I think the fact that we do have so many visible rights now as women,' argues Nicola Roxon, Labor's thirty-something Shadow Attorney-General, 'many people have been made to feel like it's unfair to ask for more. I think we've got a much harder job ahead of us now.' And she's right. Senator Stott Despoja cites the 'one step forward and two steps backward' theory: 'Maybe it is harder to move forwards when not only are you constantly protecting the gains that you have made but you're also battling this assumption that you have got nothing to complain about, that of course, it is all fine.'

Like the Senator, I too feel like a humourless feminist. No doubt it will come as a surprise to some that I call myself a feminist at all. But I do and always have. The fact that I've raised questions about the role feminism has played in over-cooking the 'have it all' quest has led some media commentators to infer

I've somehow defected. I haven't. I've just strengthened my membership by holding up some of feminism's unintended outcomes for inspection. But perhaps it's the humourlessness in my anger that most proves my feminist credentials.

Frankly, I see little to celebrate and plenty to commiserate with in the lives of women around me—the women you will meet in this book. We are not women who show any outward signs of suffering or pain; on the surface we are the success stories our feminist foremothers should be proud of. As their daughters, the beneficiaries of their hard-fought battles, we are the ones for whom the gender walls were ripped down. Unlike many of our pre-war or baby boomer mothers, we could 'have it all': a solid education; tertiary degrees; an impressive career path; a great job; a top salary; an equal and loving partnership; happy, well-adjusted children and a balanced family life. Yes, all that was ours for the taking, the doing, the making. We just had to work out how the hell to fit it all in, and make it all work. For the most part, we can't, but that doesn't stop us trying. After all, we're trained to be 'achievers and succeeders', 'doers', not 'quitters'.

We're part of a privileged social class whose first taste of that privilege came with a serious focus on our education, through high school and beyond into universities and colleges. We have been encouraged to seize every opportunity and we've been supported every step of the way—until we fall over. Until we find that yes, we do want to have children but we've left it too late, or don't have a mate. Or until we tell our boss that we're pregnant and need time off, and then watch our carefully constructed career path take a dive. Or until we try to return to work, after unpaid maternity leave, and find our position has been demoted, our confidence battered, and we're forced to hide the fact of our motherhood and juggle quietly on our own. When all the 'have it all' elements collide and the pieces lie like an impossible jigsaw puzzle before us, that's when we find we are on our own. That's when some unenlightened pain-in-the-ass will cock a disapproving eyebrow and tell us, 'Ah, but it is *your* choice!'

That loaded word: choice

Overused and at times infuriating, the word 'choice' is by no means the exclusive domain of women. Men have choice too. Rarely, though, is a man's choice used to scorn and abuse him in the same way it is used against women.

Choice is more than a word when hurled at women—and hurled it is. The phrase, 'It was your choice', is thrust at women like a metaphorical punctuation point to end all discussion when the going gets tough. Where can you go from the finality of that conversational gem? After all, it's true isn't it? You had a choice; you made it; now you wear it. It's not like there's much mileage in shouting back, 'Yes I know it was my choice, but I may have made a mistake.' How plausible is, 'Yes I know I *had* a choice, but I didn't realise it at the time?' or, even worse, 'Actually I didn't understand that I had a choice at all, I was too busy to notice?'

The problem is that 'choice' has become a double-edged, dirty word. All women want it, even demand it, but when we've used it, exercised it, sucked it for all it's worth, choice inevitably comes back to bite you. In laying out the smorgasbord of so-called 'choice' for women, telling them to gorge themselves on the buffet of exotic fruits that older women, and less privileged women, never had the chance to sniff, are we setting a trap? Are we urging women to stuff themselves and then buckle over with the belly ache of too much choice?

In theory, the women of my generation are 'the lucky' ones. We have been grudgingly given access to all corridors of power—

if we want to walk them. We can run for prime minister, lead corporate boards, be a CEO of a multinational, run hospitals, be a police commissioner, sit on the High Court bench, even host our own late-night TV variety show—not that many of us really get to do these things. But the point is—we *can*. It's *our choice!* The equal opportunity for full participation in our society is there for the taking. Or so we're told. What we're not told is the high price we will have to pay for it, nor are we warned about the burdensome and often irreversible consequences of our choices.

As women, we carry the lion's share of responsibility for our relationships, the birth of our progeny, the care and raising of our children, the feeding and nurturing of our families, the well-being of our spouses, the connection with our friends and the care of our communities. So while prohibitive barriers have been torn down, and once closed doors thrown open, and we're urged to feed from an expansive menu of choice and opportunity, we have nevertheless still got a whole stack of stuff piling up on the 'to do list'. Eventually, the cracks begin to show, and the 'have it all–do it all' plan begins to crumble. Sometimes the pieces crash in spectacular fashion; sometimes it's just a quiet, private, but nevertheless painful, concession to failure.

Grasping at choice is one thing, understanding its consequences is another. Then there's the 'process' of choice. Or lack of it. Telling a woman, 'It was your choice', suggests some logical, rational and well-plotted pathway to adulthood, with each step methodically followed until you arrive at *'your choice'*. But life isn't always like that. Over a period of years, plotlines get blurred, some of the steps are bypassed, or forgotten, pathways get messy, and in the end the grand destination 'choice' is often arrived at in the clumsiest of ways. Sure, there are the savvy ones, who manage to stick to the long-term game plan, with just minor deviations along the way, but, overall, there is a lot more chance in choice than we're inclined to own up to. That's why hurling the barb, 'It was *your* choice' at women carrying too big a load and not coping, women wracked with guilt and a sense of failure or women battling with a lonely sense of emptiness is cruel and unfair. More importantly, it's missing the point.

The ultimate choice

Women are judged and defined by the choices we make. Who we are, what we have become, and how the rest of the world sees and values us is dependent on these life choices. On one level we can label ourselves much the same as men do; by stating our profession, our job rank or our seniority; or by our partnership status—single, married, divorced, or 'in a relationship' etc. These labels, though, are just titles, hats, badges. We can wear a number of them at the one time; even drop a few or pick up some new ones as we go along. There is, however, one exclusive domain reserved for the definition of women only. It is a definition that is, by its very mention, burdened with baggage, and it also divides women into two distinctly different camps: 'mother' or 'not'.

Ultimately, every one of us will be defined as either a woman who has given birth to new life and mothered a child—or a woman who has not. This is why the choices we make surrounding our fertility are so heavily weighted with consequences. It is these consequences—how we get there, and how we are grappling with them—that is the focus of this book. It is an attempt to unpeel the truth about how, for many of us, our fertility choices are made with only a vague tilt towards fully comprehending the costs involved. Most of us have little, if any, real idea of how we will manage the complex and ever-competing demands on our lives in an age where we feel compelled to 'have it all'—lest we let the sisterhood down. As one of the women you will meet later remarked, consolidating a career while putting relationships and children on hold is 'like a huge gamble, with high stakes in a game I didn't even know I was playing'.

This book, though, is not only about childlessness. Indeed far from it. It is also an attempt to highlight the glaring inequalities women who *do* have children face as they try to maintain their rightful and hard-won place in the workforce, while keeping a grip on themselves. The stories of these women are a reminder too as to why so many younger women, those now in their twenties, will shun motherhood, or at least seriously delay it, when they see the struggle involved, and the high price some women are forced to pay for doing so. Another group of women are so disenchanted with the cost of motherhood, they are going to extreme lengths to avoid it. Their stories are included here too.

Of course, central to all women's lives when the question arises of to-be or not-to-be a mother is the issue of partnership. Some of the stories here are sad tales of the impossibility of modern-day coupling. Others are about the simple, albeit awkward, search for a jar of sperm and the right to be a single parent. In closing, I grapple with the growing divide between women: the status of mother versus non-mother. This, in many respects, is where it all started for me: how do I make sense of my life and my future as a woman apparently destined to remain childless?

Catching sight of myself . . .

Childlessness has become a major theme in my personal story, and one that has, much to my discomfort, taken prominence in recent years. At the same time, for all three of my sisters, both of my brothers and several close friends, their theme has been coping *with* children. They are blighted by a lack of childlessness.

'See, see what I have to live with Virginia!' my best friend Anne Marie bellows down the phone line, as her three-year-old screeches, 'Mumeeeeeee I'm not eating that!!' Anne Marie barks to little Lucinda, 'Look I'm the mummy so I'm the boss, not you!' She then groans down the phone at me, 'See, see what it's like? Bloody Nora, is it time for a wine yet?'

For years that's been our antidote to most of life's pressures: a good woody chardonnay. And there's been plenty of call for it. Anne Marie and I should have invested in a vineyard. We've certainly kept a few in business. We've drunk our way through my first marriage, travels, various career wins, divorce, new job offers, loneliness, the wild search for a lover, the purchase and sale of my homes, several affairs, my neurosis about commitment, the arrival of my new partner, and my sickness. We haven't quite drunk ourselves through my childlessness. Not yet. But we're working on it. It seems to me that childlessness is the hardest monster I've had to battle. Perhaps no amount of booze will drown it.

Anne Marie had just left after a weekend visit and I stood transfixed in front of my loungeroom heater, gobsmacked, as I read the comments of a woman well known and highly regarded in literary circles. She had revealed in a newspaper article how she felt about her childlessness. I read the quote out loud to my partner, Mark, prefacing it with, 'This is me—now. I could have written this.' Here's what she said:

> The most depressed I have ever been is when I longed for a
> child in my early thirties . . . the experience was intense beyond
> imagining and I would gasp in pain or cry whenever I saw a
> baby. The prosaic term biological clock was totally inadequate

to describe what I was going through. I wanted a child so much, and felt such anger that I did not have one that I was in some ways, quite mad.[2]

I finished reading and Mark and I fell silent. I couldn't look at him. In fact I couldn't take my eyes off the page. Those last few words hung heavily around me: '. . . *I was in some ways, quite mad.*'

Mark was understandably taken aback and when he spoke, he was somewhat defensive. We had never discussed this before. Not in such raw terms. I'd never peeled back the emotion to reveal the naked core of this pain. He was hurt. And I'd opened a floodgate.

Triggering a brawl: I said, you said, she said . . .

Yes Virginia, there is such a thing as personal responsibility.

Herald Sun, 20 April 2003

No Virginia, feminism is not to blame for your solitary pain.

The Age, 30 July 2002

Yes, Virginia, there is a way to have a career and kids.

The Sunday Age, 18 August 2002

You can swap with me Virginia.

The Age, 25 July 2002

With the face of an angel

A little girl called Alex occasionally approaches me at my local café as I'm poring over the morning newspapers. She's perhaps five, maybe six, with exquisite red curls and baby freckles on pale skin. Sometimes she appears out of nowhere and utters something to get my attention. At other times I happen to glance up and there she is, just staring. Each time we go through the same little routine.

'Hello, Alex!'

'Hello, Virginia.'

'Don't you look lovely in those boots.'

'Yes.'

'So what's for breakfast today?'

'Sausages.'

'Sausages! I thought toast and jam was your favourite.'

'Sometimes. I saw you on the news last night.'

'Oh did you? Did I do a good job reading the news?'

'Yes. I like your hair.'

And so it goes on. We exchange a few daily pleasantries. Me asking the questions. Little Alex giving her staccato short answers. Before long, her embarrassed dad retrieves her, always with an apology.

The thing is, Alex just kills me. I can handle any amount of public inquisitiveness, but little Alex, sweet little Alex is simply too much. I find myself scanning the place some mornings hoping she's not there.

You know the advertisements with the bare-bottomed babies, or the strong arm of a father holding afloat the fragile body of a newborn, or the young pre-schoolers trying to spell out the incomprehensible words of a product—all of it has me turning away. I know not to linger in that space. I know the speed with which a rotten cocktail of envy, disgust and pity will surge through me in those moments. I've learnt to clamp down the 'off' switch, before the toxic current travels too far.

The worst of it is the envy. No amount of self-flagellation will rid me of the disgust I feel following those stolen seconds of envy. Envy for what others around me, including my dearest friends and family, have—and I don't. Maybe that's why I did it. Maybe that's why I outed myself as childless, barren and frustrated. This thing was thrashing around in my heart and my head, at times sending me off balance. I needed the people closest to me, the people I love, to understand the magnitude of this pain. I needed to express it. So I did. Out loud in a major metropolitan newspaper. One thousand words of my misery.

And the result—a public king hit!

The sins of our feminist mothers

If success means a career and no children, women have been duped, **writes Virginia Haussegger**.

A few years ago, in my mid-thirties, had I heard Malcolm Turnbull pontificate about the need to encourage Australians to marry younger and have more children ('The crisis is fertility, not ageing'), I would have thumped him, kneed him in the groin, and bawled him out.

How dare he—a rich father of two, with a perfect wife and perfect life—presume for a moment to tell women, thriving at the peak of our careers, that we should stop, marry and procreate. The sheer audacity of it.

Yet another male conspiracy, a conservative attempt to dump women out of the workplace and back into the home. A neat male arrangement: a good woman to run the household, and a workplace less cluttered with female competition.

A win–win for patriarchy. And precisely the kind of society I was schooled against.

As we worked our way through high school and university in the '70s and early '80s, girls like me listened to our mothers, our trailblazing feminist teachers, and the outspoken women who demanded a better deal for all women. They paved the way for us to have rich careers.

They anointed us and encouraged us to take it all. We had the right to be editors, paediatricians, engineers, premiers, executive producers, High Court judges, CEOs etc. We were brought up to believe that the world was ours. We could be and do whatever we pleased.

Feminism's hard-fought battles had borne fruit. And it was ours for the taking.

Or so we thought—until the lie of super 'you-can-have-it-all' feminism hits home, in a very personal and emotional way.

We are the ones, now in our late thirties and early forties, who are suddenly sitting before a sheepish doctor listening to the words, 'Well, I'm sorry, but you may have left your run too late. Women at your age find it very difficult to get pregnant naturally, and unfortunately the success rate of IVF for a 39-year-old is around one in five—and dropping. In another twelve months you'll only have a six per cent chance of having a baby. So given all the effort and expense, do you really want to go through with this? Why don't you go home and think it through? But don't leave it too long—your clock is ticking.' Then he adds for comic value, 'And don't forget, the battery is running low!'

For those of us who listened to our feminist foremothers' encouragement; waved the purple scarves at their rallies; read about and applauded the likes of Anne Summers, Kate Jennings, Wendy McCarthy, Jocelyn Scutt, Morag Fraser, Joan Kirner, Elizabeth Proust etc. (all strong examples of successful working women); for those of us who took all that on board and forged ahead, crashed through barriers and carved out good, successful and even some brilliant careers; we're now left—many of us at least—as premature 'empty nesters'.

We're alone, childless, many of us partnerless, or drifting along in 'permanent temporariness', as sociologist Zygmunt Bauman so aptly put it in a recent *Age* article by Anne Manne to describe the somewhat ambiguous, uncommitted type of relationship that seems to dominate among childless, professional couples in their thirites and forties.

The point is that while encouraging women in the '70s and '80s to reach for the sky, none of our purple-clad, feminist mothers thought to tell us the truth about the biological clock. Our biological clock. The one that would eventually reach exploding point inside us.

Maybe they didn't think to tell us, because they never heard the clock's screaming chime. They were all married and knocked-up by their mid-twenties. They so desperately didn't want the same for us.

And none of our mothers thought to warn us that we would need to stop, take time out and learn to nurture our partnerships and relationships. Or if they did, we were running too fast to hear it.

For those of us who did marry, marriage was perhaps akin to an accessory. And in our high-disposable-income lives, accessories pass their use-by date, and are thoughtlessly tossed aside. Frankly, the dominant message was to not let our man, or any man for that matter, get in the way of career and our own personal progress.

The end result: here we are, supposedly 'having it all' as we edge forty; excellent education; good qualifications; great jobs; fast-moving careers; good incomes; and many of us own the trendy little inner-city pad we live in. It's a nice caffelatte kind of life, really.

But the truth is—for me at least—the career is no longer a challenge, the lifestyle trappings are joyless (the latest Collette Dinnigan frock looks pretty silly on a near-forty year old), and the point of it all seems, well, pointless.

I am childless and I am angry. Angry that I was so foolish to take the word of my feminist mothers as gospel. Angry that I was daft enough to believe female fulfilment came with a leather briefcase.

It was wrong. It was crap. And Malcolm Turnbull has a point. God forbid!

(Virginia Haussegger is an ABC TV news presenter in the ACT. She has been a television journalist for fifteen years, hosting the 7.30 Report in various states and reporting for Channel 7's Witness and Channel 9's A Current Affair.)

The Age, 23 July 2002

Now cop it sweet!

Picture this: you're sitting propped up in bed on a glorious sunny Saturday morning with a few favourite luxuries—coffee, croissant and the weekend newspapers—spread out around you. A lazy day is stretched out in front of you. Perfect. So far.

You flip open Melbourne's *The Age* newspaper and there you are. In dramatic black and white, a rather large photo of yourself, looking pathetically sad and lonely. And the headline screams, '*Meet Virginia, the woman many love to loathe*'.

Funny, huh? Well I thought so the moment this happened to me. Frankly, it *was* funny. The woman in the photo looked ridiculously miserable. It was a sort of studied *faux* misery, like she had just pulled her best 'poor me' face on cue as the cameraman said 'cheese'. And this woman—surely it couldn't be me—sat at the bottom of a tall staircase in an empty television studio; her back leaning against the wall, head staring down the barrel of the camera, a heavy slash of light creating a chiaroscuro effect with ominous shadows lurking behind her. All that, coupled with the killer headline—well, it just made me laugh.

Then the phone rang. It was my Dad.

'Darling, don't you take any notice of that nonsense. Those people don't know what they're talking about. I can't believe they'd print such rubbish.'

Dad did what he always does when the situation is too confronting; he handed the phone to Mum.

'Virginia, I wish you'd stop writing these things.'

'Mum, I didn't write it. Someone has written it about me.'

'But if you would just stop writing . . .'

'Mum, *I* didn't write it. The *journalist* wrote it, after she spoke to me.'

'Well darling, I wish you'd stop talking to people.'

Shut that girl up!

What began as an angry article, written in haste, and dashed off—unsolicited—to the opinion page of *The Age* newspaper, had unleashed a Pandora's box of emotion. Suddenly, my childless state and the choices I'd made in my life were the subject of talkback radio, letters to the editors, daily newspaper commentary, nasty columns in national magazines and, from what I'm told, heated office and classroom debates. People who didn't know me at all were suddenly instant experts on my life, my views and, importantly, my mistakes. Everyone who wrote, spoke or bellowed, took issue with some aspect of what I had said. Many took issue with what I *hadn't* said. And many more simply made up what they *thought* I had said. Several commentators who engaged in lengthy critiques of my position purported to *know* me well. They didn't.

My right to feel miserable was howled down. How dare I? I had a great job on television, supposedly a glamorous life and rich trappings. How dare I bemoan my lack of family. What's more, how dare I suggest that my feminist foremothers wrongly encouraged women of my generation to focus on career at the expense of child-bearing.

'Shame on you Virginia', screeched one of the first of several dozen emails I received over the next few days—the start of a steady stream that would continue over the following weeks and months. 'I am incensed by your article', railed another. Women— and the critics were all women—were furious at a blatant display of free speech and were quick to exercise theirs. By the week's end my email 'inbox' was clogged:

> How dare you blame any woman for your anger at being childless . . . What a perverse perspective, and how very petulant of you. I would expect as much from my fifteen year old.

> I feel dreadfully sorry for your mother and I am so pleased that you are not my daughter!

> Stop acting like a spoiled, immature brat and start aiming your darts where they belong . . . Show a bit of backbone and own responsibility for the consequences of your choices.

I was frequently reminded of my 'responsibilities', both as a woman, and as a journalist, to acknowledge my 'errors of judgment'; accept the choices I'd made, and shut up about the consequences:

Every step of the way YOU have made choices in YOUR journey in life . . . You chose not to take [the motherhood] path, no one else did it for you . . . I detect a bit of selfishness in your regretful words.

For several weeks after publication of 'The sins of our feminist mothers' (a racy headline which, by the way, was not written by me) I was hounded daily by a hungry media clearly looking for a feminist catfight. I was determined not to give them one. Eventually they got it anyway.

Frustrated women harbouring anger, sorrow, fury, impatience and occasionally pity, had suddenly found their voice. A stream of opinion let fly. Initially much of the anger was aimed at me, as I was interpreted by some women to be laying full blame for my busted biological clock and my barren state on my 'feminist foremothers'. 'No bub? It's not our fault' (*Herald Sun*) was one of the nastier headlines that shot back. But perhaps what shocked and disappointed me most was how quickly the 'kill the messenger' mantra went into overdrive.

I have not reached for my box of tissues while reading the bleating of some high-profile childless woman blaming her elders, her horoscope, the zeitgeist, anything, anyone but herself for the empty cradle in the middle of her wretched empty life.

Dorothy Porter, *HQ* magazine, Oct/Nov 2002

I have three responses to Virginia Haussegger: 1. Stop bleating. 2. Acknowledge you've been lucky enough to have choices, and have been free to make them. 3. Get some psychotherapy to work on your inner life.

Letter to the Editor, *The Age*, 24 July 2004

Apparently my life wasn't just 'wretched', it was brainlessly ignorant too. On the thorny issue of the biological clock, I was quickly reminded 'that concept didn't suddenly just drop out of the sky in 2002' (Letter to the Editor, *The Age*, 25 July). One woman wrote and told me she'd learnt all about her ticking clock in high school: 'Yes, I knew that at seventeen. Where the hell were you?' Well as a matter of fact, I was busy pashing boys, slugging tequila and dragging on Marlboro reds. I certainly wasn't thinking about my biological clock, or hearing any messages about its use-by date.

It wasn't all bleak and vitriolic. Some of the private calls, letters and emails I received were overwhelming in their compassion. Embarrassed, I didn't know what to make of these kind and loving words from strangers. Some people, both men and women, took the time to write reams of personal anecdotes and stories that were touching in their shared intimacy. A few even confessed details of their own journeys never before shared with anyone. 'I don't know why I'm telling you this', one faceless young woman said down the phone line to me, both of us sniffing away as she poured out her battle with infertility.

I guess it's the comfort of strangers who can share a sorrow.

In the public arena the loud and demanding voices of anger and frustration, which I hoped would just fade away, were getting louder. This wasn't about me. And I knew it. So for some time I kept quiet and went about the private business of getting on with my public job as a news presenter. But those voices didn't go away. When yet *another* pile of mail was dumped on my desk, many weeks later, it became starkly apparent that something was going on. And women desperately wanted to talk about it.

I set about trying to reply to all the people who had written to me. Months later I wrote a couple more articles, sending them to the *Sydney Morning Herald* as well as *The Age*. This time I turned my attention to a wider field of inquiry: modern-day relationships, lack of commitment, the dirty secrets of working mothers, the family unfriendliness of our workplaces and the questionable success rate of feminism in Australia. They were all given a guernsey. Then the so-called 'media catfight' turned up a notch.

Had I really, as one columnist put it, 'driven a red-hot stake through the heart of the sisterhood'? It would seem I had. And just in case I hadn't noticed, some male acquaintances, obviously energised by the whiff of a feminist fight, were quick to remind me. As I sat down to a business lunch one brilliant autumn day in Canberra, one of my companions leaned over and said, 'I've been reading your columns and boy you've set the cat among the pigeons!'

'Or,' his mate chipped in, 'the cat among the cats!'

Ho, ho, ho! Boy that was a blast. There were belly laughs aplenty.

While it was the fury in women's voices that reverberated loudest in the public domain, I knew that something much more important had been unleashed. By now the words, 'this isn't about me', had become my daily mantra. Once my 'wretched' life was dissected and chewed over, something much more interesting emerged. It was as if a little finger had wriggled out of the dyke, and the trickle had given way to a furious and gushing stream of women's pain. Suddenly every woman I came across wanted to talk. They wanted to share *their* story, and vent *their* spleen. It was as if my name had become synonymous with lifting the lid on a modern-day Australian version of Betty Friedan's 'problem with no name'. And in all of this, some very private and personal frustration found a voice:

> It feels blasphemous to think this, let alone write it for publication, but here goes: Some days I wish I'd never had children . . . some days motherhood feels more like grief and anger than fulfilment . . . I love my three boys overwhelmingly . . . (but) the frustration is intense. I can barely think clearly to write . . . I have had to abandon my PhD as an impossibility. The only play I've seen in years stars Bob the Builder.
>
> Lucy Hamilton, Opinion Page, *The Age*, 25 July 2002

> When I became a mother, aged 35, I too felt I had been duped. Suddenly and dramatically, I was no longer independent; worse, I was not equal. Not just angry. I was furious. Instead of waves of contentment and joy, I was experiencing waves of boredom, frustration and loneliness. I was delirious with exhaustion and felt on the edge of madness most of the time. Motherhood impoverished me, both financially and socially. My life seemed reduced to endless rounds of menial chores, and the isolation was terrifying. The reward? Well, my baby was happy. But I was miserable and angry.
>
> Zelda Grimshaw, Opinion Page, *The Age*, 1 August 2002

> You can swap with me, Virginia. I'm only too happy to admit I thought babies were enchanting; I was silly enough to have three . . . I feel unappreciated and devalued . . . I would have been slimmer and richer with a good job and superannuation (and all that great stuff you've got, Virginia) if I hadn't had

children . . . To have kids in your mid-twenties is akin to financial and career suicide. I'm angry too Virginia.

> Letter to the Editor, *The Age*, 25 July 2002

Virginia is rightly angry with the feminist mothers . . . But, by way of consolation, those who refused the feminist gospel have not had an easy time of it either. To put relationships with husband and children ahead of a career has been regarded as heresy. Women who made this choice with the cooperation and support of their partners have been subjected to a virtually endless torrent of scorn and derision. They have been told that they are 'letting down the side' . . . that they are a burden on society, that they do 'nothing', or that their work as mothers is worse than useless.

> Jennifer Sinclair, Opinion Page, *The Age*, 25 July 2002

I'm 42 and have four kids. As I was growing up I found girls were often presented with a polarised view of available choices: either you can be an articulate, suited Jenna Jetset, who isn't weighed down by kids . . . or you can be Darlene Dagface, the overweight, soapie-watching, floral-dressed vegetable brain, who stays home with her kids, has a vocab of wee wee and poo poo and uses herself to mop the floor.

> Email, 16 October 2000

While for some mothers the choice open to them felt as miserable as a dirty, old kitchen mop, for others, the flipside—childlessness—was even worse. No mystique here, just mistake.

I too feel that I was sucked into thinking that life—long partnership and procreation wasn't as important as defining who I was as a career woman. What a crock!

> Email, 29 July 2002

That sense of being sold 'a crock' was a common theme among the outpourings. What fascinated me about many of these letters, emails and commentaries was that it seemed no matter where a woman stood, be she mother, mother-to-be or non-mother, something was wrong. It was as if a scabby old scar had been ripped off a festering wound. Now that the murky mess was exposed, we were all going to hear about it.

And, thankfully, once women are emboldened, we won't be silenced.

While a number of young women contacted me, perhaps the saddest message came from a 19-year-old Queensland university student who wrote: 'I always saw women's lib as *choice* so why do I feel like I don't have one?' She went on to say that at the private girls' school she attended she was 'indoctrinated' with the 'late-millennium mantra of "career"'. Then she revealed her 'disgust' at seeing women drop children off at child care early in the morning, not to see them until they pick them up some eight hours later. Somewhere in all this, even before this teenager has reached twenty, she is lamenting a perceived contradiction in the choices open to her. She ended her letter with, 'Feminism needs reform, too many women feel cheated by the promises'.

It was a sign-off that left me feeling flat and frustrated; then pretty quickly, just downright furious. What is going on here, when even young women—barely out of their teens—view their choices as bleak when they look at women five or ten years older than them and cringe, thinking, 'I don't ever want to live like that'? How have we got it so wrong that some young women, or indeed any women, think they have been 'cheated' by the promises of feminism?

It's high time to *re-think* feminism's messages and the 'have it all' mantra that's been thumped into the brains and parlance of post-feminist women. I've long believed this. Clearly, I'm far from alone. A number of women who responded to my outpourings revealed they not only shared the belief that we need to review, re-think and, perhaps, re-group, but they've been stewing on it for some time:

> I have long tried to argue that as feminists we need to be honest about the issues feminism might have got wrong, even if it was unintended. While there were plenty of feminists who championed motherhood in the 1970s and 1980s, those who championed career (and often disregarded motherhood) certainly had the loudest voices.
>
> Email, 16 Aug 2002

> It's been my pet theory for some time now that our generation of women (35–45) are the ripped-off generation . . . We are part of a massive social experiment that's worked for some and not for others. Heaven forbid we go back to the bad old days when we had such limited choices—but if we're to make life better for the women (and the men) coming after us we have to be honest about the pain as well as the gain.
>
> Email, 25 July 2002

> I feel so strongly that we need a new way to look at life—a new feminism if you like that doesn't force us to buy into the whole male 'I am defined by my career' mentality.
>
> Email, 23 July 2002

> The freedom was an illusion . . . Certainly, the feminist movement opened up alternative choices to traditional women's roles, and as such it has been successful, but its intolerance to views other than its own has brought about some darker consequences.
>
> Letter to the Editor, *The Age*, 26 July 2002

It seems weird that a lifelong feminist such as myself should be so strongly arguing for the joys of motherhood, when I was brought up to believe that children were the tools of women's oppression!

Email, 21 August 2002

There was no cultural space available for questioning whether the pleasures of a career could be adequately compared with those of raising children. Nor was there space to question whether career and material success were actually sufficient to sustain a meaningful life. Women who stood against the feminist 'one suit fits all' model have been beleaguered and belittled . . . Feminism's heart was in the right place . . . Feminism saved women from the 'biology as destiny' argument . . . But we still have more thinking to do . . .

Jennifer Sinclair, Opinion Page, *The Age,* 25 July 2002

There is no question that we have plenty of 'more thinking to do'. Thinking, questioning, debating and acting—the need is urgent. Nevertheless, some women with whom I've discussed this at length, and others who have written about it, believe the argument about feminism is misplaced. For them, the issue is broader, as Erina Reddan explained in her article, 'No Virginia, feminism is not to blame for your pain':

Where we have got it wrong is in thinking we can have it all—both the high-powered and sustaining public life as well as the intimacy and depth of a well-nurtured family life. But the misconception is not feminism's fault; feminism never said it was possible to pack all of that into the one moment . . . What is marked about our generation is that it is much harder to make long-term commitments to love and respect one another enough in order to make it possible to have children

together . . . The explanation is a much bigger social shift . . .
Yet too many women are now blaming themselves, and looking
for answers in the wrong places.

The Age, 30 July 2002

On the subject of blame, commentator Virginia Trioli agrees that
women of our generation have swallowed a bitter pill—but that we
should all shut up and suffer in silence. In her article addressed to
'Childless and Angry' (*Bulletin,* 6 August 2002) she suggests the
complaint should not be with feminism, but rather the 'assumption—
the one we made for ourselves—that the best part of our lives
would be our careers'. She goes on to suggest that '*that* was the
delusion'. But whether it was a private delusion we created for
ourselves, or one imbued by our social conditioning and education,
Trioli fails to explore. Nevertheless, her conclusion—although
useless—is quaint: 'Some of us are now seriously considering staying
home and growing roses or working on a croc farm. And our biggest
fantasy is being a kept woman.' Nice, maybe, but being a 'kept
woman' isn't an answer. If anything, such a fantasy feeds a backlash.
Many of those who spoke up, did so with two key purposes: the
hope of being heard, and to add their voice to a call for change.

Women will not move further until they join forces with all
women and men to fight in a 'humanist' revolution that
meets *all* our needs. Interested in starting such a revolution?

Letter, 24 April 2003

In a way, our generation forms a mass social experiment . . .
One of the few benefits to come out of all this pain will be
if we can join together to re-infuse parenting with its value.
We need to design models for mothering that enable most
women to do it with the least pain and anger.

Lucy Hamilton, Opinion Page, *The Age*, 25 July 2002

It's the lack of those so-called 'models', or support structures, that would appear to be failing women. Structures that even our feminist foremothers would have to concede have never been put in place: leaving young women to race forward hopeful of achieving career success, lasting partnership and motherhood, with no idea, no plan, no pathway, map or guide as to how to make it all happen, and how to make it work. Yet it came as no surprise to me that Morag Frazer, one of the most gracious and heroic of all the feminist trailblazers I know, was quick to concede this in her article, 'Yes, Virginia, there is a way to have a career and kids':

> We have still not worked out the balance and distribution of labour between men and women, even in prosperous egalitarian Australia. We have still not made space in our daily lives for children, and for what makes life rich (Virginia is right—a briefcase and the Collette Dinnigan frock just don't rate).
>
> We have still not established structures that enable women and men to be fully themselves, to contribute their knowledge and skill to their communities and still find fulfilment and happiness, whether as partners, parents, or as single men and women. Worse, we have dismantled some of the structures that made fulfilled equality halfway possible 20 years ago . . . Feminism has always had to be opportunistic, but opportunism does not found structures.
>
> *Sunday Age*, 18 August 2002

How to build those structures and why we don't already have them in place, remain the illusive, slippery, awkward questions. Morag is typically sharp in her conclusion:

> Have it all? Male or female, none of us can. It's the wrong ambition. 'Have' is the wrong verb. The 'must have' imperative makes us all miserable, eventually.

If 'misery' is the measure, obviously too many of us have been chanting the 'must have' mantra. While the disturbing noise of frustration, disappointment, even anger is perhaps what's come through loudest in many of these outpourings, there is also a dose of sisterhood solidarity. So much so, that I couldn't help but laugh when writers such as Clare Boyd-Macrae, (Opinion Page, *The Age*, 2 August 2002), boxed the field! 'I feel equally for the bitter career women, the bitter mothers, and those in between'.

While plenty of people have had plenty to say, in public, about the issues surrounding my childlessness, no-one has addressed childlessness itself. No-one has laid a hand on the grief. No-one has asked how this might feel. All of which caused a female PhD student who interviewed me, after studying the media fallout, to ask 'Don't you think they all missed the point?'

Expressing this sadness and inherent frustration, is not about a search for sympathy. I find that both embarrassing and disempowering. Nor is it about being a victim. That horrifies me. Despite an overexcited male shock-jock yelling to his audience that 'Virginia is a victim of Nazi feminism!', I have never felt a victim of anything, least of all feminism. I'm clearly a beneficiary of that. Nevertheless, it strikes me as odd that the actual thing at the very heart of my pain—the reason I wrote out loud in the first place—sort of slipped under the radar.

However, there *were* a few private exceptions. One of those came by way of a carefully hand-written letter from a man who had himself made a personal discovery that caused him to deeply question his career, and his purpose. It was one of the most beautiful letters I have ever received.

> I just wanted to say how much I appreciated the piece you wrote and how I heard what you were saying—I heard some of the pain and I thought it would be dreadful to write such a thing and not at least have that acknowledged.
>
> These are painful discoveries.

A short while after reading these words of enormous compassion, I read the words of another man whose long letter filled me with sadness. The writer was a single father with three kids, aged between ten and sixteen. He spoke of his confusion over the role of women, and the value of being 'just a mother'. His question was quite simple: 'My dilemma is what do I teach my children?'

How could I respond to that: Tell your daughter it's '*her* choice'?

Drop the baby—put it in the 'possibles': unravelling my own story

Kate Aide looks like she's turned up in costume. She's buttoned up in a crisp, pale suit, a Sloane string of pearls tugs at her neck, and below the fashionable hemline she's sporting sheer stockings and heels. It's an odd look for Aide, the BBC's chief news correspondent and doyenne of broadcast journalism. This is a woman more at home in a flak jacket, hard hat and crumpled shirt. Aide is one of those journalists who doesn't waste any of her precious time chasing the small stuff; she goes where the news is big, and where the bombs are about to drop. It's no wonder then that British soldiers are said to know they're in trouble if Kate Aide turns up at base camp. She was one of the first women to provide television reports from the front line of war, and Aide has been at it, relentlessly, ever since.

Despite her exceptional career and pedigree as a globe-trotting correspondent, right here in Canberra, right now, what's more fascinating is watching Aide, queen of journalist inquisitors, become the uncomfortable subject of an inquisition. She is addressing a packed audience at the National Press Club. From the moment she takes the microphone you can smell the power. This woman is commanding, daunting and mesmerising—until the subject turns to Aide herself, and suddenly the great communicator is flummoxed.

After a long and powerful speech that ranged over the media's coverage of the war in Iraq, the rapid changing pace of news delivery, and the rise of 'celebrity journalism', Kate Aide agreed to take questions. A predictable line of inquiry followed, until a young female journalist from the *Sydney Morning Herald* stood up: 'What sacrifices have you made along the way to have such a fantastic career, putting yourself at the frontline all the time?' she asked, clearly and confidently, despite a TV camera moving in on her. Then we all watched, and waited, as Aide's face hardened.

'I'm going to ask *you* a question back,' she retorted. The young inquisitor shot to her feet again, standing to attention. The famous journalist eyeballed her, saying, 'Have you ever asked that question of a man?' To her credit, the young woman's reply was equally swift.

'I've never interviewed a man who has been a war correspondent like you,' she said.

'But,' pushed the imposing Ms Aide, 'Would you ask that of a man *anyway*?'

Again a quick reply from the young journalist. 'Yeah. I think I would.'

Aide seemed to stifle a grimace. It was that damn 'women's issues' stuff again.

Why is it that so many women of power and influence, when speaking in public, shy away from gender politics, or curiosity about female sacrifice? Are they afraid a straight answer might badge them as a gender 'victim'; or worse—feminist? Perhaps they don't want to stake a position because they're not interested, or just don't care. Or, maybe they're over it: over the uninvited admiration and carrying the can for womankind. Maybe they never wanted to wave the flag for other women in the first place. Will that stop eager young women from asking the trailblazers about their road to success? No. Thankfully never!

The brilliant British actor Helen Mirren once snapped furiously at me in an interview when she thought my questions were leaning too much towards some kind of feminist agenda. I was interested in how she had managed to play, almost exclusively, roles in which all her characters were strong, independent, ballsy women. At the time we were sitting on a film set in Manchester. Back home in Australia, *Prime Suspect* was winning the TV ratings around the country. It was a gripping series in which Mirren starred in the lead role as a tough, ruthless and formidable senior detective. Her character was a woman of guts and substance— yet a wimp compared with the woman who played her! The fury of Mirren's response to my line of questioning almost knocked me off my chair.

'What strong women?' she shot back. 'They weren't strong women! They were hopeless, weak, pitiful. Who was strong? Name one!' I did. Or so I thought. The comeback was instantaneous.

'She wasn't strong. She was a pathetic, miserable creature. A shadow of a woman . . .' And so it went. I think you get the picture.

Perhaps Mirren too was tired of being held up as a role model and being asked to comment on 'the women' thing. I'll never know. She stood up, plucked the neck mic from her blouse, and walked away.

Unlike Helen Mirren, back at the Canberra Press Club, Kate Aide did agree to engage with her inquisitor. Despite a visible irritation with the question, it seems Aide made a conscious decision to take the issue of 'personal sacrifices' head on: perhaps, if nothing else, to highlight what she considered to be the absurdity of the question. However, her initial answer was curious.

'Gosh, sacrifices. I never thought about sacrifices. I never made sacrifices. I think that everybody has to make choices. And I think that women, having come into the working world with a vengeance since the 1960s onwards—my generation—have *felt* our way through it.

' . . . Each decision is a personal one. And I don't think they are tremendously dramatic, they just come along.

' . . . I have never felt that I had a dramatic sacrifice to make. I just took decisions.'

At this stage the journalist who asked the original question, piped up again: 'I guess I should have phrased the question better.' To which Aide and the audience responded by laughing. But the tenacious reporter continued; 'What I mean is, what *choices* did you make?' This time Aide's answer wasn't just curious—it was curiously comforting.

'I didn't,' she shot back. 'I didn't! I didn't make choices. I didn't even think about it. I didn't ever think, "No, I shan't do that". Life just unrolls, and you grab the opportunities as they come.'

Right then and there I wanted to get on my knees and bow down to this goddess of plain-speaking truth. What a relief to hear someone, who has carved out a considerable career for herself, bluntly say, 'I didn't make choices. I didn't even think about it.'

Since outing myself as miserable about my childlessness at 38 years old, I've spent a long time wondering just what I was thinking during my twenties and early thirties. Did I think about the choices I had? Was I aware of the decisions I was making? Did I consider having a baby? Did I wonder how I'd fit it all in? Or did I simply assume I would get all that I wanted and in the order I wanted it? Which, mind you, didn't seem like an entirely unrealistic assumption, given I had grown up believing that if I worked hard enough I would always achieve what I set out to do, and would get what I wanted. I *thought* the pendulum swung both ways for me. Sure I had missed out on jobs I thought I should have got, I'd failed to conquer some career challenges, and I'd been axed a couple of times. But, by and large, I felt pretty lucky. I'd had a great run, with every knock-back proving to be a blessing in disguise, as a better, more challenging and lucrative opportunity was always waiting around the corner.

Now, on the threshold of turning forty, I find myself stuck on the question of 'choice'. Since I first publicly spoke about my sadness and frustration over my childlessness, the loudest and most persistent protestation hurled at me has been . . . 'but it was *your choice*, Virginia'. That retort almost became a theme song. 'It was *your choice* to pursue a career'; 'It was *your choice* to live the busy life you have'; 'It was *your choice* to strap yourself to the feminist sail of fulfilment-through-paid-work and identity-through-job'; 'It was *your choice* . . .' On and on it went.

'Yeah, yeah,' said my no-nonsense American friend Carrie, in her Jewish, New York accent. 'Just tell 'em "yeah, I know already!" Then tell 'em to beat it.'

What did I really know about the choices I had, or the choices I was making along my way? Like Kate Aide, is it possible I just wasn't thinking about them? Perhaps, like her, I too am one of those people who just grab life's opportunities as they come along, only to marvel, or commiserate, at how things turn out some time down the track?

Recently I addressed a couple of hundred schoolgirls on International Women's Day in Queens Hall at Victoria's Parliament House. Afterwards they asked me questions about career paths; then this gem popped up from the far back corner: 'Do you think we should talk to our career advisors about wanting to have a family?'

Oh good lord! This eager and anxious face was all of sixteen or seventeen years old. I felt knotted with contradiction. Such a question would never have occurred to me at her age. What's more, if I had heard one of my fellow classmates ask it, I would have laughed at her with the full force of schoolgirl sarcasm. Back in 1980, as year 11 students with the world at our feet, none of us were thinking like this. Families and babies couldn't have been further from our minds. Now here I am today, being asked for advice about the one area of life in which I consider myself a spectacular failure.

'Yes,' I replied to eager-eyes. 'Yes, I think it's a good idea to discuss *all* your long-term plans with your career advisor.'

I kind of choked on this one. Will the career advisor, on hearing about motherhood desires, dampen this young girl's career aspirations? I hoped not. At that moment I just felt sad and sorry that I had no useful words of encouragement to offer these girls about how they might make it all work, if they are to choose career *and* children.

What would I have said if one of the girls had asked what 'sacrifices' I had made to pursue a career? Would I have responded like Aide with, 'Gosh, sacrifices. I never thought about sacrifices. I never made sacrifices?' Sure, I had choices, but did I choose to find myself at 38 aching with a ferocious emptiness and a desperate sense of longing, so overwhelming that at times it sent me quite off balance? Did I choose to avoid discovering, until late in my thirties, that my chances of having a child were bleak, and about to become much bleaker? Did I choose to fall in love with a man whose child-rearing days were over?

Yes, I suppose I did.

In the matter of love, I certainly chose within days of a chance meeting to allow this love to grow, and I consciously committed to honour and nurture it as best as I possibly could. As for the rest, well, these things were the fallout of previous actions, decisions, and inactions, but is it what I wanted for myself? Is this where I wanted to be?

No.

So how and why did this happen?

Explaining our life story, its various plotlines, the twists and turns, and the 'big picture' moments, is a bit like structuring a television news bulletin. We cast the big moments as banner headlines up the top; the worthy and important, but less sexy detail follows; and half-way down we throw in a bit of human interest colour, to liven things up. In every TV bulletin prepared in newsrooms around the country each night, there is also always a list of 'possibles' or, at least, you hope there is.

As reporters, not every story we set out to do each morning will make it into the evening news. Throughout the day stories get dumped and bumped out by bigger, better or sexier ones. If you are lucky and the story you've been slavishly working on has genuine merit, it may not be killed off altogether. If it has a faint chance at a run, some cranky news producer will bellow out across the newsroom to the PA, 'drop that story'. Then the words you sweat on hearing next, those sweet words, 'put it in the "possibles"', means you can sigh with relief. There's still life in the sucker! Just not today.

'Possibles', though, don't hang around for long. Usually the idea gets stale, and the news producer's impatient attention span moves on. Nevertheless, it does give us a fall-back position if we're suddenly stuck. And it also serves as a great parking place for ideas. A holding ground for stories that we're not fully convinced about, or stories with endings we're unsure of. Perfect place for a baby really.

The idea of having a baby was dropped into my 'possibles' queue for years. There it sat, undeveloped and unexplored: out of sight, out of mind, but, most importantly, still within reach. Or so I thought. I could, if I wanted to, elevate its priority into the main game. Better still, I could dump it at the bottom of the pile, faintly ahead of the 'dead' queue. That way I could bury it, without actually killing it off altogether. The fact that I had a baby in the 'possibles' queue at all was quite remarkable in itself. Throughout my teens and most of my early twenties I had assigned the idea of a baby well and truly to my 'dead' queue.

At seven years old I had an epiphany of sorts about mothers. It was all because of Anne Marie. My family had just relocated to a new suburb and I moved to a new school. It was Anne Marie's eighth birthday and, given that the 'new girl' is always a novelty, I was invited to her party even though I knew no-one. As can happen with a bunch of good Catholic girls in their best party dresses, there was a fight; or at least a division of friends. All the party-goers took off to play at another girl's house and Anne Marie and I were left alone. She claims I stayed only because her mother brought out the ice-cream cake. She's probably right. As a well-brought up Catholic girl from a family of six children, who had manners drummed into her, I maintain to this day that I stayed because I was being polite. Either way, our solid and unspoken pact to stick together was cemented. It still binds us, over thirty years later.

Back then, as seven- and eight-year-olds, reasoning was a whole lot simpler. I hoed into the luxurious ice-cream cake while Anne Marie ripped open the present my mother had chosen to mark her auspicious year. With the smiley face wrapping paper tossed aside, Anne Marie held up the large cardboard box and read out its bold title, 'Mother's Little Helper'. I think I might have screwed up my nose—or at least stuck it in the air. Inside was a board game in which players won points for completing household chores. The quickest and most efficient 'mother's little helper' climbed the ladder of goodness; while the slow, lazy housework-averse player lost points and slipped down the ladder to the household equivalent of badness. Very instructive, aspirational stuff really. Funnily enough, Anne Marie seemed to like it. I remember feeling it was an odd and slightly embarrassing gift. Who wants to play with something that's all about housework? I hated housework. I hated the fact that my mum was always doing it. And I hated, more than anything, the thought that as I got older, I was going to have to do it too. That's what mothers seemed to do—housework.

When my mother wasn't running around after us, holding church fundraising meetings; entertaining the Catholic women's Magellan group or doing some kind of pastoral community work, she was doing housework. Either that or she was banging around in the kitchen cooking for the flotilla of people that filled our family life. Our home was always noisy with visitors, and our dinner table was always full. My mother would think nothing of throwing together a meal to feed a dozen or more. My parents were gregarious and generous, so much so that as my older brothers became teenagers, our house became something of a drop-in centre for the neighbourhood youth. Rock bands were formed, concerts were held, parties were had, meals were served, and somehow we all seemed to thrive in the chaos. No-one was excluded. My dad once invited four carloads of non-English-speaking young Indonesian men into our house for a barbeque, after I met one of them at a local disco. I wasn't so keen on the invitation, but Mum said we had to be kind to 'new Australians'. That's what my parents were like.

In all this happiness, love and 'normality', we were pretty much a stereotypical family of the times. My parents married in 1958. Dad, a graduate of Melbourne University, rose to become general manager of an engineering firm. Mum, a graduate of Windsor College, was never expected to work in paid employment past her early twenties. She would marry a good man of good stock and raise a family. All of which she dutifully did. By the time my mother was my age, 39, she had had six children. As Mum now says, 'That was simply how it was back then. That's what women did.'

My mother, who is the most selfless and giving person I know, and who will one day be canonised if the good Lord catches up on his paperwork, didn't ever complain about her lot. She complained about us kids not doing the dishes, not putting the milk bottles out and not making our beds but, in reality, she never complained. Her life was full: it was rich with purpose, abundant with activity and full of people who needed her. It was, I suppose, the textbook case for marriage and motherhood, as written in the apron-clad 1950s. Back then, post the shock and chaos of World War II, the 'housewife' was reinvented with vigour. Gender roles were unambiguous. Men were to be men: workers, breadwinners, decision makers. Women were to be women: wives, mothers and homemakers. The plotlines of my mother's life were clear cut and she felt no particular need to change things. It was good enough for Mum. But I knew it would never be good enough for me.

By the time I hit my late teens and early twenties I equated suburbia with mediocrity, and 'wifedom' with suppression. I wanted none of it. Up to a point, I would echo convincingly the words of Betty Friedan, who wrote in *The Feminine Mystique* in 1963, a year before I was born, 'In my generation, many of us knew that we did not want to be like our mothers, even when we loved them'. I would part with Friedan when she went on to say, 'We could not help but see their [our mothers'] disappointment'.[1] My mother was, and fortunately remains, a happy, fulfilled and enriched woman. My obsession with a room of my own, a career of my own and a life of my own was not a reflection on any loss or deficiency experienced by my mother. Rather it was a reaction, I believe, to the wider world in which I grew up: the feminist-powered 1970s, the careerist, femocrat 80s and the selfish 90s.

I arrived at Catholic Ladies College in 1976. It was a convent-run school for middle-class, well-behaved girls. We wore hats and gloves and smoked behind the toilet block like all other good girls. Although run by the Sisters of Charity, all bar one of my teachers were lay people, mostly women. They were largely wonderful women—progressive, inspirational, smart, independent, creative and, above all, enthusiastic about girls' education. Soon I became well aware of the growing strength and noise of the women's movement that was shaking and rattling the community around me. The previous three years of a Whitlam Government, committed to social reform, had heralded in a whole lot of 'firsts' for women, including the appointment of a Women's Advisor to the prime minister—a world first. The University of Melbourne, where I would later set my sights, had held the First National Feminist Conference. While I was obviously too young for any of these things to have an immediate impact on me, clearly the momentum of social change was pumping at full throttle, and its effects were permeating the world around me.

It was probably a few years later before I caught up with the TV and newspaper images of International Women's Year in 1975—the noisy rallies, demonstrations and women's gatherings that set the scene for sweeping legislative changes that would later reform the lives of Australian women. By the time I reached my senior secondary school years in the late 70s, the list of women's 'firsts' had blown out to what seemed to be—at least to my eager young eyes—a full-scale revolution. Women were winning at everything. A woman had been made Chief Justice of the Family Court. An Aboriginal woman had been made a barrister! There was now a federal portfolio of Women's Affairs, paid maternity leave had been introduced for Commonwealth employees, and, most importantly, women had flooded into universities and tertiary education courses without a hitch. Given that all this change took place while I was still at school, is it any wonder that by year 12 I was convinced I could be and do anything I wanted? The future was nothing but rosy and welcoming, and I couldn't wait to get out there and start living.

The biggest battle I faced, or so I thought, was maintaining my independence. I wanted to sail into a career seamlessly, unburdened by traditional ties. I would never need to be freed from 'domestic tyranny'—as the famous Canberra femocrat Sara Dowse had put it years earlier—because I would simply refuse to embrace domesticity. I would not make that mistake. I would be independent, unencumbered—and free. I could indeed have it all!

By the time I lost my virginity, at age seventeen, I was well aware of the blight of motherhood and how much I didn't want it. I was living in Mexico as an exchange student. I had travelled to Las Vegas for my official 'deflowering' and was high on new love, plenty of alcohol, Marlboro reds and illegal gambling. I was on the threshold of a brilliant life and no maternal responsibility was going to get in my way. Which makes it odd then that I took so little care about contraception.

I had already spent my year 11 art classes expressing my abhorrence of biological determinism by churning out black-and-white ink images of what I called 'The Baby Machine': a sort of square mechanical contraption with breasts, which forced out egg-shaped babies through a long intestinal pipeline. Perhaps I had been reading Betty Fridean's description of women stunting their intelligence by becoming an 'anonymous biological robot in a docile mass'.[2] Maybe 'The Baby Machine' series was a literal interpretation of that. While I can't be sure why such angst filled my teenage mind at the time, I do know my driving preoccupation was disgust with the idea of women behaving like breeding robots, when clearly we all had better things to do.

My time at Melbourne University doing an Arts degree in the early to mid 80s served to further bury thoughts of babies. It was there that I began reading and discussing the texts that gave form and argument to my own gut feelings about the subjugation of women. I started with Simone de Beauvoir, eventually working my way through her volumes of biography. *The Second Sex* resonated the most. Although written in 1949, my now yellowing 1983 Penguin edition seemed crisp with revolutionary zeal. I was fired by the stuff. Particularly de Beauvoir's confirmation of what I had already begun to suspect: wifedom and motherhood sapped the life out of women. On this I understood de Beauvoir to be unequivocal:

The tragedy of marriage is not that it fails to assure women the promised happiness—there is no such thing as assurance in regard to happiness—but that it mutilates her; it dooms her to repetition and routine . . . mistress of a home, bound permanently to a man, a child in her arms, she stands with her life virtually finished for ever. Real activities, real work, are the prerogative of her man . . .[3]

Although I wasn't doing a women's studies course, I was encouraged to work my way through, among others, Virginia Woolf, Betty Freidan, Anne Summers, Dale Spender, Jocelynne Scutt and pretty much anything I could get my hands on. Later Steinem, Wolfe and Faludi all joined the collection on my shelves. Germaine Greer's *Sex and Destiny* hit the bookshops in 1984 and I think I secured one of the first copies. I had already poured over Greer's *The Female Eunuch* in my early teens when I found a 1972 edition stashed away in my mother's wardrobe. When she was out I would take a kitchen stool to her room, climb up to reach the top shelf of her closet, grab the book in hiding and then prop up on her bed to read the secret thing. Thing is, it was so secret that it remained a secret. It may as well have been written in Chinese. I was too young to make sense of it and my older sister, Louise, showed no interest in interpreting. Years later I pinched the book and carried it around from student house to house. By then I had become a sponge to the cause. I was enthralled by Greer's call for women to 'humanise the penis', agreed with the need to throw the 'baggage of paternalistic society' overboard, and was fascinated by her 'denigration of sacred motherhood'.

By the time I finished my BA in 1985 a genderquake had ripped through politics and society. The noisy but enigmatic Susan Ryan had become the first woman to be appointed a federal minister in a Labor government and had succeeded in getting the revolutionary federal *Sex Discrimination Act 1984* passed. The heroic women's liberationist, Dr Anne Summers, was head of the Office of the Status of Women, rattling the corridors of power and addressing large mobs of enthralled students like myself. By 1986—my first year out of university—equal employment opportunity for women was finally elevated to an issue of national importance and enshrined into law via the *Affirmative Action Act 1986*. Now large companies and institutions were legally obliged to address issues of inequality in the workplace.

It was on the back of all this that I began my life as a journalist. The ABC's Melbourne TV newsroom employed two cadets that year: one male, one female. It was the luckiest break I have ever had.

I knew very quickly I had landed in the best place possible. I loved journalism and I thrived on the competitive spirit of the place. The fast pace, the stress, the adrenalin and the deadline of a newsroom suited me. By late 1987 I was working in the Victorian Press Gallery covering politics. During the following couple of years I watched with fascination the decline of the then Premier John Cain, and the rise of Victoria's first woman premier, Joan Kirner. On the day Cain resigned in August 1990, media speculation immediately turned to his successor. Kirner was a favourite, but she had an obvious impediment: she was a woman. Following Cain's announcement the media calls began to flood into Kirner's office with interview requests. She refused to talk, saying it was, 'John's day'.

By this stage I was reporting for the *7.30 Report* and had developed a more aggressive, stop-me-if-you-can approach to my work. I travelled downtown to Kirner's office at the Rialto building, despite being told she was unavailable, and walked in on what was clearly a private party. A bunch of women—I don't recall any men—were clinking champagne glasses, hugging and smiling. Joan was in! That very gracious woman saw me standing there and beckoned me in. She then gave me an exclusive interview.

As a journalist I've had a number of lucky breaks in both stories I've chased and jobs I've won. Perhaps the biggest career break I got was in the partner I chose just as I was starting out. Somewhere in all those odd 'one liners' a journalist collects, I recall Mary Easson, a successful, hard-working federal member of parliament, saying, 'The best thing I did was the spouse I selected', and she went on to warn young women to 'pick your spouse wisely'. In terms of my career, it would seem I picked the perfect spouse: an ambitious workaholic with feminist sympathies.

Greg was 24 years old and work working on a PhD when we met. I was eighteen. Within a couple of years we'd set up house and were playing grown-ups. We were married just after I turned 23. By then Greg was working as a stockbroker and I was churning out current affairs stories, chasing awards and had my eye on presenting roles. From the outset Greg was an enormous supporter of mine and was furiously gung-ho about my career. He took great pleasure and pride in my work and my wins, and he was always on the lookout for stories for me. In what I saw as proof of his feminist credentials, Greg was prepared to stay at home in Melbourne while I upped stumps and moved around the country chasing job opportunities. In our first eight years of marriage I set up home in four capital cities; three of them alone. The moves were largely about me climbing the television ladder, paying my dues, working on various programs in order to build up my scorecard of credits that would eventually help me manoeuvre into a position where I could pick and choose from plum offerings. Greg appeared happy to support me in all of this. The freedom of my long absences also gave him plenty of time to work sixteen-hour days, and all weekend, in order to build his own thriving career as a stockmarket analyst. We both worked ridiculously hard, and we no doubt thought we had a very grown-up and sophisticated kind of partnership, albeit a distant one.

One of my interstate contracts included a provision for a flight back to Melbourne every third weekend for a year, to 'visit my husband'. But, right from the beginning, we shared an unspoken agreement that children were not on our busy agendas. Given that babies were still in my 'dead' queue, and my abhorrence of domesticity and 'wifedom', one might wonder why I married at all. It's not as if living together wasn't an option. We had already been living together for a couple of years. In some slightly perverse way, however, I think I thought marriage—without any of the traditional baggage—would be good for our careers. It would mean I no longer appeared simply young and single. Marriage would make me serious and unavailable. I could get on with it; which I did. Greg and I didn't refer to one another as 'husband' or 'wife', and marriage didn't change our domestic arrangements. Greg still did all the cooking and maintained control of the household, and I did most of the socialising. Alone.

Eventually one of my male bosses plucked up the courage to tackle me on my baby plans, now that I was married. The event was a Melbourne press club dinner which we had hosted the then prime minister, Bob Hawke, who was the evening's speaker. The night had gone off well and Hawke had left when the stayers—of which I was always one—moved on to a late-night bar. The bloke in question plonked down onto the couch opposite me, raised his glass and toasted my many babies yet to be born. Well . . . that was the beginning of what developed into a furious, loud and what I imagine was a rather obnoxious debate. At one stage, after I forcefully explained that I had no interest in having children, my boss jumped to his feet and started jabbing his finger in my direction: 'That's unnatural!' he yelled, for the benefit of the whole bar. 'You're bloody unnatural!'

The next time a male boss tested the waters on my baby plans, I knew to be a little more 'feminine' in my empathy; but I was nevertheless clear about my unencumbered position, and my intention to remain that way. On this occasion it was important to get the balance right as I was being interviewed for a job on a commercial TV program that I wanted badly. 'The problem is,' the well-known executive huffed, 'we get these smart sheilas in here and they keep going off and having kids.' I had no illusions about this gruff, falsely flippant comment. It was a test. One I was going to pass. This time I artfully made an equally flippant attempt at mocking maternity, enough to secure the job but not enough to appear 'bloody unnatural'.

Not suprisingly, that network was the most patriarchal workplace I've ever experienced. On one occasion, after I had indulged in yet another round of complaining that the men on the program were being assigned all the best stories—the overseas trips and the war jobs—while the women were stuck with the 'colour' stories, I was told to shut up and pull my head in. So off I went on yet another soft story, only to return hours later to find a present in my office. It was a very large, long, thick, black rubber penis, sitting upright on my desk. For a moment I was floored, and awfully embarrassed. What to do in such a situation? I mentally weighed up the pros and cons of rage versus humour: to be a victim or victor? Then did the only thing I could think of. I put the wobbly rubber penis on my head, walked into my boss's office and said, 'Well, look at this, I've got one too! So now do I get an overseas assignment?'

To my surprise I received a phone call within days to check that my passport was in order. I was to pack my bag as I was heading overseas. I flew to Hawaii for ten days . . . and covered the 'Supermodel of the World' competition.

During the 1980s and early 90s, as I was thrashing away at building my career, I was acutely conscious of the serious dearth of role models for women journalists working on television in Australia. There were growing numbers of women on the lowest rungs, but I could count on less than one hand the senior women—the women past their mid-thirties—who held serious, prime broadcasting positions. Even now, mid-decade into a new century, we still lack role models. Sadly and frustratingly, the one thing that marks most of the few women you do see in prominent TV journalism roles as commentators or correspondents is their childlessness—with perhaps the exception of a few feisty women on the ABC's *4 Corners* and a couple on Channel 9's *Sunday* program. As I was working my way up the slippery ladder of television journalism, none of this was ever lost on me. The few women I looked up to seemed to be continuously dropping off the ladder and disappearing out of the system—inevitably to have children. Rarely, if ever, did I witness the return of a female journalist to a key high-profile reporting role after she had a baby.

By the time I was 31 I had moved from Melbourne to Adelaide to take up the role of presenter of the *7.30 Report*, in the days before the ABC nationalised the program. I had already spent the best part of a year in Darwin in 1989, working on the same program in the Northern Territory, where I took over the presenter's role from Claire Martin (who many years later became the Territory's chief minister). She had left to have a second child and never returned to television.

Although married, I lived in Darwin alone, and when the move to Adelaide came up my husband once again didn't move with me but stayed on in Melbourne. By now Greg had set up his own business and he felt a move interstate was simply not feasible. The timing was all wrong for him.

That year, living on my own in Adelaide, something inside me began to shift. Here I was with a great job, doing precisely the kind of work I had always wanted to do, on a prime-time program that often set the agenda for political and social debate, yet something was nagging at me. I was alone, although not lonely, but I felt unsettled about my aloneness. It was a sort of gnawing feeling. I managed to mask it by constructing a rigorous routine around my work—easy to do given my time was entirely my own. However, I was becoming increasingly aware that without my work—I had nothing. And I was nothing. Or so it felt at the time. Gradually I realised the baby issue had moved from the 'dead' queue to my 'possibles' queue. It was a quiet, unheralded move, but a move nevertheless.

By the time Greg and I were in the same city and got around to discussing this change of status he surprised me. I thought he would be thrilled and jump at the idea of starting a family. Instead he suggested, as he had with my move to Adelaide, that the timing was all wrong. What about the business, the unsure finances, the insecurity of the future, etc? It was all too hard. As always, Greg's position was well argued and persuasive. I couldn't help but agree with him. It *was* all too hard. Thoughts of a baby were quickly pushed back down to the bottom rung again.

Later that year I was restless and ready for another move. I needed distraction and wanted to test myself in tougher, bigger and noisier terrain. Sydney beckoned, and I once again boxed up my belongings and jumped on a plane. This time Greg said he would come too. I think we both knew we had left it too late. With too much time apart, too much time spent working so hard and furiously chasing very separate dreams, I had lost sight of why we married in the first place. We had become very separate people living very separate lives, with little to hold us together. Our sad and painful divorce, after ten years of marriage, took a couple of long and protracted years. I thought I would never recover from the grief.

The day I packed my car and held Greg to say goodbye we cried and cried. He was shattered. So was I. The months droned past in a foggy stupor. Eventually the all-day and all-night head thrashing subsided and in its place a dull, grey and joyless state took hold of me. I thought that was how I would live for the rest of my life. By then the idea of a baby was well and truly in my 'dead' queue. It felt like I was too.

There is only so much emotional self-flagellation and soul searching a person can endure. I had exhausted myself. A good year or more after our separation I made a conscious decision to ditch the endless analysis and try going with acceptance instead. Acceptance that a union based so clearly on love, mutual respect and regard can unravel and dissolve.

Finding myself single, in my mid-thirties and living alone in Sydney in the late 1990s, proved to be the perfect cocktail for reckless self-distraction. I furiously dated and bedded a long string of inappropriate and impossible men. I tried not to think too much about what I was doing, or where I was heading, and limply convinced myself I was 'just having a good time'. What I was really doing was keeping myself frantically busy in the hope of screening out the noise growing within me.

I had a reporting gig with a new show that was taking me around the world, paying me well, and keeping me distracted from my growing loneliness and despair. While I kept moving, I could keep a lid on my 'possibles' queue. Eventually, I convinced myself I had killed off the baby thing altogether. The more whacky and irresponsible my bed partner, the less likely I was to even consider exploring that option.

Then everything changed.

After repeated poor ratings, the show I was working on was unceremoniously axed and, along with an elite bunch of highly skilled and highly paid journalists and producers, I was suddenly unemployed. Given that my unhealthy, co-dependent attachment to my job was well known, most of my colleagues thought I would be the first out of the pub and back to work, but I knew I couldn't do it anymore. The party was over. After a long trip through Burma and weeks spent in silent and painful meditation at a forest monastery, I returned to Sydney, ended the on again–off again relationship I was having, and got a regular day job with a small corporate communications company.

The job was weird and wonderful. Everyone there was so utterly normal. No-one drank too much, no-one took drugs, everyone got along and everyone genuinely cared about everyone else. And they cared about me. As I said, it was weird . . . and wonderful. Although I did have to learn to stop saying 'fuck' all the time and curb my language, especially after my new boss suggested calling a client a 'prize dick-head' over the phone was not his preferred style of client–consultant relationship. As I sank into my new leather chair, in my beautiful office with its magnificent sweeping harbour views, I knew toning down my language was a tiny price to pay for the opportunity to finally get myself back on track and my life in order. Under the gentle guidance of the company's two principals, both exceptionally patient and compassionate men, I began to thrive again. Soon, with a briefcase full of organising gadgets, I became part of the corporate set, celebrating our client wins with Bollinger, speeding through Sydney's CBD in my boss's Lotus, and devouring the *Financial Review* for breakfast.

Then something utterly unexpected happened. I fell in love. Deeply, hopelessly and utterly. Just when I least expected it, my 'possibles' queue exploded its lid.

Mark walked back into my life after a six-year absence. He was wearing a funky shirt with its tail hanging out, a gorgeous smile and laughing eyes. He came for a short visit and never went home. We had first met when I was presenting the *7.30 Report* in Adelaide. Mark had been working in the medico–legal industry and had asked me to address a conference of doctors to talk about the media. Sometime later I ran into him during a live broadcast I was doing at the Adelaide Show. He was there with his son Sascha, who was nine years old; a beautiful young boy who held his dad's hand and threw me a sweet, boyish grin. Together the two of them looked like Irish brothers. They had the same broad smile, the same inquisitive, intelligent and gentle eyes and, as I would learn later, the same wacky wit. They were both shy in front of me and I think I fell in love with Mark right then. As is often the case in life, the timing had been all wrong. Mark *was* single, and had been for some time, but I wasn't.

Now the timing was perfect. Within months of Mark arriving in Sydney, we packed up my apartment and moved to Canberra for a fresh start, new jobs and a new life. I had been offered a role back with the ABC as the presenter of a new local TV news service. It was a fabulous opportunity to get in at the ground level and help establish a newsroom from scratch. It was also, I thought, the perfect job in which to start a family, given that it was office based, highly routine and involved very little on-the-road work.

Mark and I didn't discuss having a child. We didn't 'make plans'. But then we hadn't made plans about anything. Having both been battered and bruised by previous relationships and failed marriages, we were careful not to jinx this thing with the burden of expectations. Also Mark's son had just turned sixteen when we moved to Canberra and the strain of separation from him was a daily factor in Mark's life. It broke my heart to see Mark get off the phone from one of his numerous conversations with Sascha and see his eyes filled with tears. Not that the conversations were ever sad. Even at that very young age his son's maturity and worldliness was evident in the encouragement he gave his father. He wanted his dad to be happy. Young Sascha could see that here was a chance for that. I was, and remain, eternally grateful to that extraordinary boy for allowing his dad to move away from him. From the outset, I intuitively knew and accepted that Sascha must be a major priority in our relationship, in fact, he must always come first. Mark was, after all, first and foremost, a father—well before he became my lover and partner— so we agreed Mark would fly back to Adelaide to be with Sascha every third or fourth weekend. Watching this exceptional and unconditional love between father and son has only served to deepen my own love for Mark.

So, what about me and my baby love?

It's hard to begin to describe what happened next. Unlike some of the other women you will read about in this book, I didn't ever seriously contemplate motherhood on my own. With

Mark in my life I was now not only no longer alone, I was deeply and safely in love. My life was rich with an impassioned love that suddenly made everything possible. I was lighter, the world was clearer and, the best part of all, I heard myself laughing louder than ever before. Finally I could unscrew the tightly closed lid on that thing that had been gnawing away at me over the years. What took me by surprise—and this is where it begins to hurt—as soon as I felt comfortable enough to loosen a few of the screws, I realised the stuff just below the surface was on the boil. The lid didn't just come off, it blasted off. The contents of my long, pent-up and continuously quashed desire came screaming out of its hiding place like a mad woman let loose. It was then that a ferocious pain—the force of which I have never experienced before—took hold of me. I wanted a baby. Desperately. I wanted Mark beside me. And I wanted our baby in my arms. I wanted to be a family. And I wanted it now.

Then I got sick.

Or rather, I gave in to my sickness and my long-ignored stomach pains.

For many months I had been grappling with intermittent pelvic and abdominal pain, but the intensity of it had steadily increased. It was particularly bad in the mornings when I went for my regular run along Lake Burley Griffin. For a while I just put it down to my exercise routine. Eventually, though, the pain began to seriously interfere with my work. As I sat in the television studio minutes before presenting the 7 p.m. news, I would undo buttons, zips and loosen anything tight, hoping that I would make it through the next half hour without any shooting pain. I had stopped breathing deeply for fear of exacerbating the pain, and had developed a technique of quick, short, chesty breaths, in between reading sentences to camera. I even started taking private voice lessons to try to disguise the 'breathiness' in my delivery. Eventually I couldn't get away with it anymore, as the sudden jabs of pain were causing me to grimace, live on air.

The first GP I saw made me feel angry and foolish. After poking around, he suggested it might be something to do with my ovaries and casually asked if I had any kids. He scoffed when I said no, but that a baby was a possibility.

'How old are you?' he asked, squinting as if he couldn't hear me.

'I'm 37, almost 38,' I replied.

'Well!' he exclaimed with no attempt at subtlety, 'You may have left your run a bit late. I mean at your age. You know 38 is sort of getting over the hill for a woman's eggs.'

I was gobsmacked and furious. I couldn't quite believe what I had just heard. All my life I've been *young*. I was a 'young achiever', one of the youngest women to present a serious current affairs program, 'young' to get married, 'young' to be divorced. Just plain *young*. And now for the first time in my life, a man with no hair and a paunch was telling me I was *old*!

But baldy not only made me angry, he made me worried.

I began a round of tests, more prodding and poking, and eventually admission to hospital. I underwent a laparoscopy to investigate the state of my *aged* fallopian tubes and ovaries. The worst-case scenario was that I would come out of all this minus my tubes and possibly my ovaries; the best was that I would wake to find all my fertility bits still fully intact.

Prior to the operation, my gynaecologist counselled me about infertility and IVF. I left her rooms with a bag full of pamphlets from the Sydney IVF clinic, which I studied when I got home. The only brochure I was interested in was titled—somewhat unambiguously—'Success Rates'. It said the chance of a successful live IVF birth for a woman my age, between 38–39 years of age, was around twenty per cent. If I was to delay another year, the rate of success fell to just over six per cent. During a long phone conversation with one of my brothers, I read him the list of statistics. When I got to the stats on a forty-year-old woman's chance of IVF success, he said in his typical dry-witted way, 'Oh gee, Virginia. If you were a horse I wouldn't back you with those odds.' We laughed and laughed.

When I woke up from my operation no-one was laughing.

A nurse was fussing around the end of my bed and I asked her straight away, 'What happened? Do you know if they took my fallopian tubes out?' She just looked at me, as if she was deciding whether or not to answer, and then she blurted out, 'Yes. Er no. Ahh, I don't really know love. You'll have to ask the doctor,' then off she went. I read on the chart that she left behind that I had undergone a 'complicated operative laparoscopy' and a 'hysteroscopy'.

'Oh we did some awful things to you,' my gynaecologist said cheerfully as she breezed into the room. She screwed up her nose as she said, 'So how are you feeling?' She didn't wait for a reply. 'Oh it was awful,' she said. 'You were a mess in there. You shouldn't have left it so long. That right tube of yours was buggered. Buggered! We had to yank it out in bits. Here, I've got some photos. Do you want a look?'

I took a look, turning the card around and around, as I didn't know at what angle I was supposed to hold this thing to make sense of it. I couldn't understand what it was. I had never seen grotesquely diseased fallopian tubes before, so the image in the photo just looked to me like some sort of bloody carnage. I still have that photo, and as I look at it right now, it continues to fascinate me. It's a view inside my abdomen showing a very swollen, distended and distorted, bruised looking fallopian tube, in the state of being 'yanked' from what might be my ovaries. I know this may sound odd, even perverse, but I often pull this photo out of my filing cabinet and stare at it. For a while I wondered about sticking it on my fridge, like expectant parents do with their first ultrasound photos.

The prognosis on my left tube—the one that wasn't yanked out—was poor. It was probably buggered too the gyno told me, but because it wasn't showing severe signs of disease like the right tube, she had left it in situ. She told me that my tubes had probably been decaying over years as a result of an episode of chlamydia or pelvic infection. She also said the problem may not have prevented a pregnancy, if I had got in early enough. Then before she left she told Mark and I that we needed to think seriously and quickly about any plans to have a baby. I already knew she was a staunch believer in IVF as we'd had long discussions about the process involved. Her parting words to us both, with a raised eyebrow directed at me, were, 'But you really should get moving. Don't wait.'

This is probably when things got really tough.

For me—and for all the women I've spoken to about this—IVF is a huge commitment, at a frightening emotional and financial cost. I knew the strain of it would have enormous ramifications. Frankly, I'm not sure I could cope with ultimate failure. Would I be strong enough? What about my aged eggs? Again, my very blunt GP—who had skipped the student lecture on 'bedside manner'—had already reminded me about the increased risk of chromosomal abnormality at my age; not to mention the high incidence of miscarriage. To further complicate matters, there was always a risk the disease that had distorted and distended my tubes had already affected my ovaries, and rendered them rotten. I could see myself looking down the barrel of a couple of years of endless medical appointments and long stretches of hope and anxiety, thwarted by repeated failure, disappointment and heartbreak. I searched for a breath of optimism within me, but couldn't find it.

Given my trepidation, I knew that for Mark and I to embark on a path of infertility treatment and IVF, I had to feel convinced he was fully committed to it. I needed to know that he wanted a child as desperately and as completely as I did. In a moment of aching honesty he told me he didn't.

I was 38 and childless. Mark was 40 and far from childless. Apart from his own adored son, who would be starting university in a year or two, he had raised, loved and cared for stepchildren. Living with me was the first time his life wasn't focused on kids, and he was enjoying this new-found freedom. Knowing this, though, did nothing to quell the ache and longing I had. There were perhaps even periods when the knowledge of Mark's experience with children made my pain and sense of emptiness seem worse.

Mark's honesty was nothing short of honourable. We both knew what was at stake. While I knew Mark would go to any length to try and bring a child into our life, if that is what I asked for, I also knew his longing for children was well satisfied.

Around the time I had my surgery I was reading Wendy McCarthy's autobiography *Don't Fence Me In*. I first met Wendy years ago when I interviewed her for a story on child care for the ABC and I've long been a fan. While sitting up in bed recuperating, I reached chapter six of Wendy's life story. It began with this:

I cannot find the words that best describe the joy, the sensuality and the power of being female that childbirth confers. To experience the brain and body so perfectly synchronised and the rush of a profound love for a person you have just met is to feel life on a higher plane.[4]

With furious force I chucked the book across the room. It thumped against the wall before sliding to the ground. Right then I hated Wendy McCarthy. Hated her book. And just hated.

Furious and heaving I pulled out another book from under my bed. A book I'd tucked away there, hiding its confronting title. It was *Baby Hunger*, by American author Sylvia Ann Hewlett. I'd already read most of it, so I went straight to the bit I'd marked up for quick reference. It said:

This thing has a terrible power . . . the desire to have a baby before it's too late can kick in with ferocious intensity. It can become a non-negotiable demand—a veritable obsession—that rides roughshod over every other aspect of life.[5]

By the time Mark arrived home that night and came upstairs to our bedroom to check in on me, I was wild. My eyes were burning with all the tears I had howled. I was full of fury, rattled with jealousy and raving mad. I had in my hand a crumpled clipping from the *Australian* newspaper. It was a story about a group of women in the media, the print media, who were all first-time mums in their late thirties and early forties. I had read this clipping over and over. I knew some of these women. Right now I hated every one of them. And I hated myself even more for feeling this way.

How had I come to this? How had I reached such a desperate and bereaved state? I knew it wasn't Mark's fault. We had been together only a short time. My life had been a veritable feast of choices and decisions well before I set up home with him. So what had happened? How was it that for so long I seemed to have the world at my feet, and a gluttonous smorgasbord from which to choose, then suddenly what I wanted most—more than anything—seemed hopelessly out of my reach?

Weeks after getting up and out of my recovery bed, I sat down one morning for breakfast with the day's newspapers spread in front of me. I opened *The Age* newspaper and began wading through an article by Malcolm Turnbull, the then federal treasurer of the Liberal Party, and a man whose arrogant powerplays get plenty of media attention. Turnbull wrote:

> The fact is that we would be a healthier, safer and stronger society if: Australians married earlier than they are doing today; had more children and had them earlier; we stuck together more often, rather than getting divorced . . .
>
> There is compelling evidence that while women are increasingly accepted into responsible and well paid roles, their acceptance is often, albeit tacitly, on the condition that they don't have any children . . .[6]

As I read on the words began to swim in front of me. Something inside me lurched forward, thumping at my chest, straining my throat. My head spun. I just couldn't stand it any more. I went back upstairs to my study, sat down at my desk, and furiously started writing. I began . . .

> A few years ago, in my mid-thirties, had I heard Malcolm Turnbull pontificate about the need to encourage Australians to marry younger and have more children, I would have thumped him, kneed him in the groin, and bawled him out . . .

By the time I finished writing the keyboard was wet. And so was my sleeve. I looked up the email address for the opinion page editor of *The Age*, pressed 'send', blew my nose, and rang my mum.

'Having it all'—a f..... up feminist fantasy?

My generation was the generation that was told, 'All the work has been done by the feminists of the 60s and the 70s and you can *have it all* now.' And I believed them! And it's only as time has gone on that it has dawned on me that we don't have it all. We have to *do* it all!

Marion Keyes, UK author, on 666 ABC Radio, *The Morning Program*, 2 April 2004

I also recognise that for many of you, being the daughters of a revolution is far more difficult than was being on the frontlines of the battle for change. I hear this in conversations with women who are exhausted with the effort of trying to 'have it all' and wonder why equality and opportunity have to be such hard work.

Anne Summers, 'Letter to the Next Generation', 1994

You've got to love Germaine Greer. Just when I'm at a low ebb and wishing that infuriating woman with the big hair and ludicrous message—'Secret Women's Business: How to Get It All and Keep It'—would shut up and go away, I'm reminded of Greer's retort to a woman who offended her: 'I decided I would smack her around the chops', she brazenly stated. And she did—with her wicked tongue! The target of her vitriol was UK columnist and feminist Suzanne Moore. Moore had repeated the erroneous claim that Greer had had a hysterectomy. The flippant suggestion stabbed at Greer's private pain and enraged her. So she smacked her with lashings of Greeresque language, describing Moore as having 'hair birds-nested all over the place, fuck-me shoes and three fat layers of cleavage'.[1] None of which went down too well with Moore—who pouted. Only to have Greer bellow, 'So much lipstick must rot the brain'. Of course the UK press pounced on the spat as the 'catfight of the year'. Greer didn't care. Later she remained unrepentant, saying 'the chastisement has done [Moore] nothing but good'.[2]

While such naked fury and colourful language is not that shocking coming from Greer, what is shocking—in its inherent sadness—is the subject of the spat. Greer was deeply hurt by the inference that she had deliberately undergone a hysterectomy to avoid pregnancy. Some four years after that initial 'chop-smacking', Greer was still hurting:

> You know, it's pretty painful when you have spent a goodly part of your life struggling to have children, to have this young woman who is lucky enough to have two children of her own suddenly announce that I had myself hysterectomised at 25 because I didn't want kids. How could she be so stupid? Who did the operation? A vet? I think that level of incomprehension is inexcusable in someone who calls herself a feminist.[3]

She's right. It's not just the indignation that is so palpable here. It's the grief at her childlessness; a grief that must largely be endured alone and in private. Here is the cruel and bitter irony: one of the Western world's greatest and most important feminist is beset with sorrow and regret about her failed fertility, or lack of opportunity to become a mother. Not even Germaine Greer can 'have it all'.

Ah! But let's just flip this around for a moment. Hasn't Greer made choices too? Come on. How selfish is this women? Does she really think she can be a leading intellectual, a trailblazing feminist, an icon of an era *and* a mother to boot? How many feminists are lining up to jab their pointy finger at Germaine and bellow the mantra, 'But it was your choice!'? How many media commentators and writers have you seen bang on about Germaine being a whinger, 'petulant' or a 'brat' because she feels sad about being childless? They wouldn't dare. But then, Germaine didn't make the connection between childlessness and feminism. I did.

As I sat at a dinner table one night, a well-known, high-profile political journalist leaned across the table and whispered to me, 'You know Virginia, some of the women in the Press Gallery say you're a whinger. Just a bloody whinger.' Funny isn't it, whenever a woman laments her lot, dares complain, or ask for more she is written off as a whinger. (If it weren't for those bloody, noisy whingers in the long skirts, we'd still be free of the obligation to vote!) So, is Greer a whinger too? Or is she excused with a special dispensation for expressing her frustration and her sorrow because she's a brilliant, eccentric feminist, who has never questioned feminism's role in creating burdensome expectations for women? Expectations that we could, should and must, 'have it all'.

What is this notion of 'having it all'? And why is it such a twisted and perverse aspiration used to exhaust, punish and belittle women? As the BBC broadcaster Kate Aide said when addressing the National Press Club in Canberra, 'How many men are asked,

"Do you think you can have it all?" I don't know any men who are asked that.' It would seem to be a male birthright, but not women's. The right to 'have it all'—or even a little piece of it— has been won through hard fought feminist battles right throughout the last century. Is it possible the glaring inequities that galvanised the second-wave feminists in the 60s, 70s and 80s meant they pushed the mantra just too far?

'You are able to have it all', says feminist author Anne Summers in her 'Letter to the Next Generation', in which she argues that neither convention or law force women to choose between marriage and family or a career in the same way it did for our mothers and grandmothers. In theory, at least, she is right. The reality, as all women know, is quite different. Summers can provide little comfort with her suggestion, 'But simply being able to do it does not make it easy. It is often exhausting and debilitating . . .'[4] Hello!

The heavy burden on the women of my generation to live up to the expectations of our feminist foremothers, and the ambitious expectations we furiously set for ourselves, has given rise to a demographic of exhausted and angst-ridden women. To be a woman aged in her thirties to mid-forties in Australia right now can be a wretched business. We are perversely guilty much of the time: guilty for failing to fully excel in all aspects of womanhood. We are the generation that should have no excuse, and no reason to complain. After all, we are the first generation who could, should and must 'have it all'! The truth is, *none* of us can. Frankly, I would like to do a bit of chop-smacking myself. I'd like to shut up, and shut down, those foolish women who keep insisting we can *have* it all, *be* it all and *manage* it all. The inference in such a ludicrous message is that if you somehow don't manage to keep all your balls in the air and all your spinning tops spinning, then baby, you're a dud. A failure. A cop-out. What's wrong with you?

'I think it's a trap,' says Senator Natasha Stott Despoja, a woman who, in her mid-thirties, would appear to 'have it all' but is grappling—like many new mothers—with the heavy costs of a woman's choice:

> I do think it is a trap because I don't believe women can have it all yet. I don't even think women, at this stage, still even have a part of it. I think there are huge expectations on women, and a false belief that 'Yeah, it's all available to you'. But then the next trap is, if you don't get everything you aspire to, it is your fault because it's available to you. It's [considered] your fault because you just haven't worked out the balance or how to achieve it.

Superwoman—patron saint of suckers!

Throughout the 1980s and 90s we were bombarded with media stories about outstanding women achievers—the modern-day Superwoman. The idea of women being 'super' was born in the mid-1970s, during the heady years of second-wave feminism. At the time, it was both empowering and liberating. Suddenly women could be strong, aspirational, kick-ass kind of broads, who existed well beyond the apron-clad confines of domesticity. Naturally the concept was pounced upon by a media hungry for buzz words and terminology to help describe this ubiquitous social change that was redefining women. So when English writer Shirley Conran penned her bestselling *Superwoman* in 1975, she gave the 'women can do it all' concept form, and the movement a role model.

The witty author, wife and mother, who made a virtue of her own lack of domestic skill and ambition, and who 'would rather lie on a sofa than sweep under it', was adored for her savvy thesis, 'Life is too short to stuff a mushroom'. Back then 'Superwoman' wasn't trying to stuff organic mushrooms; design the stuffer; write the stuffing-R-us business plan; run the stuffed boardroom; stuff her lover; or feed, bath and burp a few kids that she had managed to stuff into her life along the way. No, all that was yet to come. That was to be the life of girls born and bred in the age of the Superwoman—that was to be us.[5]

Now, well past the novelty stage, being 'super' is no longer considered spectacular—it's expected. Of course all women can be all things, to all people, at all times. Can't they?

'Unstoppable' screams the cover of Australia's leading business magazine *BRW*, 'Women heading for the top in business'. Perhaps the proudest and loudest claim in the accompanying article was: 'The notion that having children rules out a corporate career at the top does not apply to these twenty women'.[6]

It turns out eighteen of the twenty 'stars' are mothers, and the nineteenth is pregnant. The profile of each Superwoman makes a point of mentioning her mothering responsibilities, and the apparent ease of combining a woman's many roles.

Says one 39-year-old chief executive with a breastfeeding baby, 'I . . . had a supportive organisation, as I continued to feed for the first year'.

Another is said to be 'at her desk by 8 a.m. and always home by 7 p.m. The laptop is open again when the children are in bed.'[7]

A single parent, who says she wants to spend more time developing new aspects of her career, claims to have 'an understanding daughter'. She's eleven.

When Senator Stott Despoja launched a letter campaign as part of her ongoing push for paid maternity leave in Adelaide's Rundle Mall back in 2004, the local newspaper wanted a pregnant woman included in its photo. The photographer disappeared into a lingerie shop, opposite where the small launch crowd had gathered, and returned with a heavily pregnant woman who had just purchased her first maternity bra. She told the senator she would be delighted to pose for a photo as she was 'passionate about paid maternity leave', having already used up the miserly two weeks she had. When quizzed by the senator, it turned out the token photo prop was in a mad hurry, and stressed to the max. She had just dashed out of work, with laptop in hand, done some work in her car, then managed a pregnant sprint to the mall to grab the first bra with flip cups she saw—today was her 'last chance'.

'If you don't mind me asking,' the polite senator pushed, 'When are you due?'

'Oh,' the busy woman replied, with half an ear out for her mobile phone and one foot turned ready to hoof it back to that laptop propped up on the passenger seat, 'Oh, I'm pretty sure it's today.'

Photo snapped. The pending mother dashed. And one can only hope that the baby held off till mum got the work report finished and her emails cleared!

UK journalist and author, Allison Pearson, says she was stopped short when she read a Mother's Day survey that suggested the vast majority of women canvassed wanted time out for themselves, were too exhausted for sex, and felt their lives were tougher than those of their mothers:

> I thought, 'Is this where equality has got us?' I thought about my own life and that of my friends and it seemed that we were all running around like headless chickens trying to do

it all because somebody has told us, 'Oh yes, you can do everything'.[8]

Pearson went on to write the international bestseller, *I Don't Know How She Does It*, a frantic, fictional tale about the crazy life juggle of a 35-year-old high-flying fund manager and mother of two. It was hailed by Oprah Winfrey as a 'working mother's Bible'.

A real woman, who *does* know 'how she did it'—because she did it herself, lied about how easy it was, then chucked it all in—is former American high-flyer Katrina Heron. A powerhouse in US publishing, Heron's last and most high-profile position was as Editor in Chief of *Wired*, a must-read magazine that, according to American *Vogue*, 'wrote the book on digital culture'. In a profile on her in the same magazine in 2003, Heron said she was making pots of money, 'hobnobbing' with leaders of the high-tech world and working around the clock. In her private life she was a single parent with twin daughters. When they reached four years old, she threw in the job and the career and went home to play with her kids, tend the garden and cook. It was then that friends said, 'I don't know how you did it'. To which Heron admits:

> I tried to make it look like no big deal. A lot of us are like that—we have no particular desire to have others see the insane lengths we go to make life work when work is overtaking life.[9]

What is it about Generation X—women born in the 1960s and early to mid-70s—that makes us such martyrs to the cause? It is not just the mothers among us who aspire to superwoman status. The non-mothers are possibly even worse, for they have no excuse for not reaching their 'full potential', for not smashing through any real or perceived workplace barriers and claiming an assortment of career crowns and accolades.

Annette Thompson is a Gen-X non-mother. At 38 she is now working on a PhD and she simply shrugs her shoulders when she recounts the life she led until recently:

> I was working on a long-term project that consumed a lot of my thinking and all of my energy, and I was engrossed in it and didn't think about anything else. I regularly worked about 18–19-hour days. I would get up at 2 a.m., work for four hours at home, and then go into work where I'd stay for most of the day and well into the night. And I always worked on weekends. I was awful! I look back now on myself and I'm so embarrassed.

'Can't anyone see what's going on?'[10] Germaine Greer exclaimed, as we stood on the threshold of a new millennium. The answer: 'Obviously not!' So Germaine sat down and wrote *The Whole Woman*, in which she states a blunt and painful truth:

> In the last thirty years women have come a long, long way; our lives are nobler and richer then they were, but they are also fiendishly difficult. . . . The contradictions women face have never been more bruising than they are now. The career woman does not know if she is to do her job like a man or like herself. Is she supposed to change the organisation or knuckle under to it? . . . Is motherhood a privilege or a punishment?[11]

Questions for feminism . . .

Why is it that women of my generation have felt so compelled to have and do it all? Why have some of us felt compelled to keep our nose to the grindstone, furiously priming and pumping our careers at the expense of all other aspects of our lives? Why have many of us sought identity and meaning primarily through the work we do, and the positions we hold, in a working world so fundamentally structured around men? Why are we so hard on ourselves, and on each other?

I have been accused of something akin to feminist treason and driving a stake into the sisterhood by suggesting these are all questions that should be asked in the context of feminism. Certainly, no one social movement is fully responsible for shaping the way any generation thinks or functions. The rapid changes of the past several decades have impacted upon all of us—women and men. The powerful forces of market deregulation, the casualisation of the workforce, commercialisation, the speed of technological advancement, increased competition and the growth in isolation and loneliness, have all played a part in our make-up. It would be foolish to deny the combined impact such things have on the life choices we make. All that withstanding, *nothing* has changed the lives of contemporary women as profoundly as feminism, and the battles fought and won by the women's movement. Even though many—perhaps most—women claim no connection with this recent past, it has nevertheless imbued and affected every single one of us.

And yet, it would seem even today, mid-way through a new decade in a new century, we are still not allowed to question some of that movement's most powerful and lasting messages. One commentator suggested that by putting the spotlight on feminism I was cranking up the so-called 'False Feminist Death Syndrome'.[12] Another rather perversely insisted I was perpetuating a 'feminism that is anti-motherhood',[13] which of course is a gross misunderstanding of my call to question. So fearful are some of the diehards about holding feminist theories or promises up to that light, that

I've been branded 'dangerous' for endeavouring to do so, as well as 'selfish' and 'neo-conservative', even 'totally icky'.[14]

All this is but a sideshow distraction in the face of what needs to be addressed. To ask what role feminism has played in bringing us to where we now find ourselves is both fundamental and necessary. It's fundamental in understanding where we've come from—what messages shaped our thinking, our choices, and why—and necessary in order to take stock, to look at where we've got it wrong and how we might improve things so that women can move forward, and not backward.

Some of the women interviewed for this book proudly call themselves feminists and see no problem in ensuring feminist principles govern their working lives—but they were only a few. To my surprise, many expressed little connection to feminism, seeing it as something harking back to their university days. Although these women expressed 'sympathy for the cause' and a sense of obligation to appear in solidarity with the sisterhood, the truth is, in their busy and hectic lives, feminism just doesn't rate.

Perhaps then we should be asking, 'Is it all too late?' '*Is* feminism dead?' In 2002 the prime minister of Australia, John Howard, declared it all over. 'We are in the post-feminist stage of the debate,' he smugly told the *Sydney Morning Herald*. 'I find that for the under-thirties woman . . . the feminist battle has been won.'[15] So then, has it 'served its purpose and should now eff off', as Germaine Greer puts it?[16] Or should feminism just be 'flipped on its ass', as Canadian performance artist, Peaches, suggests?[17]

'I hate the word', said the acclaimed American actress Sarah Michelle Gellar—alter ego of Buffy the Vampire Slayer—when asked if she considered herself a feminist. Gellar was 21 years old at the time and riding high on an international tidal wave of fame and female adoration. Her portrayal of Buffy was applauded as creating 'nothing short of a cultural icon—a feminist hero who's smart, tough and self-reliant . . .', according to the *USA Weekend* magazine.[18] While this fearsome and lusty personification of young womanhood could cause a genderquake all of her own, any suggestion that Gellar might be a feminist was enough to make the Hollywood actress gag: 'It makes you think of women that don't shave their legs,' she told the journalist.

It's not just the Yankee star who is choking over the thought of hairy limbed feminists. Young Australian women are just as turned off, with an equally oddball aversion to body hair. When asked by the *Financial Review* if feminism is relevant today, a smart young twenty-year-old said that while *she* thinks it is extremely important, her generation of women doesn't. It's 'not a cool topic', she told the journalist. 'It's so seventies etc. People visualise underarm hair.'[19] And of course it doesn't stop there.

Hop a continent and her British sisters are equally as offended by the question.

'Would you say you are a feminist?'

'No I wouldn't,' retorted Victoria Beckham, aka Posh Spice— another international pin-up girl and fantasy role model. Beckham told *Cosmopolitan* magazine back in 2002, 'I'm a romantic. I like a man who opens doors for me, takes me out to dinner, buys me flowers. I like men to treat women like women, and I think many other women do too.'[20] Revelations of adulterous affairs by her husband aside, Victoria Beckham clearly likes men to be men, and women to be girls. For the Buffys and the Posh Spices of the world—whose iconic role-model status is pervasive and powerful—it would seem feminism not only embodies all things un-feminine, it is also irrelevant and immaterial to their lives.

For these young women, and the millions they influence, a life of inequality is simply unimaginable. They have what they believe is full and equal access to everything their male counterparts have—so what's the problem? For them feminism is not just outdated, it's 'like *so* over', uncool, and even embarrassing. Yet, as we know, there is probably not a girl or young woman out there who doesn't relish and utilise the opportunities she has to participate equally with her male peers. I have never met a young woman who does not agree with the principal tenets of feminism—a right to equal opportunity in all aspects of life including education, work, financial independence, equal pay, career choice, the right to own property, the right to run or create a business, play sport, lead a team, sit in parliament, or run the country. All this stuff is taken for granted by young women. They assume, wrongly, that all battles for equality have been won, and that the gender war has been put to rest.

Such an outcome, such disinterest or disdain for what's been fought and won, is in itself a matter of feminist failure. That's not the key problem, though. The bigger and much more damaging problem is the fact that women of my generation–Gen Xers—are a failed and failing generation. We are the ones who have not got the mix right. We have unintentionally given rise to a rapidly expanding demographic of successful, independent, childless and miserable women.

It started around the time we were born, when Betty Friedan's 1963 literary hit, *The Feminine Mystique*, threw a polemical bomb right into the epicentre of the world of women. Its reverberations sent shockwaves of fear through the wider world—the world of men. Agitated and dissatisfied with the way things were, Friedan, a frustrated journalist, who had passed up the opportunity for a career in science for the lesser job of housewife and mother, went in search of uncovering 'the problem with no name'. In the almost hushed tones of a gripping mystery novel, Friedan begins her groundbreaking book with just a faint whiff of the revelations to come:

The problem lay buried, unspoken, for many years in the minds of American women. It was a strange stirring, a sense of dissatisfaction, a yearning that women suffered . . . Each suburban wife struggled with it alone.[21]

The 'problem', of course, was the psychological and emotional oppression felt by women who were herded by the social mores and expectations of the times to forego education and careers and settle instead for a lifetime occupation as housewife and mother. A role that for many women proved to be vacuous and inadequate. 'The feminine mystique', according to Freidan, erroneously suggested women could find fulfilment only through their femininity, 'sexual passivity, male domination and nurturing maternal love'.[22] 'The mystique', she lamented, had already 'succeeded in burying millions of American women alive'.[23] Thus blighted, and utterly oppressed, Friedan argued there was no way women could 'break out of their comfortable concentration camps . . .'[24]

It was powerful stuff. Friedan had documented a miserable litany of tales of women wastage. The underlying message was a screamer: marriage, wifedom and motherhood were a curse on women. They were the very things that would stunt, shackle, and thwart a woman's ability to grow, flourish and achieve her true potential.

If Friedan's messages were screamers, Germaine Greer's were howlers.

By the 1970s the subjugation of women was all pervasive and Greer didn't mince her words in writing about it. 'Women represent the most oppressed class of life-contracted unpaid workers, for whom slaves is not too melodramatic a description', she wrote in her conclusion to *The Female Eunuch*.[25] By now there was no equivocation; women were the most miserable of all men. They were wasted as wives and had the life sucked out of them as mothers. 'The plight of mothers', wrote Greer, 'is more desperate than that of other women, and the more numerous the children the more hopeless the situation seems to be'.[26] While mothers were clearly the most wretched of women, their maternal status was nevertheless the source of conflicting focus. They were at once pitied for their suffering yet despised for their complicity in performing their role. There was no let up. Years later US writer and academic, Camille Paglia, burst onto the scene insisting motherhood sapped all creativity out of women, rendering them useless as artists, and drowsy as humans.[27]

Given such a rotten and depressing view of the role of mothers, is it any wonder that those of us who grew up during these times—times when the institutions of marriage and motherhood were hailed as the greatest source of women's oppression—is it any wonder that we felt reluctant to embrace it?

Of course, not all women of Generation X bought into these powerful messages and the dominant mood of the time. Many passed through high school, tertiary courses and work keeping well clear of the more radical, noisy and bullish feminists on campus, in lectures and agitating in the workplace. There was one spin-off from the social revolution that had taken place that no-one could avoid, however. That was the re-positioning of mothers as an underclass, and motherhood as a waste of talent. Far from being a career option, motherhood was a career killer.

What about the push for child care during the late 1960s, 70s and early 80s? Isn't that proof of a feminist commitment to motherhood and evidence of an inherent support of mothering? This is a common enough argument but it belies the obvious motive behind establishing childcare facilities. I tread cautiously here because clearly this is one of the most divisive issues among women today, as it was back then.

Certainly in the early days of second-wave feminism in Australia, child care was almost unheard of. It took some well-organised campaigns, sophisticated lobbying, and a good dose of feminist tenacity to finally get governments to support and subsidise childcare facilities. Significant gains were made but even today the battle is far from won. We have a screaming, urgent need for more affordable, reliable, flexible and safe childcare facilities and options for working parents. There is no question about that. Nor should there be any question about the fundamental need for child care at all. In this new century we are well and truly past the time of one-income families, and one stay-at-home full-time parent.

That said, it's time to be honest about the early motives behind establishing child care in Australia, as this is instructive in understanding how a woman's sense of worth and identity became subsumed by the same stuff men rely on—their success and position in the workforce.

Prior to the genderquake brought about by second-wave feminists, it was unclear just how the emancipation of women could be achieved. While shackled and oppressed by tradition—a tradition that saw women only in a feminine context, as wives, mothers, and carers—it was unclear how to undo all the chains *and* remain woman. But in the post-war world run entirely by men, one thing *was* clear: the power of money! Money bought freedom. Therefore the need for women to achieve economic independence was paramount. If women could become financially independent they could, in a sense, buy their way out of oppressive circumstances. Once in control of their own money, women would finally have real choices *and* the means to choose.

Of course to achieve such an end, women needed to join the paid workforce. Once there, it became clear that in order to survive they needed to morph into would-be men, adopting the same values that motivated and anchored their male counterparts. Before long, women were led to believe that it was there—and only there—that they had a meaningful 'identity'. And in the heady climate of hard-won gains, as women were encouraged to relish their newfound 'equal' status as paid employees, it became necessary to downgrade all other seemingly 'lesser' female identities. This is where motherhood suffered, and in its place paid employment took over as the only meaningful occupation.

The initial push to establish good and reliable child care, therefore, says little about the positive value of motherhood but a lot about the primary value of paid work. Child care was a way of helping women escape the devalued existence of homemaker and enter the much more highly valued world of men—the workforce. It was only in the world of paid work that woman could derive a sense of worth, value and, most importantly, an identity that mattered.

Unfortunately, some leading Australian feminists are *still* stuck on the notion that employment is what gives women 'an identity'. This wrong but nevertheless powerful message contributes to the sense of failure, or sense of opting out and 'letting the side down', felt by some women today who choose to stay at home and be mothers rather than paid employees. It both horrified and embarrassed me to hear a women I approached about being interviewed for this book say, 'Oh, but why would you want to interview me? I'm just a mum.' It turned out the mum in question also happened to be an Australian fluent in Japanese, who'd given up a sterling career in Tokyo to become 'just a mum'. Such is our continuing sense of the lack of value in mothering that even a woman well accomplished in the world of work feels devalued, and a loss of identity, when she steps out of the paid workforce.

So pervasive and powerful have been the social messages that only paid employment can give women a sense of identity, fulfilment and meaning, that many of us have opted for career success at the expense of everything else. Of course, some of us now feel all the poorer for it. Some are devastated by it. For childless women who have left their run too late, it can be an enormous shock when we're forced to accept that indeed we cannot, and will not, 'have it all'. Feminism, it would seem, may be a useful scaffold from which to construct a career but it is, of itself, an inadequate structure from which to build a life. Unfortunately, many of us are realising this too late, and our sense of failure is profound.

This is not about a backlash. It is not a call to turn back the clock. As commentator Pamela Bone put it, 'Women's improved position is non-negotiable'.[28] And she is right. Those things which *are* genuine improvements in women's lives must never be up for grabs again. But what about the broader web of women's lives? The whole experience of womanhood is rich and multi-faceted. It spans the world of children, partners, careers, community, family and creativity. Being a woman is a heck of a lot more than just succeeding in the workforce. For women to really be liberated we require something much better than the model of a male worker on which to fashion ourselves. That is what feminism has failed to recognise.

Perhaps the last word here should go to Anne Summers who, after decades of tirelessly slugging it out for the betterment of women, is gracious enough to concede that we have not yet got it right when she says, 'We are not providing women with real choices if the price exacted from them is so steep'.[29]

A child-riddled career . . .

Raising children may be the most important job in the world, but you can't put it in a resume.

> Ann Crittenden, *The Price of Motherhood*, 2001

Second-wave feminists changed a lot of things for the better, but we had no reference points for how to manage a career and motherhood.

> Dr Louise Watson, academic researcher, February 2004

We've all seen women arrive at the office door and do that thing that women do as they fumble for the security pass. It's a moment of mental adjustment, disguised as body correction. We straighten our shoulders, tug at our skirt and grow a few inches before plowing through the door—chin first. Is this the point at which women say 'Unsex me now!', as British author Allison Pearson suggests all women entering a corporation are obliged to do?[1] How many of us take Lady Macbeth's entreaty one step further, beckoning the spirits to fill us with 'direst cruelty!

Make thick my blood'? Come on. We've all done it at some stage. Maybe some more than others. While the rush of cruelty is perhaps a bit outmoded and unnecessary, I've no doubt a dash of thickening—of blood, skin *and* sense of purpose—still comes in handy.

For several months I watched with fascination as a client of mine did the daily 'unsex me now' thing just moments before walking into a regular weekly meeting. She was the boss; the men around the board table were the stakeholders; and I—the only other woman present—was the communications consultant. The project was huge. It was the nation's most prestigious construction development at the time, worth more than half a billion dollars, and all eyes were on us. Not just because of the size of the deal, but because Kim, the team leader, was a *sheila*. Never before in Australia had a woman headed a construction project of this magnitude. On paper it looked tough: in person it was even worse. Not only was Kim female but she was Asian, short, diminutive and, to top it off, she fell pregnant.

That's when I noticed Kim perfecting her act. She was so good at it that the day she gave birth, which happened to be on the day of our weekly meeting, the male stakeholders revealed their complete and utter blindness to her sex.

'Where is Kim?' they asked politely when a substitute took the chair.

'She went into hospital this morning,' they were told.

'Oh, is she ok? Did she have an accident?' they enquired.

'Err no,' the new chairman explained. 'She had the baby, an hour ago. It was a few days early.' The proverbial pin clanged to the ground.

'What baby?' was the startled response.

Many of the dozen men present hadn't noticed Kim's growing rotundness, which she had kept secret, hidden under rather fulsome swing jackets. Earlier, when Kim confessed her pregnancy to me, her biggest concern was a clash of dates. The baby was due on the day of the official launch of the development project. Over three thousand people were expected to pour through the new doors, and I had arranged a heavy schedule of media interviews with Kim as the star talent. She assured me she had the matter 'in hand' and that everything would go according to plan. None of which I believed. Instead, working on the assumption that when the day rolled around Kim would be lost somewhere in the fog of new motherhood and unable to function, I set about briefing a stand-in spokesperson. Bad move. When Kim heard about it, she was neither impressed nor forgiving. Nor was she going to let go. This building was her baby; the other one would just have to fit in. And it did. At around 8 a.m. on the day of the launch Kim was on deck, ready to roll, in a neatly buttoned-up business suit, with a three-day-old babe in arms.

I still didn't get it as over a week later I made another wrong assumption about working mothers. As I thought our regular weekly meeting would be cancelled, while Kim was on maternity leave (of some sort) I failed to show. I got an agitated call from her asking my whereabouts. When I arrived late and took my place at the table, Kim was centre stage and in full flight. Half an hour or so later there was a faint murmur from under the table. Kim ducked her head down to take a look, then slid off her chair and disappeared. We all looked at each other. In a jiff she was back on her seat, cradling her now nine-day-old baby, who had taken up residence under the board table. When I asked Kim much later if she intended to take any time off work now that she had a new baby, she shrugged. 'Maybe, when things aren't quite so busy,' she said.

There are a couple of issues at play in a case like Kim's. Is this a superwoman in action, or is it a woman working in a man's world driven by the all powerful Fear of being Female? In Kim's case it was possibly the latter, although we publicly applauded her as the former. In fact, I even arranged a 'superwoman' media story, stressing to the journalist, 'Don't forget the fifteen-hour days and the fact that Kim has a brand new baby.' In a working world structured by men, and modelled on *men*, a sheila needs to be a bloke. Or at least a worker needs to become less sheila, and more bloke. In this sense we are no different to our American sisters, as author Ann Crittenden puts it:

> The unwritten requirement for success in corporate America is to be a corporate man . . . When and if [women] do give birth, they are expected to treat the event like an appendectomy, take a brief time-out for recuperation, and then resume the truly important business of business.[2]

What about those successful working women who don't treat the birth of their baby like an 'appendectomy', and instead embrace it as a change in their life's course. A change that demands dedicated time, focus and a rescheduling of priorities. What about those women who put their careers on hold, only to experience demotion, loss of opportunity, side tracking or backward sliding, in among the joys and trials of motherhood?

When Sophie and her husband had the first of their two children, they decided to follow a dream and head for the country, quitting their busy inner-city Sydney lifestyle. Resettled in a rural village in southern New South Wales, they built a home, raised their family and became an integral part of the local community. As a film-maker Sophie was ill-qualified, indeed over-qualified, for any work to be found in the village. But, in need of bringing home some bacon, she took a part-time job in the closest town. Several years passed in a rich wave of child-rearing—schooling, pony club, parents and citizens meetings—and playing host to the endless stream of friends who loved to escape the big city pulse and take refuge at Sophie's rural haven. In all of this busyness, Sophie maintained an extraordinary discipline, spending a couple of years banging away in the early pre-dawn hours, writing and re-writing a film script she had been mulling over in her head.

When completed, the script had no trouble in attracting a New York-based producer and cinematographer. The duo flew to Australia to scout the locations, and they liked what they saw. When Sophie's executive team was due to meet with a film financing organisation to discuss funding, Sophie made an extraordinary decision. This was a vital meeting: they needed the support of the financing body to help move the project on to the next step, and the pitch had to be faultless. So Sophie, mother of two, rural housewife and part-time worker . . . stayed at home. She sent along her team of men, without her.

Why? This was her baby, her film, her brilliant script, and it represented years of hard, silent and lonely work. So why would she stay out of the process at the most crucial juncture? Sophie's answer shocked me:

> Honey, the meeting is with a groovy young woman who arrived at film school years after me. She only knew me by reputation, we never met. But how can I suddenly reappear on the scene with a resume that says 'last ten years—Mother'. I mean, hello! She'll just immediately read 'loser'.

It seems Sophie was right. The meeting went well; very well. Ms Finance loved the film script and agreed to back the project. As for the film's absent director/writer, Ms F turned to one of the team as the meeting was breaking up and said, 'Funny, isn't it. Last I heard of Sophie, the talk around Sydney was that she'd gone off out bush, to breed children. Imagine that!'

'Imagine that!' we all laughed, as Sophie banked her first film cheque. With the kind of rat-cunning found on Sunset Boulevard, Sophie knew the image of her as a 'mother'—and a rural one at that—was enough to destroy any prospect of her project being taken seriously. Her tactic of 'mysterious absence' proved to be smart, sassy and sophisticated. It ensured she wasn't sideswiped.

Not all working mothers can hide their motherhood. Many simply won't. Some will purposefully throw it into the work arena, expecting that their solid reputation, previous success and years of career investment, will override any negative attitudes about the 'diversion' of mothering. Not an unreasonable expectation when you're riding high and near the top of your game. But, as the next couple of women's stories reveal, even well-founded expectations are vulnerable to entrenched workplace prejudices.

Demotion and lost opportunity . . .

Giuliana's first child, Allegra, was a long time coming. She was born just before Giuliana turned 36. We all knew about Allegra—or at least the idea of her—from about the age of twelve. Among my group of school friends, Giuliana was a stand-out star with a glittering future. The first time I laid eyes on her she was on stage enchanting a school hall full of kids as Dorothy in *The Wizard of Oz*. A year later, when I found myself sitting next to her in a maths class, she was still just as enchanting, beautiful, smart, multi-talented . . . and clucky. Within our group of girlfriends Giuliana was always one of the clearest about babies. She loved them and wanted plenty of them. Like all of us, Giuliana also wanted lots of other things. She wanted career success. She wanted to become an academic, a researcher, a scientist, a lecturer, a doctor, a paediatrician and a specialist. And she did. She did all of those things. In fact when I remind Giuliana that since we left high school she has spent the best part of 22 years studying, she rolls her eyes.

'That sounds so depressing, Virginia. Thank you for adding that up for me!' We both laugh.

The only explanation Guiliana can give for leaving the birth of her long-awaited child until her mid-thirties is, 'I got distracted.' The fact is, with a killer drive and a brilliant mind, it seems there was always another Everest to climb. Two weeks after completing her PhD in science, Giuliana began studying medicine.

> I was aware [of my ticking biological clock] but it didn't translate into something sensible. Also, I'm a goody-two-shoes. You have a job to do and you do it well. Distracting myself from the path, or even allowing myself to say, 'Well, if I have a child, I'll just drop out of medicine for a year and drop back in' . . . I couldn't do that.

Alongside the pursuit of knowledge and qualification, Giuliana also managed to find and nurture an exceptional love, on which she built the foundations of a wonderful marriage. Both she and Michael wanted children.

'Once I finished my medical degree, I thought, "When I'm an intern or a second year, I'll have a child". Then I thought, "No, I want to do paediatric training, I really should get the exam out of the way".' So she did. 'By then I was 35. I suppose part of me thought, "Oh, my God. I can't leave it any later".' Once Allegra was conceived, though, a few new fears set in:

> I had no doubt it would potentially have a negative effect on my career. It's interesting, because I was really excited about

having this baby, and yet I was really worried about my employability.

Giuliana is quick to point out that there are plenty of role models of women working at the top echelons of medicine, who manage to have a family as well. 'We have these extraordinary women who have children . . . and do these fantastic things. But I suppose I knew I wasn't superwoman in that way.' Nevertheless, as Allegra grew inside her, so did Giuliana's focus on pending motherhood, a focus that soon overrode any career concerns: 'I was really excited about it and eventually I didn't give a toss.' She put the word out that she intended to return from maternity leave on a part-time basis, and set about finding an appropriate position. A job came up and the interview panel had an 'informal' chat with Giuliana. Without hesitation, she was upfront and honest about her intentions to work part-time, for a while at least, while adapting to life with a new baby. The panel didn't need to hear anymore. She was crossed off their list of suitable candidates.

Consequently, after a month of frank consultation with various colleagues and mentors, Giuliana decided to ditch the part-time idea. It just wasn't going to work. The only part-time positions available to her were either not satisfying, involved stepping backwards, or would penalise the continuation of her specialist training. So she returned to the interview panel and formally applied for the full-time job vacancy, explaining that she had changed her mind about the feasibility of part-time work. But it was too late.

I wasn't given the job. Later when I asked why, two of the members of the interview panel said they didn't give me the job because they didn't believe I would work full time. Even though I said I would and addressed that first thing in the interview, because I felt it was really important.

Why is it that a woman's commitment, focus and professionalism are suddenly up for re-evaluation by employers once she becomes a mother? Guiliana stresses that the doctor who did win the position deserved it, but nevertheless it was a harsh blow to become the victim of foggy old patronising prejudices. 'I had worked with these people before,' she says, still a little stunned that this happened. 'I felt that they knew me. But somewhere in people's minds they don't see you as the prospect that you are, because you have children.'

So what does a girl do? In typical style Giuliana pushed on. Determined to prove her point—to both herself and those who said she couldn't or wouldn't do it—she accepted another position and continued to work full time after Allegra was born. A couple of years later, at the age of 39, she achieved a long-held career goal by being awarded the position of Fellow at a major children's hospital. Once ensconsed, and using her experience as a starting point, Giuliana set about trying to fix a cranky, old-fashioned system. Along with a colleague she established a part-time workforce committee in order to attract funding for part-time Fellow positions. A radical move, but a timely one. Funnily enough, the first objection came from a senior female colleague:

> She really struck me when she said, 'You know, I just don't think it's fair to have to work with women who are mothers and who work part-time because basically they are unreliable.' It was an incredible slap in the face because she knew I was a mother. But she expressed what a whole lot of people are thinking. We have to deal with it, not just be pissed off about it, but deal with it.

The cruel irony is that, as you would expect, Giuliana— doubtlessly along with many of her working mother colleagues—is one of the most reliable, efficient and organised people I know.

'Damn organised, incredibly organised!' laughs Giuliana when I point this out. Of course she has to be, because despite a gradual improvement in the availability of part-time work in hospitals, Giuliana has maintained a full-time load:

> One of the younger male consultants in my department, a lovely bloke, has chosen to be at home with his children two days a week and come into work three days a week. And we sometimes laugh about the fact that if people were to look at the two of us and say, 'Who works full time?' he would be perceived as the full-time worker and me as the part-time worker, whereas it's the reverse.

Unlike Giuliana, Rosa has never, ever considered working part-time. I've known this exceptionally talented woman for most of my life, and I've always known her to be ambitious, committed and more than capable of taking on a full load. In fact she thrives on it. At 38, after fifteen years working for one company, it was no surprise to any of her friends that Rosa was at the top of the game. She was confident, successful and had a golden touch for turning a profit. As the head of a sales team, she raised $10 million in revenue in 2004 and the future forecasts were looking even better. Just when she thought her reputation stood her in strong stead, she made the critical career mistake of opting to work from home—one day a week.

It was hardly a big ask, but it had a profound effect on perceptions. Suddenly this workaholic was putting her family first. 'Most people referred to it as my "day off",' she says groaning. 'So I had to correct them and say, "No, it's my working from home day".' In fact, it became her weekly working day from hell:

> I found it the most stressful period in my life. Even though I had two kids at home who were really happy to have me

here, I was running to the computer every two minutes to respond to an email, whereas if I had been in the office I would have been quite happy to have left it for a couple of hours if I was in a meeting.

Rosa says the enormous pressure to prove she could do this, and that the working-from-home option was viable, was more self-imposed than employer-dictated.

I think it's my natural kind of working paranoia or worth ethic, which is diligent, conscientious, hardworking, all those kinds of very nice Catholic schoolgirl things that I have not managed to escape, even in the workplace.

Despite such attributes, and being a dream employee, it counted for little when 'Rosa the sales executive' morphed into 'Rosa the mother of two'. However, the metamorphism was gradual and the souring of perceptions was slow.

Initially Rosa's first pregnancy was not only tolerated, it was celebrated:

I became a bit of a poster girl for people wanting to combine career and family. Because I was the only one who did— anybody who did have a baby at my work didn't return. But that didn't set off alarm bells, I didn't think, 'Gee, this is not going to be a good place to have a baby.' I just thought they were lucky to have well off husbands to support them.

Even so, Rosa was mindful from the outset not to bring her family into the workplace:

I was quite careful not to talk too much about my daughter at work. I worked with a lot of single women under 35 years old. I didn't think they would be interested and I didn't want the fact that I was a mother to change anything about how I was operating or how people saw me.

But eventually it did.

Two weeks after having her second child, Rosa was back in the office for meetings to discuss her next new challenge: a more senior role was going to become vacant and Rosa was in line for the job. However, it was all about perception. Now she had *two* children. Surely her commitment was fading and her attention lagging. Her focus *must* be foggy with family. After a bit of head office discussion, no doubt based on ill-informed assumptions, Rosa was reviewed and revalued. None of it was to do with her bottom-line balance sheets. This wasn't about productivity or profitability. As any woman who has worked in a competitive environment knows, even unfounded perceptions can be powerful persuaders. Yep, Rosa was a goner. She had hit the 'mummy ceiling'.

Needless to say, Rosa didn't get the job. Instead it went to a childless woman, unburdened with family responsibilities. Blind Freddy could see what had happened. So too could Rosa; although for a while she chose not to. Under such circumstances the brew of office gossip and intrigue can spill over. 'I was being told things that probably shouldn't have been told to me. It became quite political,' she says, frowning with the memory. Eventually Rosa had to concede that despite her decade-and-a-half of dedication to the company, she had been passed over because her commitment had been questioned—although never directly to her. Given the mounting evidence, Rosa knew she had a case to argue if she wanted to highlight the discrimination and inherent hypocrisy behind what was occurring:

I could have, but I chose not to. Was it going to be worth it? Was it going to change the fact that I wasn't going to get the job? Again, it was a weighing up of ambition and outrage and family.

So who won? Rosa smiles gently at that. 'Family,' she says as if stating the obvious. Rosa had still taken a hard knock. After what seemed like a lifetime of loyalty, she quit. Within a week she was settled in a new workplace, with a big new desk, a big new title, working for a new company. This time it was to be five days a week—in the office!

One of the things both Giuliana and Rosa say in defence of why they feel they *should* be able to combine motherhood and full-on careers is that they know they're not alone. It's the hoary old 'other women manage to do this, so why can't I?', which of course is useful fodder for a bit of self-flagellation. Rosa says she clung to a belief that juggling motherhood and a busy job would work by reminding herself that 'millions of women around the world do this every day and everyone survives'. Although she's quick to add:

> But, prior to having my first baby, all the ideas, all my thoughts about how things would happen and how I would manage were made in the context of not having a child, so essentially it was a matter of having no idea.

Naturally, in ignorant bliss everything and anything is possible. With an ever-increasing number of mothers in the workforce, combining roles should not only be possible, it should be *workable*—or so the 'pre-baby' logic goes.

According to the 2001 Census there are 1.2 million working women in Australia who have dependent children under the age of 15.[3] Almost 480 000 kids aged 0 to 4 have working mums.[4] Like Rosa and Giuliana, around one in five women with children of pre-school age or younger work full time, and more than a third work part-time.[5] The ranks of part-time working mothers quickly swell with each year their children get older. Yet, despite the clear preference for this choice, part-time work arrangements nevertheless continue to be a major stumbling block and a viciously vexed issue for Australian women.

Dr Louise Watson, an academic and director of an education research network, is unequivocal about the need to 'hide' the fact that she works part-time. 'There is just that assumption that people who work part-time, even though they work the same hours, possibly harder and more efficiently than full-timers, don't deserve anything,' she says. Louise sees this in terms of a backlash against the rapid rise in the number of women in the workforce.

> It's the idea that women can join the workforce but they join on [male] terms. If you're a token male, you're accepted. So if you don't have photos of your family on your desk, or don't tell anyone you're going home to cook dinner, if you act neutered, act as if you haven't got children, then you're seen as professional.

In another spin on the 'un-sex me now!' mantra, Louise says, 'Women have to face really hard choices. If they want to be taken seriously at work, they have to renounce their family, or outsource a lot of the caring.' It is the 'outsourcing' that brings many mothers unstuck.

Louise began her PhD six weeks before her first child was born. She was, by her own admission, fiercely ambitious and academically competitive. After three months' maternity leave, the plan was to put the baby in child care and get back to full-time work and study. When that time came, suddenly her 'mother buttons' were pushed:

All my instincts went against it. I didn't realise there was all this emotional stuff with children. I thought that everyone puts their kids in child care and works full time. 'Other people do it. I should be able to do it.' But I hated it and my daughter hated it. I struggled with a huge amount of guilt.

By the time her second child was born, Louise and her husband had given up on the pain of outsourcing the care of their children. It wasn't working for either of them, so they decided to get a nanny. 'She was gorgeous and the kids loved her.' But the guilt and frustration only worsened for Louise:

I just felt that I was missing out on motherhood. In effect, the nanny met their emotional needs. I felt quite emotionally cut off from them. In a sense, I think it confused them if I stayed home too often or tried to get too involved. I was sort of interested in them and I liked them but I didn't feel tied to them.

After living like this for a year and a half, both Louise and her husband paused from their frantic, full-time jobs to re-assess. Neither liked what they saw:

We had high-profile, high-status jobs. We had the cars and the travel and it just seemed a really stupid life to be living when you had two little children who just wanted you to be at home with them and you wanted to be with them.

So they both made a critical career choice . . . they quit, to take up part-time academic jobs at a university in another city. While it was an equal solution to a shared problem, Louise nevertheless had to battle hard to make this choice work for her.

I found it very difficult to let go of my job, my status. My ego was much more tied up with my work than his was. There was a big 'identity' issue for me. Especially because I was in a new city and no-one knew me, and I just felt . . . I felt just like a mother: low self-esteem, lack of confidence. I found it very hard, very hard to feel like a person.

So where does such a drive come from? And why is feeling 'just like a mother', such a rotten ride? Louise takes a deep sigh before answering this. It's painfully difficult:

I think it's partly the values of the society that we live in, that you're brought up to believe you have to become something, be something. The whole career drive comes from thinking there's something better around the corner and that you're nothing if you're not meeting the next challenge.

'So why isn't motherhood seen as that challenge?' I ask.
'Because it is so humbling, I suspect.'
'Humbling?'

If you have children late, or in your thirties, you're so used to being in control of your life, and motherhood is all about coping with not being in control. I always found there was at least one time during the day when I would feel absolutely hopeless and helpless.

Clearly for a woman who can whip out a PhD, take on a senior role in the public service, and establish a lucrative commercial research network for a major university, feeling 'hopeless and helpless' at the hands of a toddler is pretty confronting. However, Louise is obviously made of tough stuff. She has managed to bring up three children and remains firmly committed to working part time, for the sake of her family. But it is a hard choice, and one that needs a regular wax and polish to stop the rust setting in. 'I still have my antenna out for the next opportunity and I find it very, very hard not to pursue work. It's very hard to say no,' she says.

At this point Louise glares down at her coffee mug, as if some fountain of wisdom might spring from the dregs. Here is a woman hot with the sort of talent and ability that score big time in the world of professional work. There, where the parameters of success, achievement and victory are clearly drawn, women like Louise thrive. At home, the accolades, pats on the back and congratulations are lost in the murky mess of motherhood. Understandably Louise, like many women, is torn between both worlds. When I ask if she ever feels any resentment against childless women in the workforce her answer is immediate: 'No, I wouldn't be a mother if I did, or I wouldn't be this sort of mother.' Her face opens and lightens as she smiles broadly, looks me in the eye and says, 'Motherhood is pretty great too. So I wouldn't want my life to be different now.'

Rex I love 'ya chips!

Anne Marie wouldn't mind her life being different. She'd like it to be a bit more organised. But that's unlikely. In her household, with husband David and their two gorgeous little girls, Lucinda aged five and Emma aged three, life is a daily circus. It's wild, it's fun, it's loud—very loud—and it's eccentric. Even her goldfish are eccentric. Not to mention the multiple personalities of her cats. It's a household built on the strongest foundations of love and there is always a warm welcome, plenty of room to stay and a quick knock-up feast for anyone who drops by. Consequently plenty of people do. Me included.

Anne Marie and I have been best friends for over thirty years, and we've ridden the waves of most of life's dramas together. Yet our experiences are vastly different. I always knew Anne Marie would have children. She'd laid out the plan when we were kids. Like many of us, Anne Marie had trouble finding the right man, having wasted years with the wrong one. In the end, I found him for her and arranged a 'business meeting' between the two of them. The business of falling in love began that very night at the Sheraton Hotel in Brisbane. I know this because Anne Marie rang me in the middle of it all. And she rang her mum. And I rang my mum to tell her she could stop praying to Saint Jude— patron saint of hopeless causes—Anne Marie had finally found her man.

But the thing about Anne Marie is the extraordinary ease with which she made the transition from senior manager and boss, to home, hearth and full-time motherhood. She takes great delight in seeing little triangles of vegemite toast being squashed into her briefcase, and stuff like that. Unlike Dr Louise Watson, Anne Marie couldn't wait to chuck in her big job and push her business suits to the back of the wardrobe.

Now, at forty, and after a few years of part-time positions and plenty of full-time mothering, Anne Marie is ready to take a serious plunge back into the workforce and resurrect her stalled career. A move I always expected. What I didn't expect or anticipate was to witness my smart, successful, accomplished and highly qualified friend open the classifieds and eye off low-level jobs well beneath her abilities. This comes from a girl who once had 'Director' after her name, and was riding high at the senior level of the public service. Now, having moved house and family to another state, she is grateful for a two-day-a-week, pen-pushing gig that pays a miserly portion of what she used to command. The fact is, after being out of the fast pace of full-time corporate work for so long, Anne Marie's confidence has plummeted and her contacts have dwindled. Dabbling in lower level part-time positions while her children were toddlers has only served to undermine her sense of career achievement and mess up her CV. That alone is enough to worry me. Then we had a conversation like this:

'Virginia you'll never guess what your best friend has just done. Are you sitting down?' Anne Marie is in full flight. It's Friday night. I'm in Canberra; feet up on my desk in an empty newsroom with a tumbler of cheap 'social club' plonk in one hand, the phone in the other. Anne Marie is in Melbourne; a long-stemmed wine glass in one hand, the other swishing detergent around the kitchen sink, the phone tucked under her chin.

A small interlude for a drum roll of clanging pots follows.

'I think I've found myself a new career. Now, just wait for it . . .'

'I'm waiting. What?'

'Your best friend has just been on the . . . you're not going to believe this, but I have just starred on the *Rex Hunt Show*!'

'Rex Hunt. You mean that fishing show?'

'Exactly.'

'On TV?'

'No. The bloody radio. You *do* know who Rex Hunt is, don't you?'

'Yes, that fat fishing bloke, who kisses fish.'

'Not fat, Virginia. Well fed. Anyway, I think Rex has got the hots for me. We really had something going . . .'

'Why on earth were you talking to Rex Hunt?'

'Well, I'd fed and bathed the girls and while I was waiting for David to come home from work, I was listening to Rex on the radio . . .'

'Anne Marie, why would you be listening to Rex Hunt? You live in inner-city Melbourne, nowhere near water and you don't even like fishing.'

'I didn't ring up about fishing. I rang about his flashy fish 'n' chips shop down in Port Melbourne.'

'Why?'

'To tell him I really like his chips . . . well actually "love" is what I said, "Rex I love 'ya chips".'

This was too much.

'And you know what he said Virginia?'

'What? "I love 'em too?"'

'No . . . He said . . .' Anne Marie could barely spill this one out she was laughing so much. 'He said, "Thanks Anne Marie. Gee, I need people like you working for me".'

'And you know what I said?' Anne Marie was triumphant.

'What? Thanks Rex, when do I start?'

'I said, "Rex, I don't want to *sell* your chips, I just want to *eat* 'em!"'

We both buckled over, hooting with laughter. Neither of us could say anything for a few moments.

'See, Virginia, see what my life has come to?'

'And all this from a woman who used to jointly run a well-oiled state government department, was responsible for a large staff and was in control of a sizeable budget.'

'Ah yes,' a fake sigh of whimsy came from Anne Marie. 'You forgot the bit about the big office, large whiteboard and very, very big leather chair. Now look at me.' The whimsy again. 'Now I'm responsible for a department of three. Two little girls, a husband who is always at work, and two cats—one with schizophrenia. And two bloody fish that stare at me from their algae-infested bowl every time I walk past.'

'Anne Marie I don't think fish can stare.'

'Speaking of fish, what do you think of that job offer from Rex? How'd I look serving fish and chips?'

'Gorgeous.'

'I'm in! Hey, Virginia?'

'What?'

'Do you think Rex will call me back after his show?'

The postscript to this episode of Anne Marie's story is that no, Rex didn't ring back. And no, she isn't serving fish and chips. However, we are still workshopping her plummeting confidence and the emotional value of purchasing a smart, new business suit and changing her hairdo.

Meet Maya—she folds underpants . . .

When she first went to the Bar and set up office in the plush surrounds of Melbourne's Owen Dixon East Chambers, on its famous tenth floor, Maya Rozner had one clear ambition in mind: she wanted to be a QC. And why not? This extraordinary motor mouth of a woman, who probes and jabs at each thought before leaping onto the next, has an intellect that would rival any QC. She is a barrister of a rare breed. Most of her life Maya has been a rising star, catapulted from one victorious challenge to the next. But right now, surrounded by piles of washing on a kitchen table cluttered with children's gadgets, dishes and half-opened packets of food, I can see why Maya the Great has become Maya the Grateful.

'Yes,' she thumps the table between us, 'I wanted to be a QC. That's what I was working towards. That was my ambition.' Then as she throws her arms wide up into the air, as if petitioning the Gods, she adds, 'But now, I'm just happy for someone to give me a brief!'

It's not that ambition has died, far from it. It's just that Maya's life has taken a dramatic turn since she made the difficult choice to hang up the horsehair wig for a while to concentrate on being a full-time mum to her two young children. Life is now consumed by domesticity. The mundane madness of it, though, is sucking Maya dry:

> I wake up, I pick up the dirty underpants off the floor, I put them in the washing machine. I take them off the line, bring them inside, fold them, take them upstairs and put them in the cupboard. And I wake up the next day and pick up the same pair of underpants off the floor. It's the most thankless, God-awful existence. I never wanted this role. I hate housework. I hate being at home. It's completely toxic. I went from being the primary breadwinner in the household to being the person responsible for doing the domestic duties. I'm completely affronted and incredibly angry at the thought that this is expected of me. I'm a liberated intelligent woman who's used to working in a male-dominated industry and here I am picking up underpants off the floor, and I'm miserable! What's going on here?

The beaut thing about Maya is that she doesn't mince her words. She says what she thinks and she thinks a lot. In fact she doesn't stop thinking. Beautiful, gorgeous Maya with her wide, dark-chocolate eyes and lush black hair is an exotic mix of Israeli and Polish heritage. Just when I'm thinking what a formidable and intimidating barrister she must be, one of her two children appears from under the makeshift tent pitched in the family room and comes to her with arms outstretched. It's five-year-old Aurelia. In that moment I see the full force of Maya's focus shift, wholly and utterly, onto this child. She holds her daughter's little face in her hands and envelops her with gentle love, talking to her softly. She squats down, sweeps her up into her arms and they dance around the kitchen for a moment, oblivious of me, the piles of washing, the dishes or the mess. They sing the words of a song I can't understand and then, when her daughter is sated with attention, she disappears back under the tent. Maya looks at me, as if suddenly remembering I'm sitting there. She slides back down onto a kitchen chair and says:

> My daughter is going to be a preppy this year. It's a new thing, a new experience. And I'm seeing it through her eyes and thinking, 'Oh my God! Who is going to be there to talk to her about her day at 3.30 p.m.? Who's going to be there to hear the little Greek song that she has learnt? Can I divest that role to somebody else, or do I still want to try and have my cake and eat it too?'

This is a difficult time for Maya. She's just turned forty. She has two adorable children, Aurelia and her two-year-old brother Zephyrine, and a devoted husband, and she's also hungry to revive her career. But how? The work of a top-end barrister can mean sixteen-hour days, sometimes for weeks at a stretch during a big case. 'I love working like that,' Maya stresses. 'I'm an adrenalin junkie. That is my ultimate.' And she's not kidding. Before 'dropping' her first baby, as she puts it, she ran a highly public medical negligence case against a doctor accused of bungling a forceps delivery. It was a stinking hot Melbourne summer. 'I was sitting in this unrenovated house, in my bra and undies, with holes in the ceiling, my laptop on the kitchen table and the sweat pouring off me. It was just bizarre,' she recalls. But she did it. She finished the submissions on her due date. The case was a corker. And the baby was beautiful.

Initially, Maya's return to the Bar after her first baby went well. Her husband Alex, a junior solicitor at the time, was clearly proud of his brilliant and highly regarded wife. He was supportive, encouraging and very domesticated—more so than Maya. They got a nanny who doted on their daughter and took charge of organising the household. For a while life ran smoothly. Maya says her career was 'blossoming' and her husband was also kicking goals, 'Then I buggered it all by getting pregnant with the second one.'

Juggling one child with two busy careers was just manageable, but throwing another child into the mix made it impossible. By the time the second baby was due, Maya's husband Alex was heading towards partnership at his law firm and regularly clocking twelve and fourteen hour days. In fact, he almost missed getting her to hospital for the second birth as he was held up at work. Both Maya and Alex knew there was only room for one 'star' career in a household with a toddler and a new baby. When Zephyrine was born Maya chose to relinquish any notion of returning to work for at least a year. That's when things got ugly. 'I got depressed, very depressed,' she says. Eventually Maya found herself battling against the powerful tide of resentment. 'It was huge, huge,' she says:

> I was sending Alex off in the mornings and sometimes he couldn't come home until 9 o'clock at night. All of a sudden, this was his dream. His career was at a very seminal point and I was watching mine go down the toilet. I was sitting here thinking, 'People are never going to brief me again'. And it shocked me to my very core. I hadn't anticipated it.

It's important to pause in Maya's story and point out—if this hasn't already been made clear—that like all the mothers I've interviewed who have struggled with this 'brewing resentment' as they watch *their* careers take a hefty pounding while their partners' careers continue largely undisrupted, none of them, Maya included, lay the blame at the feet of the men they love. Nor do any of them, Maya included, harbour a jot of resentment against the children they adore. Rather, it's just the immense frustration of 'having it all' swiped from under you when you weren't looking.

> I knew my life would change but I didn't think that I was going to have to give up what I wanted in life and what I was enjoying, which is my work. I didn't think it was a choice of one or the other. That never occurred to me.

The choosing only gets harder. All the buttons are pressed and Maya is now feeling torn from another direction:

> I'm getting an enormous push from my mother now that Zephyrine is two-and-a-half. She says, 'Get a nanny. Go back to work' because that's something that she really would have wanted for herself. My mother never had a career. She puts pressure on me because I am the fulfilment of her career ambition.

The pressure is clearly weighing heavily. Maya knows her mother is proud of her, and that she has trouble understanding why her exceptionally talented daughter would not push on and upward in a career that her mother could only have dreamt about. Maya's mum is quick to remind her that she spent seven years at university, succeeded in a well-respected and tough profession and then went on to 'nail it' by becoming a barrister. 'She can see for me it's been a great progression and to turn my back on that, for her . . . she just doesn't "get it".'

Maya is well aware that it's not only the emotional pull towards her children that is thwarting her career, it is also the sheer practicality of it all. 'How am I going to juggle and keep all the balls in the air?' she asks, looking at me expectantly. I have to remind her that I'm the wrong person to ask, as I wouldn't have a clue. 'But how am I going to do it?' she persists, as if an answer might miraculously present itself right here in front of us. 'How am I going to try to fool everyone into thinking that I'm a supermum?' The best I can do at this stage is shrug, which is next to useless under the circumstances because I can see this is a painful struggle, and these are serious questions. Then Maya drops her voice and for perhaps the first time in hours, slows right down. It's as if she has just realised something. What she says next shocks me, in its twisted, dark and brooding sadness.

'I'm heading for a big crash,' she says staring hard at me. 'I will make a mistake. It's inevitable. I will make a big mistake in my career.' I ask her if she means a mistake in the choice she makes. 'No, no, no,' she fires back. This is about making a major, irreversible mistake at work, when she returns to the law and her role as a barrister. 'I'll be too tired,' she says, 'And I'll overlook something.'

'Why?' I ask her. 'What makes you think you'll make a big mistake and crash?'

Maya looks at me as if the answer surely must be obvious. 'Because,' she says, 'I will be trying to do it all.'

Helen's corner office at Lollipop's

Frankly, the office chairs at Lollipop's Playland suck. They're tiny, weenie things, big enough only for a toddler's bottom. And the wobbly plastic desks aren't much better, but Helen Vatsikopoulos couldn't care less. Sure it's makeshift, but it works.

Any Monday afternoon you'll find Helen in a far corner of Lollipop's Playland with notepad, files, mobile phone and electronic gadgets cluttering the surface of one of these baby tables, while she presses her phone's earpiece hard into one ear and her finger in the other. She could be talking to someone in Japan or Hong Kong; today it's probably Jakarta. It's likely she's lining up a satellite link for a television interview with an Indonesian academic to talk about that country's presidential elections. For a moment her focus is a million miles away from the hoards of noisy kids playing around her, until one of them tugs at her.

Helen has two children, Andreas aged five and Clio aged two-and-a-half. They love going to Lollipop, and so does she—but not for the same reason. For the kids it's a giant, noisy, colourful playcentre not far from their home in Sydney's Bondi Beach, with dozens of kids, clowns and distraction. For Helen it's a 'time-out' haven where, despite the deafening squeals of kids, she can set up a makeshift office on her 'non-working' days. She looks at me a little stunned that I'm not familiar with Lollipop's.

'All working mothers know about this. You pay $25, you enter, the door is closed and they can't escape. Then I find a little table in the corner and get to work. I can stay there for three hours and prepare for the next day.'

Helen, at age 43, is one of Australia's most accomplished television journalists with a long list of awards to her name, including the industry's highest accolade—the Walkley Award for outstanding international reporting. Hers is a stellar career in which she broke new ground. Until Helen's arrival on the scene, no other Australian woman had consistently reported for television news and current affairs from such a wide range of international locations and dangerous hotspots. Helen was everywhere—which never really surprised me. From the outset she couldn't wait to claim the globe.

Helen's arrival in the ABC's Melbourne newsroom—back in the mid-1980s when I was a cadet reporter—sent ripples of expectation through the station. She was different from the rest of us. Not only because she was beautiful, Greek and exotic, but she seemed electrically charged. She was hungry and impatient. Her star was destined to rise rapidly—and it did. After making a name for herself at the ABC she went on to become a powerful journalistic force at SBS where she clocked up nearly a dozen years. In a blink she was in Rwanda, doing a piece to camera surrounded by human mounds of dead bodies. Then she was in India during the assassination of Rajiv Gandhai . . . then Kashmir, Taiwan, Yugoslavia, Russia, Azerbaijan, Cambodia and so it went on. For over a decade Helen's feet barely touched homeground, before she was off again.

At SBS she presented various news shows, eventually becoming the face of *Dateline*—the network's flagship current affairs program. As host, Helen continued to travel the world, reporting on international affairs. Perhaps not surprisingly, along the way she fell in love with another award-winning, international journalist, Mark Corcoran. They married a few years later and, yes, they literally passed each other in the dark of night for years, as stories broke around the world. 'In fact I always put work before my life, my relationship,' says Helen. Fortunately her husband understood.

Although they both wanted children, Helen delayed, and delayed. 'I knew that I would be giving up a high-flying career and the travel and excitement of this sort of job. That's why I held off for as long as I could get away with it.' Helen was lucky. At 39 years of age she gave birth to a beautiful boy, Andreas. Naturally both new parents were thrilled and for a while it seemed life had blessed them. Helen knew that her role as a globetrotting reporter would have to be put on hold, for some time at least, because travelling on the road with a baby would be impossible. Travelling *without* her baby would be worse. As the show's host, she could see her way clear to remain office-based and work part-time. With that arrangement in mind she took a minimum maternity leave of three months:

I was even nervous about taking three months off, which I guess has a lot to do with my upbringing, coming from an ethnic family where you've got to work, work, work, otherwise they might throw you out of the country.

Well, she wasn't thrown out of the country.

Two weeks before she was due to return Helen was told she was no longer required in the role as presenter of *Dateline*. 'I have to say it was the biggest wake-up call in my life,' she says. At the time the story of the ousted Helen Vatsikopoulos 'on maternity leave' ran for days. 'Was she pushed, or did she jump?' was the question the media asked. It was a question Helen refused to answer, despite journalists knocking on her door and photographers hanging around outside her home. Throughout the ordeal she chose to remain silent. 'I was in shock,' she says. SBS insisted she still had a job as an on-the-road reporter with the program.

At one stage, during the height of the media fray, a network executive told me over lunch that Helen had chosen to 'stay at home and raise her child'. Eventually Helen agreed to the issuing of an SBS press release that stated she had indeed chosen the 'stay at home' mothering option.

After a period of long service leave, Helen quit SBS. She was readily snapped up by the ABC, where she arranged a job-share deal with another senior journalist. For a while life and work ran smoothly, and eventually, she had another baby.

'I thought, "Bugger it. I am going to have another child and I'll just soldier on",' she says, laughing now at her own fierce determination. But wasn't she afraid of the risk to her career?

'Nothing is forever,' smiles Helen, obviously older and wiser about the fickle nature of a high-profile career. 'You can't place your ambitions in one basket because eventually someone is going to come and tip it all out.' However, her hard-working Greek mother wasn't quite so philosophical:

> When I confirmed the second pregnancy, I told my mother and there was silence. 'Don't you want to go back to work?' she eventually said. And I remember thinking, 'I can't believe my mother said that'. I think she probably thought, 'It's impossible now. She won't be able to do it'.

Helen smiles with the memory of that response, because in a sense, her mother was right:

> I didn't think it would totally exhaust me, or that it would be such a balancing act and that in the end the person who would miss out is me, because it's true. I have missed out on everything. Of course I have my beautiful children and I have a very good and stable marriage and I have a really good part-time job . . .

So what is she missing out on?

> Time for myself. I work three days a week. I have the children seven days a week, but there is no time for me. You miss out on feeding your soul basically, or enriching yourself. In order to make myself still valuable here in the workplace so that I don't have a problem with missing deadlines . . . I'm going to go home tonight and stay up until four in the morning writing this goddamn script so it is there on their desk at nine o'clock in the morning. So you can't have your arrangement— your choice—affect your career and your career prospects, and the children as well.

Like many working mothers, it's Helen who keeps the household rolling and all the family balls juggling in the air. Therefore it's *her* working day and *her* deadline that is thrown into chaos if any one of those balls loses its spin and crashes to the ground. That's when she earns her stripes in the 'bad mothers' club':

> Your child is sick, even though you've doped them up to the eyeballs in the morning and hope they don't notice [at the childcare centre]. And then you get the phone call saying, 'Your child is sick, she's got a temperature', and you think 'Bad mother! Bad mother!' And you say, pretending, 'I didn't know that. When did she get this?' So you have to go and pick them up and that's when it all falls apart.

Not even the hefty payment of $20 000 a year in childcare fees can buy immunity from the realities of life. As Helen says, sometimes it just all ends in tears—hers:

> I had an episode a few weeks ago where it all just got too much. My son couldn't believe it and he said, 'Mummy, grownups don't cry'. Then he hugged and kissed me and went off and made me a present, a Lego contraption. It looked like a hammer. 'Yeah', I thought, 'I'll just go and bash something'.

When I ask Helen how having children has affected her husband's journalism career, she is uncharacteristically blunt: 'A big fat zero, I would think.' However, she is quick to concede, 'I think that he suffers emotionally.' Mark recently returned from an exhaustive seven weeks working in Yemen, Somalia and Eritrea, to find two little people sitting under a Christmas tree waiting for him. It was Christmas day and his children had refused to open their presents until daddy was home:

> So it hurts him, but there isn't enough room for two high-flyers in the family. I think it's an unwritten, unspoken contract. I'm the one who had the baby so I guess I'm the

one with the nurturing, biological genes perhaps. There is no point in having both of us at home wishing we had better careers.

While that all makes sense, I'm nevertheless a little startled to hear her say it. This is a woman who, along with nearly all the women I've worked with in television, appeared to identify herself primarily by her work. Her success and the plum roles she won were worn as a personal badge of pride. So how does she define herself now?

'A woman with two children who works when the work is available,' she recently told a journalist. When I remind her of this public comment, asking if she really meant it, Helen laughs so loud someone in a nearby office pops his head in to see what's so funny. 'It's true!' she says, slapping her knee.

'But what about all those years of hard slog, all those awards and all those runs on the board? What about all that hard-earned experience?' I ask. Helen shrugs, still smiling:

In the end, does it count for much? I don't know. My husband has said to me, 'Don't expect to get any of those high-flying jobs any more, Helen, because they know you've got kids and they know you've got a husband who travels.' And I think, 'Hang on. They can't do that'. But deep down, [I know] it's the truth.

'Hang on!' Now it's me doing the protesting. 'This isn't the way it's meant to be. This is not what we wanted for ourselves. Nor is it what our mothers fought for—on our behalf.'

'It's interesting you bring mothers into it,' Helen responds:

I've always wondered, 'How did my mother do this?' Am I just being precious? Am I having some sort of middle-class anxiety attack? Why is it my mother and her generation didn't complain? They were brought up to expect that love will fulfill them. We were brought up to expect that career would fulfill us.

'In other words,' I butt in, 'What you're saying is you can't have it all!'

'No bullshit!' laughs Helen.

The mummy backlash

Even if it had been real, equality would have been a poor substitute for liberation; fake equality is leading women into double jeopardy.

Germaine Greer, *The Whole Woman*, 1999

On an individual level, women are looking for liberation from judgement of their choices . . . Some of this liberation will only happen in the short term if women can individually understand and then refuse the impossible model of 'intensive mothering' and instead opt for reasonable personal standards.

Barbara Pocock, *The Work/Life Collision*, 2003

Anne Marie roars with laughter when I read the above quote from Barbara Pocock. '*Reasonable* personal standards! Lord, *any* personal standard will do! Who cares whether it's *reasonable* or not. Just give me back some *standard*s!' It's not that Anne Marie's standards have dropped. They're just temporarily on 'maternity leave'. She assures me they're there somewhere—

possibly squashed under her three-year-old's playdough, or put out to soak with her five-year-old's Barbie pants, whose hot pink colour is slyly penetrating the pile of white socks and running shorts swimming in days-old soapy goo. But hey, it's been a busy week.

Her husband had to jet off at short notice to Singapore. She's had to prepare a presentation for a full-day training workshop she's running tomorrow. On the weekend, she and husband David are heading off to London for a week of meeting and greeting board members of an international firm trying to poach him for a new job. David is flat out with his own presentations and Anne Marie's mother is on her back about buying new clothes for the trip, insisting she grow up and bypass Witchery and Sportsgirl. No wonder Anne Marie rolls her eyes at the suggestion of simply opting for *reasonable* personal standards.

Professor Pocock is right, but even the many, many mothers who know she is right have tremendous trouble heeding the message. Maya, who finds housework 'toxic' and folds underpants while she is trying to resurrect her career as a barrister, is flummoxed over the 'standards' issue:

> I'm not going to sit around and make the model house in the way our mothers felt they were duty bound to do. Mothers before us were considered a failure if you walked into their house and the house was a mess.

That said, Maya is the first to admit she feels the heavy weight of judgment from both her mother and mother-in-law when she allows the domestic 'standards' to slide. 'Both those women are outraged at the thought that my husband Alex might have to iron his own shirts because I do not iron. They're horrified,' she says, almost with disbelief at the scent of a double standard. Mothers like Maya's actively encourage their smart, successful, high-earning

daughters to get back into the workforce after having children—
'Get a nanny', she said—and yet they look for their own domestic
standards and pride to be replicated. It's a double whammy.

Rosa, on the other hand, doesn't need a mother's pressure to
make her feel bad about slipped standards on the household or
family front. She is her own harshest critic: 'You can't have a
fantastic-looking house. You can't have kids and ironed clothes
all the time, the gourmet meals, the entertaining—it's impossible.'
Yet, boy, does she try! Like many successful women, Rosa seeks
success in all endeavours, even though it might mean running
herself into the ground. For her—and thousands like her—the
tedious mantra of 'having it all' means 'doing it all', which Rosa
says is akin to making a 'martyr' of herself. Martyrdom, mind
you, is something she is prepared to embrace if it means things
get done in the right order and with the right outcome. 'Doing
it all,' Rosa says, 'means that everything happens the way I like
it to.' Yet not even a control freak can control every aspect of a
working mother's life. Inevitably, at times it all goes belly up and
the prewritten—or imagined—script doesn't go according to
plan—anyone's plan.

After Rosa had her first baby and returned to work she was
plagued with guilt. 'I was abandoning her,' she says. Even though
her daughter was safely in the care of her doting grandmother,
Rosa was wracked with feeling 'selfish'. The stress wore her down:
'I was being a very inattentive mother and also not a very good
employee.' Sadly, Rosa is far from alone.

Pocock says, 'Australian motherhood is suffering an epidemic
of guilt.'[1] After hearing *every* mother I interviewed talk about
the 'guilt' they feel, I'm beginning to think it must be a key
ingredient in breast milk. Mothers are sloshing around in the
stuff by the time the toddler becomes a pre-schooler. You only
need to turn sideways to the woman sitting at the desk next to

you to hear about it. 'Woman's guilt does not seem to abate,' says Pocock.[2]

'Guilt?' says Giuliana, 'Gosh, guilt is a natural state for me. I don't know a guiltless state. I'm Catholic, Italian and I'm a mother, please! Guilt is my middle name.' Without any prompting Giuliana launches into a tirade of her failures as a mother, despite the fact that I've just canvassed her many outstanding achievements as a doctor. 'I will never forget,' she says, 'Just the other day when I was running late again to drop Allegra off at kinder— I'm always late—and she said, "Mummy, please don't make me lucky last again".' Giuliana screws up her face as if wincing with the pain. I remind her that all mothers run late.

'My mother was the worst; she's still running late to pick me up from ballet class on Tuesday 4 May 1976! I know she'll get there. Eventually.'

But Giuliana isn't hearing me now. 'Sometimes,' she says as she stares out the window, 'I sit down and I think of my three jobs—i.e. being a mum, a doctor, a partner–wife–lover—and I think I do a crap job at all of them because I'm stretching everything.'

Of course I can't imagine Giuliana being 'crap' at anything, but the thing is . . . she really believes she is. Worst of all is when she feels she's being a 'crap' mother. 'Crap' being an entry card into the 'bad mothers' club' that most of the working mothers I've interviewed are secret members of.

When pressed on what constitutes a 'proper mother', Giuliana says it's all about having time. She hates the way her working week, with an early morning start each day, means she wakes up singing the 'hurry up' song. She says her daughter hears the same tune each day. It goes like this: 'Got to get up. Got to hurry. Mummy's boss will get mad if she's late. Come on, hurry, hurry, hurry. Eat breakfast in the car. Hurry, hurry, hurry.' Most mothers know the chorus. In fact 1.2 million Australian women probably know this tune, because that's how many mothers with children under the age of fifteen are juggling work and family demands.[3]

Most mothers don't wait—or have the luxury to wait—until their children are settled into school before they plunge back into the workforce. Over a third of new mothers return to work before their child turns one. According to Pocock by the time their youngest child is two, more than half are back working. By the time that child is a pre-schooler, aged between four and five years old, 59 per cent of mothers are juggling work and family demands.[4] 'Juggle' being the operative word. As Australian author and academic Susan Maushart points out, 'juggling' carries all the connotations of some kind of 'trickery'. Why has motherhood become a clever performance that requires the extraordinary dexterity and quick nimble gear shift of a juggler? Whatever happened to the more gentle and blended phrase of 'combining motherhood and work'?

Well, for a start, juggling has clearly become the rule, not the exception. By 2001, according to Australian Census data, 61 per cent of mothers with dependent children under the age of nineteen were in the paid workforce. Since then every labour force indicator has continued to suggest that proportion is increasing, not decreasing. Yet you would never have gleaned a sense of that when listening to the Federal Treasurer Peter Costello back in mid-2004 prior to the Budget announcement. In an interview with journalist Laurie Oaks, on Channel 9's *Sunday* program, the treasurer repeatedly referred to '*Mums*' who want to do '*a bit of part-time work*'. By his third reference to '*Mums*' who want to '*do a day or two's work*' you could be forgiven for thinking the mothers of Australia are incidental to the labour market, and that '*Mums*' are quite happy to pick up the office scraps, doing '*a bit of part-time work*' on the side for kicks.

The fact that women's participation in the workforce has skyrocketed since the mid-1960s, and that we now have over four million women in the labour market, seems to have eluded not only the treasurer, but possibly the rest of the populace.[5] And the fact that more mothers work than mothers who don't is part of the reason the so-called 'juggle' is the norm and not the exception.[6] The juggle isn't the only problem, though. It's *how* mothers juggle that lead many, like Giuliana, to think that they are 'crap' at everything.

Australians are working harder and longer. The standard full-time 35-hour week is becoming something of an oddity. By 2002, the average working week had increased to 44 hours for full-time workers. The biggest growth, according to the Australian Bureau of Statistics, is in the proportion of people working between 50 and 59 hours per week, which, incidentally, goes *against* the trend in other OECD countries where work hours have seen little recent change, or are in fact reducing.[7]

A report by the International Labour Organization released late-2004 found that Australians now work twice as hard as most Europeans, with one in five of us working at least 50 hours a week. On the Continent they must think we're crazy. In Greece for example, less than one in every sixteen workers put in 50 hours or more; in the Netherlands it's less than one in twenty workers.[8] Perhaps this will come as no great surprise to many of the Australian women clocking on extra hours at both ends of the day, but the proportion of women who work 50 hours or more has almost *doubled* over the past couple of decades.[9] What will certainly come as no surprise to all working mothers with dependent children at home is the disparity between their working week and that of their partner.

Women, 'regardless of their participation in paid work', still do the lion's share of housework—a whopping 65 per cent.[10]

Professor Pocock says on average women do 33 hours a week of housework, child care and shopping compared to men's 17 hours.[11] On aggregate, the average mother in a full-time job is clocking up a 77-hour *working* week. No wonder they feel 'crap'!

'I'm a feminist,' says Helen Vatsikopoulos, 'because I *chose* to work and I also *chose* to have a family.' She pauses, and I can hear a 'but' coming. 'But I'm having a tough time of it. I wish that the women of my generation lobbied harder. I think we need to, on the homefront, bring men into the child-rearing job as well.' When I interrupt her to say I thought that had already happened, Helen's answer is fast and flat. 'It hasn't.' She then repeats the modern woman's mantra: 'What I need is a wife.'

At a distance, the lack of gender equity on the domestic homefront among most of the mothers I've interviewed is curious, if not a little disturbing. It's curious in that all these smart, sensible, liberated women insist they have great, loving and supportive partners. So what's going on? Giuliana says it's obvious.

'I think women have to recognise that they behave in a particular way . . . *because* they are women. To me there are intrinsic differences,' she says. Although she works longer hours than her husband Michael, Giuliana says she takes on most of the domestic 'organisational' issues, which she insists is more about her wanting to be in control, than it is about Michael not pitching in. A sentiment echoed by Rosa, whose need for order—and a possible predisposition for perfection—means she willingly takes on the heavier load.

'I have a supportive husband who will do anything. He'll do the shopping, but I can't stand him doing the shopping because he won't buy the things I like and the brands I like. So I do it.'

It's an ongoing battle over priorities. Recently Giuliana's husband spent a rare day off work playing with his daughter, making chocolate crackles and pancakes. When Giuliana arrived on the scene after a heavy day of hospital rounds, she admits her first thought was, 'Oh shit. Now I have to do more work and clean up after them.' The paradox is not lost on her.

'Who's making the better choice?' she asks. Knowing that I'm not going to answer, she goes on: '*He's* making the better choice, because he's had a really quality day with his daughter doing nice things, and maybe I should do that more often.' Then she adds, 'But the house has got to keep functioning and you just can't live with shit.'

We may be a generation of house renovators, but we clearly could do with some major work on our models of motherhood and fatherhood and our models of work. Professor Pocock suggests we've been duped by a range of 'cover stories' that distort and obscure the truth about our lives. These stories include suggestions that:

> . . . domestic work is now shared and the egalitarian household has arrived; that paid work has meant liberation and equality for women; that 'family friendly' work-places now smooth the way for parents; and that flexible work practices now facilitate flexible parents.[12]

Pocock says, 'The "cover stories" obscure the truth'. I say she's right, but she's being over polite. The so-called 'cover stories' are crippling women and sending us backwards. In the false belief that these 'cover stories' are true, women themselves believe they have no right to complain, no right to occasionally stand up and say, 'Enough! This is too hard, too unfair, I want to get off.' In the absence of expression, in the absence of a call for help, women push on, bearing the brunt of 'doing it all' alone and in silence.

A lifetime free pass to the 'bad mothers' club'

Emma's face is ashen. I've just walked into the make-up room next to our news studio for my daily session with the ever-serene, ever-smiling Emma. She does my make-up, my hair and provides free therapy while I'm caked in powder. She also operates the auto-cue, occasionally corrects my grammar, often corrects my spelling and generally pulls me into line—ever so gently. Today she's a mess. Bent over the wash basin, energetically wringing a hand towel and without looking up she says, 'Oh Virginia, I'm a terrible mother. Poor Angus. I'm just not a proper mother.' I brace myself for yet another sad and sorry tale of failed mothering; a tale that will inevitably end in the rotten mother hurling herself smack-bang up against the front door of the 'bad mothers' club'.

Emma's story is neither shocking nor unusual. It's just another tale about a stubborn two-year-old boy who threw a tantrum in a toy shop, flung himself down the shopping mall escalators, raged at the world and then lay dead flat and immovable across a pedestrian crossing, bringing traffic to a halt: all for the very simple and understandable reason—Thomas the Tank Engine wasn't coming home with him. The fact that Angus can stiffen his limbs, refuse to budge and howl like a wolf—all at the same time—shows talent. Or so I try to convince Emma. She thinks all it shows is that she's a 'bad mother'.

Like many working mothers Emma takes on a double load. By necessity, her adoring, but absent, husband works in another city. Theirs is a 'weekend' family. Therefore, Emma's working week, which occasionally starts at the crack of dawn and always ends well into the night, centres around childcare support. The rigours of dropping off and collecting her son, packing lunchboxes full of home-cooked vegetables and curries for Angus's Sri Lankan palate, as well as providing clean clothes to cover a day's worth of gumboot activity, means Emma has to be meticulous in her timing and super organised. On the odd occasion when she might try to squeeze into the routine a bit of extra shopping activity and it all goes pear-shaped, what does it matter? So what if it crosses her mind to leave her howling son prone on the road, pretending he is someone else's child? All pretty normal I would have thought. But not to Emma.

She argues that the temper tantrum was her fault; that she should never have entered the toy shop in the first place, knowing that Thomas and his evil bloody Tank Engine paraphernalia lurked there. 'I should have thought it through, Virginia. It wasn't fair on Angus.' I try to reason with Emma that not only is it not her fault, but she is trying to juggle more than her fair share of parenting, working and household management, and she should go easy on herself. She's not convinced. Emma rarely gets upset, yet right now I can see she is deeply troubled. It's not just about the tantrum, it's about this absurd business of being 'a proper mother'. Where has this impossible and unrealistic standard of 'proper' mothering come from? How has it pervaded otherwise smart women's thinking?

As Emma prepares to lay out the day's make-up, we both eye an old pile of well-thumbed women's magazine scattered on the bench in front of us. Australian actress Claudia Karvan beams from the front of one: 'Gorgeous first photos, Claudia shows off her beautiful baby girl', screams the cover. Inside, surrounded by the casually chic furnishings of an immaculate home, Claudia's cute baby in her little designer number wriggles over squeaky clean floorboards, as Claudia explains how, 'happily [her] life off the set has fitted in perfectly with her on screen life . . .'[13]

Another one boasts a relaxed and perfectly groomed Antonia Kidman—mother of three—hugging her seven-month-old baby in tropical sunlight by a backyard pool. Antonia is 'very much a modern woman' we're told, 'used to juggling the demands of home and work'. Despite her extensive list of work activities, which include hosting a couple of TV shows and a busy charity schedule, Antonia insists mothering comes first. One of the charities says it chose Antonia to represent them because, 'She's such a marvellous mother . . . such a caring mum.' This wondermum doesn't do it all alone, though. Antonia says she employs a nanny to allow her to help 'make time for herself': her fit, tanned and toned body glowing proof of her commitment to an exercise routine.[14]

The praise for perfect motherhood doesn't stop there. Singer Kate Ceberano's gorgeous face beams from another glossy. This great Australian talent is sitting poised at the piano, supposedly writing lyrics, as she burps her bonny new baby on one knee.[15] The messages here are clear: motherhood is beautiful, babies are giggling cherubs and all mothers have glossy hair, a healthy tan and an ethereal goddess-like glow about them. Emma tosses the magazines off the bench and out of our way. 'Why don't they do profiles on the nannies?' she asks.

Well, why don't they? Simple. It would spoil the myth. We don't want to know about the nannies, the carers, the support teams and the tens of thousands of dollars spent on buying domestic services. Nor do we want to know about the pitfalls, the mistakes or a celebrity mother's misery and depression. It would ruin the image—the heavily hawked media image—of womanly fulfilment, which clearly is found only in blissful motherhood. Or so a staple diet of women's glossies would have us believe.

In the face of such a powerful and pervasive image of perfect motherhood, there must have been an audible sigh of relief across the United States when the book *The Mommy Myth*, hit the stands. In it, authors Susan J. Douglas and Meredith W. Michaels identify a ruthless and pernicious modern-day malaise afflicting mothers, would-be mothers and even non-mothers. They call it the 'new momism': a trend where the bar on motherhood has been raised so high that 'to be a remotely decent mother, a woman has to devote her entire physical, psychological, emotional and intellectual being 24/7 to her children'.[16] The authors, who bravely admit they've pondered the idea of locking their kids in the basement, insist they love their kids:

> But like increasing numbers of women, we are fed up with the myth shamelessly hawked by the media that motherhood is eternally fulfilling and rewarding, that it is *always* the best and most important thing you do, that there is only a narrowly prescribed way to do it right, and that if you don't love each and every second of it there's something really wrong with you.[17]

No doubt the American women who read these words whispered a quite little hallelujah! Across the Atlantic, Australian women must do too, because even though we don't have 'mommies' in this country, we certainly have 'mums', 'mummies' and 'mothers', and they are all copping the same raw deal.

Douglas went on to tell the *Washington Post* that 'new momism' suggests that motherhood is continuously presented as something of a perfect science when, in fact, the message to mothers should be that it's okay to be *imperfect*. Douglas is unequivocal in laying the blame on the mass media in general and women's glossies in particular:

They were telling me how to feel. And the way I was supposed
to feel was eternally ecstatic and joyful and thrilled. I wasn't
feeling any of those things. Did I adore my kid? Of course,
I adored her. But I didn't love getting up with her at three in
the morning.[18]

No sooner has the problem of 'new momism' been identified,
than we've got a solution. Rather than complain and rail against
the impossible standards set by 'new momism', American women
are said to be chucking it all in—the career success and the high-
powered positions that is—to heed the call of the mommy. *Time
Magazine* caused something of a sensation when, in March 2004,
it ran a cover story on 'The Case for Staying Home: Why More
Young Moms are Opting Out of the Rat Race'.[19] The article
identified a growing trend among high-earning women in their
thirties who are choosing to opt out, stay home, bake cakes and
be what Emma would call 'proper mothers'. News of this so-called
'trend' infuriated author Susan Douglas. 'The chic thing to do
now,' she told *USA Today*, 'is to be able to work but to *choose* to
stay at home with your children. That is seen as the morally superior
thing to do. But very few mothers can do that.'[20]

I detect the acrid smell of a backlash—the mummy backlash.
What a murky mess we've got ourselves into. After decades of
encouraging women into the workforce, and creating a powerful
economic imperative for them to stay there, we then turn our
attention back to motherhood—and crikey, standards have slipped!
Too many women are too focused on paid work at the expense
of families. Enough! By the turn of the twenty-first century the
bar has been raised and mothering is once again—in 1950s
style—promoted as the womanly ideal. Just at a time in history
when women's participation in the workforce is at its highest

ever! Motherhood, the once debased and discredited state, is back in fashion again, with a vengeance. Here is the backlash: the *good* wife, the *'proper'* mother, the *best* woman is the one who will 'opt out' and put on her apron. While there is little evidence of such a trend occurring in Australia, *yet*, we are only a few media stories away.

In March 2004, I was asked by *60 Minutes* to participate in a story on the 'new wife'. The producer explained it was based on the 'American idea' that 'more and more successful career women are giving it all up'. I declined to be involved. No doubt soon someone else will, and the notion of the 'new wife' will be off and running in Australia too.

In the Unites States it has already got a foothold. In her book, *The New Wife*, American academic and author Susan Shapiro Barash says Generation Y is turning its back on the kind of lifestyle forged by Generation X. She insists young women of the twenty-first century are putting marriage, partnership and family first, and deliberately choosing to 'worry less about high-powered careers'.[21] She told *The Age* newspaper, 'Young women can see how women in Generation X have left it too late to have children, or are being torn between the office and their babies.'[22] It seems the 'haggard looks' of the juggling working mother is a turn-off, and striving for the motherhood ideal and the 'inner housewife' is the new turn-on:

> The twenty-first century wife has taken a good look at the errors of her predecessors, especially her mother's generation, and has decided to revamp the role. If the fairy-tale life of the wife is being reinvented, it is performed in a fashion that offers young women a chance to get it right . . .[23]

This is by no means just an American phenomenon. Our British sisters are falling for it too. The British equivalent of the Country

Women's Association, the Women's Institute, is reportedly enjoying a surge of interest from young thirty-something wives, who are supposedly happy to dump careers in fund management, law and the like, for 'the joy of jam bottling and baking bread'. A new thirty-something recruit of the Fulham's Women's Institute told the *Australian* newspaper: 'Now my generation is saying "hang on a minute". We've seen what that [career-orientated] life did to our mothers and we don't want it for ourselves.'[24]

As the mummy backlash percolates in Australia, it's vitally important to probe the truth here. How much of this apparent 'opting out' of careers is about women discovering the blissful joy of full-time motherhood and the 'inner housewife', and how much is because the workplace can't accommodate the full range of a woman's roles? If we turn back to Professor Pocock's 'cover stories' for a moment and ponder a few key ones again: 'that "family-friendly" work-places now smooth the way for parents; and that flexible work practices now facilitate flexible parents',[25] isn't it clear that a probing spotlight should be shone on the workplace?

In May 2004, an OECD (Organisation for Economic Cooperation and Development) study found Australia to have 'some of the least family-friendly policies for working mothers in the developed world'.[26] In terms of 'the generosity of family support', Australia ranked way down towards the bottom of the OECD scorecard, next to Mexico and Turkey, but even those countries scored higher on the issue of paid maternity leave.[27] These findings are a disgraceful admission and should be a source of red-faced embarrassment to our government and business bodies. Perhaps Australians just aren't easily shamed. The Business Council of Australia (BCA) in its 2003 report, 'Balancing Work and Family', boasted that 'More than 90 per cent of BCA companies offer flexible working hours', however, just like the report's glossy cover, it is a glossy statistic. Any Australian worker who has broached the possibility with their boss of adjusting their work schedule to make it more 'flexible' around personal needs, knows all too well how *inflexible* and uncomfortable the discussion can become. Despite every company or corporation I've ever worked for including rhetoric about 'flexibility' in their mission statement, I've watched countless women fall off the ladder—and many disappear altogether—because part-time options and flexibility in the workplace are really just rhetoric, not reality. Despite the numerous photos of happy faces peppered throughout its report, even the BCA had to admit that 'company culture' has a nasty habit of getting in the way of implementing flexible workplace policies:

> Resentment from managers having to become more adaptable as their staff take up more flexible working options, and resentment among other employees, were also identified as difficulties to overcome in implementing work/family policies.[28]

One of the survey's respondents stated, 'Family-friendly initiatives are often seen as "soft" by some managers, who expect 100 per cent dedication by all staff to their cause.' Another added, 'These policies are still seen as "women's business".'[29]

In the spirit of Australian 'women's business', we seem content to keep the messy truth 'secret'. Until such pressing and fundamental issues stop being 'women's business', little structural or cultural change will occur. Meanwhile those Australian women who *do* 'opt out' will continue to battle—some painfully—for their place in a society that sends such confusing and mixed messages to women.

Me? I'm just a 'mum'

The first time I met Jenny we chatted politely across a boardroom table about each others' work, our busy schedules, and the property market—as you do. I was in the process of buying an apartment in Canberra and the details were weighing on my mind. Jenny told me she and her husband had just purchased a couple of penthouse apartments at one end of Collins Street, right in the heart of Melbourne's CBD. They were thinking of gutting them and joining the two together: a sort of upstairs–downstairs penthouse. Suddenly, my little two-bedder didn't seem that interesting anymore. She also mentioned they were selling a one-hundred-acre property at Apollo Bay on Victoria's south-west coast. Knowing the area well I asked if they were into farming or cattle. She laughed and said certainly not!

Jenny explained the property had a beautiful old homestead on it and they had bought it as a holiday home. The trouble was, she said, they never had time to go there. I think by now I must have flushed green, knowing that if I had a hundred acres down by the beach on one of the world's most glorious coastlines, I would have no trouble getting there—regularly! Then I learnt a little bit more about Jenny and her passion for work, where a lazy Sunday was a 'late' start around 8 a.m, a café breakfast with her husband, and both in at the office by about 9.30 a.m. The more I heard, the more I understood why a rural property for weekends away was probably wishful thinking for this couple, both in their early thirties.

That was a while ago. Jenny is now 36, has a three-year-old daughter Bethany, and lives minutes from the beach in Auckland, New Zealand. There are no more Sundays at the office, or Saturdays. In fact there are no more days at the office for Jenny at all. Instead her life has been transformed by a whole new career—motherhood.

> I have a momentary pause every time I have to complete a departure or arrival card at the airport, as one of the questions is 'What is your occupation'. I hate putting 'mother' or some other suitable descriptor, but cannot fully explain, even to myself, why it is such a problem!

Pre-motherhood, what Jenny could have proudly filled into the blank space (but her modesty would forbid it) is:

> The youngest and first female appointed as head of an internal audit group for one of Australia's major retail banks. Star performer with outstanding technology skills, frequently head hunted, a stellar track record with inexhaustible energy, a high earning bonus hunter, willing to clock up eighty-hour weeks.

Instead, she now simply writes 'mother' and leaves it at that. It's not easy. Jenny's is a complex story of identity crisis and a clash of two very different and demanding cultures: the workforce and motherhood.

> It took me a good twelve months after having Bethany to really identify myself as a mother. I would look at other mothers and think, 'That's not me'. I was so determined to hang onto the career. I think I was impacted by the broader philosophical issues about the way society thinks about mothers, and didn't see myself as being the second-class citizen that a lot of people think mothers are. That is why I tried to shun any linkage I might have with that group.

Like many highly successful women, Jenny loves a plan—a thorough, meticulous, well-organised plan, where everything works to schedule. Any potential problems are weaned out well before they get a chance to grubby the slate. Perhaps it's the skilful accountant in her, but she can spot an errant number a mile away. In typical style she crunched the numbers on childbirth and drew up a long-term maternity plan: give birth at 33, take three months off, employ excellent nanny, return to work full time and continue sixty- to eighty-hour working weeks. You can probably already spot the problem in the numbers, but Jenny didn't. 'I think that was a fairly naive plan,' she now says softly. We both laugh. 'I wasn't expecting the physical issues that some women have to deal with upon giving birth, nor was I expecting the emotional,' she says. So, with a bit of whiteboard calculation and rescheduling, Jenny extended her maternity leave to five months and arranged to return to work in a part-time capacity for a few months, before resuming a full-time schedule. But she still hadn't got the numbers right.

Once back in the office, Jenny threw herself into her former role with gusto, anxious to display the same 'pre-baby' levels of energy, effort and success that she was known for; but on a three-day-a-week basis. However, three doesn't fit neatly into five, or seven for that matter—at the executive level at which she worked a seven-day week was not uncommon. Jenny found out quickly that it was almost impossible to 'carve up' her job, but that didn't stop her trying, no matter how exhausted she became. Like so many other young guns that have only ever known success, this was the first time in her life she was seriously struggling to nail a challenge to make her choice work. The baby pull just didn't fit Jenny's pattern of calm and studious control.

On the homefront she became miserable, and on the work front she felt wobbly. Typical of so many women like her, Jenny blamed herself. 'I have to say, however, that it was me putting on the pressure; it wasn't my boss or the organisation,' she says. Then a bolt out of the blue completely shattered her already shaky work–family plan. A major corporate restructure within the bank meant a level of management was lopped off . . . including Jenny and her job. The bank wanted to keep her on in some other role, but after fruitless negotiations over a flexible job structure and suitable pay, Jenny accepted a redundancy. Shortly afterwards she was diagnosed with postnatal depression, which came as no great surprise. She says she was devastated by the redundancy and the 'identity crisis' that followed:

> I was so career focused; I pretty much identified myself 100 per cent by what I did for a living. After the redundancy I felt I didn't have a hook to hang my hat on. My emotional reaction to it was mixed up with the whole issue that you go through when you are a first-time mother, which is, 'Who are you? What are you doing? Where do you want to head?' I took it all pretty badly.

Given her exceptional credentials, Jenny had ample opportunity to take up a range of similar paying, high-flying, full-time jobs. But she held off. The internal chaos she felt within forced her to undergo some serious introspection, particularly about how she was handling her role as a mother:

> I was a real perfectionist at work and in the career context and I translated that perfectionism into motherhood, so I was expecting myself to be the 'perfect mother' . . . I wanted a work program and something to measure myself by. In your career you have your short-term plan and your long-term plan, and you know whether you have achieved enough to get your bonus etc. I was trying to convert that kind of structure into my role as a mother, and you just can't ever make that happen.

Despite being part of a social group where nannies are the norm, and watching a friend juggle no less than three—a day time, night time and a weekend nanny—Jenny says working the sixty- to eighty-hour weeks at the level she did pre-baby was no longer an option. 'You just can't do that and have a child. It is just impossible.' Her pre-redundancy experience also taught her that some work environments can't accommodate part-time roles, and that such flexible arrangements work only if it is a non-executive 'lesser job'. That was not a healthy option for this ambitious woman. Eventually Jenny made a critical, life-changing choice: she decided she would give up trying to combine motherhood and work, and would stay at home instead.

It's been three years now since Jenny 'opted out' and she says she'll give it another two before she begins to consider re-joining the workforce. In the meantime, the biggest and perhaps most challenging hurdle for this stay-at-home mum has being re-building an identity. Shortly after she made her decision to 'opt out', Jenny's husband was poached for a top job in New Zealand. Now in a new country and a new social environment, no-one knows anything about Jenny the former corporate high flyer. Instead she is just Jenny, a mother and a wife—titles that sometimes get stuck in her throat:

> I am meeting people either through Bethany going to day care, or through my husband's work and it's very difficult to retain a feeling of me as an individual in that context. I hate to think that they would meet me and think of me as a 'housewife', but that is essentially what I am now, at least at the moment.

'What is wrong with that?' I ask.

'It has the "little woman" connotation to it and that is not me,' she says with an ever-so-slight edge of defiance in her voice.

The 'little woman' connotation doesn't fit comfortably with many new mothers. The idea that Jenny is hinting at here, that of being a 'kept' or 'subservient' woman, harks back to our mother's generation; the generation of women Betty Friedan found were trapped by the 'feminine mystique' and a false belief that 'sacred motherhood' defined 'a total way of life'. That was then. This is now. Today almost all women giving birth have already had substantial participation in the workforce before becoming pregnant. Given the median age of child-bearing in Australia has climbed to 30.2 years old, the vast majority of new mothers have already invested up to a decade in developing their career and are perhaps performing at their peak around the very time they interrupt it all to become mothers.[30] Little wonder then that many suffer a clash of cultures and a crisis in identity.

Of course, not all women are so torn.

But I *am* just a mum!

Annie is one of a rare group who has embraced full-time motherhood unflinchingly. For her, the choice between a well-paid Tokyo-based career and 'opting out' to stay at home was almost a no-brainer. Watching Annie while she explains the choices she's made is like watching a fully bloomed flower, shaded in blush pink, peel away to reveal something surprisingly solid at its centre. Here is a woman with an immensely strong sense of herself and what she values. Yet she is mindfully gentle and unimposing in communicating her strongly held beliefs. Annie knows her life and her choices are not for everyone, and she has an overriding respect for those women who have chosen paths opposite to hers, or whose life choices have made full-time motherhood unattainable. In fact, so much so, Annie was initially reluctant to tell her story because she says she feels so 'lucky' and 'grateful' and . . . well . . . happy. 'I'm just always a happy sort of person,' she says, in the knowledge that so many women are not. Funnily enough, Annie also thought her story of little value to

other women because of the lack of eventful drama, crisis, pain
and regret. I assured her *that* in itself makes her path a source
of fascination.

Annie has two children, Harriet who is almost five and Fionn,
aged two-and-a-half. She and her husband Andrew are both 34.
The family live in an old, single-fronted Clifton Hill terrace in
inner-city Melbourne. While it is the suburb of choice for many
professional couples with young families who can afford a
substantial mortgage, it still has the occasional 'renovator's delight'
awaiting the extension and the brass number plate. Annie's house
is one of those: long, dark in parts, with fittings that have seen
better days, and child-friendly walls and floors, all yet to be
replaced. This is a house in which children can run and laugh,
throw things and spread out. Furniture is sparse. After elbowing
open the stiff gate, I'm met at the front door by a poppet.

'Hello, I'm Harriet Audley Rose.'

'Hello Harriet, I'm Virginia.'

'Come in,' says the poppet, thrusting her body against the
fly-screened door to open it. Just then a round face on a squat
little body beams up to me, 'And I'm Fionn.' At this stage Annie
appears, all smiles and warmth.

It's a beautiful, sunny, summer morning and we take our tea
outside, sitting in the rambling garden where Annie can keep an
eye on her children as they play. If snapped for a magazine feature
right now this scene would drip with domestic bliss, maternal
calm and kids' laughter—if, of course, it had all the designer
accompaniments, which it doesn't. It's perhaps the lack of gloss
that makes it all so beguiling.

Annie surprises me when she reveals that, despite her self-
confessed maternal nature, she and Andrew never had children
on the agenda when they married in their early twenties. He was
an engineer with a bright future. She was a linguist who specialised

in Japanese. With a mother who speaks six languages, Annie knew she also had a gift for language, but how she would marshal such a talent and put it to use was never planned. It was all a bit ad-hoc. For the first few years of marriage Annie was content to pack up and follow Andrew's career each time he was offered a bigger and better position. She never had trouble picking up work as a Japanese teacher or translator. On one occasion when they were relocated to the Pilbara, Annie filled her time teaching English to refugees.

A yearning to deepen her connection with the Japanese language stirred inside her for years. At the age of 28, after quietly testing the water, Annie was offered a terrific position in Tokyo; an opportunity she couldn't pass up. 'It was something I had to do before I had children,' she explains. 'It was like this thing I had to conquer.' Her husband agreed to quit his job and throw himself into the adventure of a new life. As can often be the case on the precipice of opportunity, there was a sudden twist.

'Three days after I accepted the job, Andrew got a major unexpected promotion at work, to which I congratulated him with tears running down my face.' Now they *both* had opportunities that were too good to pass up. So bravely and somewhat reluctantly, they chose to pursue their given paths separately . . . for the time being.

Needless to say, Annie flourished in Tokyo. That didn't stop her putting a firm time limit on it though. She made a clear choice that when the year was up, her career was over.

'I knew that once I became a mother I was going to make the children my first priority.' But it wasn't easy. Saying goodbye to her life in Tokyo and her work took a toll.

'I actually came back and found it quite difficult to close that part of my life.' However an immediate pregnancy helped. Then a whole new life started.

Since having her two children, Annie has developed an interesting take on the idea of 'opting out'. Her view is that there is really only room for one star career in a family. In her case, that happens to be her husband's:

> He's done pretty well for himself so he's on a good salary, which means we can afford to do this. But I feel strongly it is a choice. We certainly don't have any money for extras. We have to be really careful about it. We don't just do it because we can. We have actually had to make this decision that financially we'll just go backwards for a little while.

Later when Annie mentions her old fridge has just packed it in and the repairs will cost $700, she laughs as she says, 'That's half the money we had up our sleeves for emergencies over the next twelve months!' 'Going backwards' clearly requires a good sense of humour.

Perhaps it's her optimism, or maybe it's just her nature, but unlike the identity crisis suffered by some ex-working mothers, Annie is proud to identify herself as a stay-at-home mother.

'I take great joy in saying that I'm a full-time mother of two who's really enjoying what I do.' She even suggests it's her way of doing something 'for the sisterhood', in an effort to overcome the 'devaluing' of motherhood.

'I think probably a lot of women think that I'm very lucky. But I guess I mix among a lot of professional people who the first thing you find out about them is what they do for a living.' Annie says a lot of the women she meets through her husband's work and his MBA studies privately tell her the same thing, 'They all say to me "All I want to do is have children".'

The only hole in what is otherwise a happy-ever-after sort of story is a nagging fear about finances and 'making ends meet'. Annie admits that she has put her youngest child, Fionn, on a waiting list for child care, 'if things do start to go too badly backwards' and she has to find work in a hurry. Then, almost reluctantly, Annie confesses that watching her husband work his way through an MBA has whetted her own appetite for further education; maybe even another degree. How would she fit it in?

'I'd probably study after hours, like in the evening. Once Andrew finishes his MBA, hopefully there'll be time for me to do something.'

Not so fast, Annie. Just as those 'what-about-me' thoughts were gaining momentum; the family game plan suddenly changed. A few months after that last chat, Annie is now boxing up the family's belongings for yet another move. Andrew has once again been offered a job opportunity that 'is too good to refuse'. This time they're off to Italy and a new home in Milan. While some mothers of two young children might cringe at such a big cultural upheaval, Annie is thrilled to bits.

'It'll be great,' she tells me clearly excited and already sounding as if she's got a foot on the European continent. Then with typical optimism and good humour she says, 'Last year my New Year's resolution was to cook more fish. This year, it's to take more risks!'

The baby strike—
a fertility crisis?

I am confused as to how it is that women my age are supposed to be failing the nation by not having kids. The nation is failing women my age in not creating conditions in which women feel they can have kids and have successful careers.

Moksha Watts, 22 years old, interviewed on SBS's *Insight* program, August 2002

The breeding creed . . . is being articulated as a social goal in this country. And if she isn't having children, then a woman is increasingly told that she's letting the whole country down.

Anne Summers, *The End of Equality*, 2003

It is Federal Budget day 2004 and Canberra is awash with the nation's media heavies. The airport taxi queue snakes slowly as cars ferry the huge cast of extras who have flown in for the day. The cafés of Manuka and Kingson are clogged as the interlopers grab a caffeine fix ahead of a long, frantic day and an alcohol-soaked night. This is Canberra's 'big day out'—an intellectual orgy for the nation's top journalists and commentators and an adrenalin rush for the myriad producers, editors, crews, techs, lobbyists, apparatchiks and all the rest. By mid-morning there's a frenzied buzz in the air. The party boys are circling.

I could feel what was coming and felt tempted to warn some of the women journos going into the budget media lock-up to take a raincoat, or a least an umbrella. Once the treasurer took to the microphone Canberra's drought would break and the place would rain testosterone—in bucket loads. And it did. Even from the safe distance of my desk in the ABC's newsroom—watching the theatre unfold on a bank of TV monitors—it was sickening to witness. What was supposed to be an election year budget was quickly dubbed the 'erection budget'. Wearing the smirk of a private school boy telling a dirty story after a swig of his first UDL, Treasurer Peter Costello told the assembled media to go forth and procreate. In other words . . . go and get f****d.

'Go home and do your patriotic duty tonight,' he told the dozens of reporters before him. The message was unambiguous: the country needs your babies!

'You should have one for your husband and one for your wife and one for the country,' he told the startled mob. Despite dressing it up as gender neutral, it was clearly a message for the girls: political talk for 'C'mon you Sheilas, what the hell is wrong with you?' It was not the first time the federal government has clanged alarm bells over Australia's declining fertility rate and our shrinking baby population, but this time the federal treasurer was pulling no punches. It was a megaphone message, loud and clear:

> Some will manage two for the country (but) two only replicates yourselves, so if you want to fix the ageing demographic— you're just square after two—you're making no net

improvement. Some of you will have to have [more] than one for the country, you'll have to make up for some of your friends that aren't even replicating themselves.[1]

It was no polite request. Nor was it funny, despite the embarrassed tittering among the crowd. It was a patronising 'father knows best' demand that 'those under-utilised and downright un-Australian ovaries be put to good use', as journalist Christine Jackman put it.[2] By way of encouragement the treasurer dangled a new lump sum maternity payment of $3000 for every woman who proves herself a breeder and pops out a baby. In an effort to redress a family tax system that has long discriminated against working mothers, concessions were also made to 'ease the burden on struggling families'—as politicians love to euphemistically put it. Just who created the tax burden in the first place is, of course, never discussed. All in all, it was a budget with an 'f' focus: family, fertility and . . .

Naturally, the double entendre proved irresistible to the nation's headline writers. 'F-word used in erection year', teased the front page of the national broadsheet, the *Australian*. Inside, the paper fleshed out details under the heading, 'Sexing up economy puts us in poll mood'. *The Canberra Times* implored women to forget about the bloody motherland, instead just 'Lie back and think of your country'. The more conservatively dictatorial *Courier Mail* called it straight: 'Go forth and multiply'. Even Prime Minister John Howard, not normally known to be enthusiastic about sex, weighed in with something absurdly akin to an excitable war-monger's cry: 'Come on, come on, your nation needs you'.[3] While the bonking metaphor got plenty of laughs and sat comfortably within Australia's very blokey business of politics, parliament and media, it nevertheless left many women on the periphery with their jaw dropped.

Little Aussie breeders . . .

Anne Summers had flagged it would happen—and she was right. A good six months before the federal government began its overt 'and one for the country' campaign, Summers had already warned of 'the breeding creed' about to come in her book, *The End of Equality*, published in late 2003. In it she details a 'powerful new ideology' that locks women into a single and primary function: that of breeders. Summers says the 'breeding creed' is about a national 'goal' and harks back to the early days of the last century when the panic about Australia's small population led to the forceful 'populate or perish' federal campaign. In an interview for ABC radio shortly before her book's launch, Summers told me the new 'breeding creed' had nothing to do with revaluing mothering or motherhood; instead, she said this new ideology is much more singular. 'It is putting breeding as the *only* choice for women,' she said.[4]

The rhetoric that has since imbued both sides of politics and the mass media, only serves to confirm this. The undercurrent of moral 'duty' has pervaded public discourse and the message is clear: Australian women have a job to do, and it's a job done in the bedroom, not the office. What is most disturbing is that the push to breed is not about women—their advancement, identity or status—it is fully focused on what women *produce*: children. More uncomfortably, it is also focused on what they *don't* produce: no children. Furrowed brows are cocking their disapproval at women who are childless.

It is well known that the man at the helm of the 'and one for the country' campaign, Australia's Prime Minister John Howard, is a lover of white picket fences. He has said so himself.[5] It's the gentle gingham image of a 'golden era'; a throwback to the idea of a happy family of four or more, waving from the neatly mowed lawn of their manicured garden, while Dad washes the wagon and Mum straightens her apron (is that home-baked cookies I can smell?). While this image probably entered the Australian psyche via American television, nevertheless it has stuck in the mind of conservative political leaders as a national aspiration. It couldn't be further from the truth.

Australia is vastly different from the picket-fence era—if ever there was one. Instead, we are a nation that has undergone a massive demographic shift and psychological transformation. But this change has been both gradual and universal, leaving most of us unaware and somewhat ill-equipped to recognise it. Is it any wonder then that women are forced to battle and anguish alone as we all struggle to interpret this new terrain, but no-one really gets it?

In tackling the question, 'Who is the mainstream now?' journalist and political commentator George Megalogenis points out in his book, *Faultlines*, just how much the tables have turned. Standing behind the white picket fence these days are more couples *without* dependent children than couples *with* children. Megalogenis, a stickler for demographic number crunching, says that across Australia in 2001 there were almost 1.8 million couples without children compared with 1.6 million couples with kids under the age of fifteen. 'The childless generation is the real mainstream couple', he concludes.[6] Slow to cotton on, the daily mainstream media nevertheless experienced a mini 'family frenzy' with numerous front-page stories when the ABS released its *2005 Year Book Australia* stating: 'Couple families without children are projected to experience the largest and fastest increases of all family types in Australia.'[7]

Also standing behind that picket fence is a rapidly increasing number of single householders. By 2003, one in four homes had just one person living in them. Over the first quarter of this century that's projected to increase by up to 105 per cent; such that by 2026 Australia is expected to have nearly four million single or 'lone' person households.[8] And you can bet there won't be much wagon-washing there. Maybe not much baking either.

The favoured choice of fertile females: *delay*

Central to the demographic shift happening around us, and the psychological renaissance occurring alongside it, is a major change in the choices women are making about their own fertility. However, all too often, when public discussion turns to the important matter of Australia's declining fertility, the media immediately swings the spotlight on to childless women. In doing so, we effectively ignore the vital first step to childlessness: fertility delay.

Back in 2002, the SBS program *Insight* rather bravely ran a television forum titled 'Australia's Fertility Crisis'. It was a serious attempt to delve into this tremendously broad and complex issue, to try and gain perspective and a little understanding. Encouraged by the producer's commitment to the subject matter, I agreed to participate along with a selection of experts, demographers, academics and various interest group representatives. After a well-researched introduction outlining the 'national crisis', and how Australians are 'losing their enthusiasm for becoming parents', the show's host then turned to her panel, and straight to me.

I could picture the director in the control room shouting to his cameramen, 'Zoom in on that childless woman first'. Once again, I found myself being asked to explain my childlessness, in particular; and Australia's growing rate of childlessness, in general.

Naturally, people are always shocked to hear one in four Australian women are childless, and that this proportion is expected to grow. However, a focus on this figure often ignores an important detail: Australia's rate of childlessness has a lot more to do with women choosing to *delay* childbirth than it does with women choosing to *remain* childless. When my mother married in the late 1950s, she and each of her girlfriends gave birth within the first year or so of their marriage. Back then, becoming a mother in your late teens and early twenties was not only common, it was expected. It was also 'expected' that a woman would have more than one child; which my mother dutifully did—she had six. In 1964, the year I was born, the median age of mothers giving birth was 26. I was the fourth child; mum still had two to go. By the time my youngest sibling, Fiona, was born in 1971, the median age of women giving birth was at a record low of 25.4. Since then, the birthing age has crept up, and up, and up. The fertility revolution has slowly, quietly—but well and truly— changed not only the age of women in maternity wards, but the face of Australian mothering dramatically.

By 2001, for the first time ever, the median age of women cradling their first newborn tipped over 30 years of age.[9] This trend continues, each year adding a month or two to the birthing age. During the 1990s the proportion of 35-year-olds giving birth for the first time doubled.[10] But perhaps even more startling is the news on 'older' mothers. During the last couple of decades, the number of births to women aged 40 or older has more than tripled.[11] In 2002 alone, 7500 women aged 40 or over gave birth. Nearly 300 of them were between 45 and 50 years old.[12]

While demographers, economists and politicians are desperately hoping this 'older mother' trend will eventually plateau—perhaps even go backwards—there are no apparent signs of women complying. As women continue to delay child-bearing until late into their reproductive years, the likelihood of having more than one and a bit babies rapidly diminishes. Eggs dry up, bodies grow old and women get tired. Continued delay means a smaller family. Or worse still, for the woman who pushes her luck, continued delay could mean *no* family. The small family/no family scenario means a shrinking fertility rate.

A worldly view . . .

For a long time demographer Professor Peter McDonald from the Australian National University was something of a lone voice warning Australia, our politicians and whoever would listen, about the perilous state of fertility in this country. For a long time our nation's leaders were of the view that there was little governments could do to give modern-day procreation a push along. By the year of my first encounter with contraception in 1981, Australia's fertility rate had already been in free fall for twenty years. By 1992, the best you could say about the propensity of Australian women to give birth was that our decline was consistent: the fertility rate fell a neat .02 or .03 percentage points every year. Some saw it as an insidious creep. Others ignored it. It took the loud clanging of alarm bells across the world for Australia to sit up and take note.

In 2003, The United Nations World Fertility Report screamed out a global truth: fertility rates were dropping around the world, and it was the developed, educated, affluent western countries that were declining the most. An OECD report of the same year echoed those findings, adding that 'in most OECD countries fertility rates have reached levels that are well below those needed to secure generational replacement'.[13]

'Generational replacement'—perhaps already a hopelessly optimistic ideal—is important if we don't want to be swamped by a sea of grey heads in a world without children. At current rates, the United Nations warns that by 2050 the world's population of old people will be larger than the population of children 'for the first time in human history'.[14] In Australia it will be even worse. By the middle of this century, the proportion of children is estimated to fall as low as twelve per cent of the population, with nearly 50 per cent of Australians aged over fifty.[15]

Currently around the world, on average, there are nine workers to each elderly non-worker aged 65 or over.[16] The United Nations calls this—somewhat euphemistically—the PSR, or 'Potential Support Ratio'. In other words, it is a way of ascertaining how many able-bodied, productive people there are to every not-so-able, non-productive, older person in need of support. By mid-century, according to UN projections, an aging world with below replacement birth rates will see the PSR worsen to around four workers per elderly non-worker. In Italy, Spain and Japan, where fertility rates are among the lowest in the world, the projected ratio is an astounding one to one: a demographic, economic and fiscal nightmare. In Australia, given current fertility rates and the trend towards further decline, it is expected that by 2050 our PSR will fall to three to one: that's three able-bodied, tax-paying, productive workers to each elderly, non-productive, non-tax paying, pension-receiving person.[17] On sheer numbers, the economic sustainability of a three to one scenario is seriously worrying. No wonder Australia was forced to read the fertility figures, look at the projections and sit up and take stock. The result—shock!

The cupboard is looking empty and supplies are low. Little Aussie breeders haven't been breeding like they *used* to—like they are *supposed* to. What is this birth dearth? A breeding drought? Or worse, a self-determined choice by women? A baby strike? Now it seems 'suddenly' Australia is gripped by a 'fertility crisis'. The ramifications, the *real* ramifications of an aging population, and the financial impost this will have on Australia's economy, is what has provoked the bespectacled prime minister to urge women to have more unprotected, uncontracepted, unadulterated sex. Just who is he barracking for with his plea to 'Come on, come on'? Is it Him, Her, the yet-to-be-conceived Baby It, or is it the treasurer's kitty?

Hitting rock bottom?

In 2001, Australia's fertility rate dropped to an all-time low of 1.73.[18] By late 2003 it had nudged back to 1.75, where it appears to have settled—for the time being.[19] That means, on average, each Australian woman is producing just 1.75 babies. This is well below the 2.1 babies per woman needed for our population to replace itself. It is well below our peak of 3.6 babies, back in 1961. It is also one whole baby below the world average of 2.7 per woman.[20] Although not reliably recorded, it is estimated Australia's fertility rate at the turn of last century was as high as four babies per woman.[21] Against that, our current 1.75 babies per woman seems miniscule. Perhaps, even miserly.

Interestingly, as the ABS points out, this is the second time Australia has experienced a long and sustained decline in fertility. The first period was from 1907 to 1934.[22] Back then, war, disease, economic insecurity, the Great Depression and fear for the future, all contributed to the creation of a giant and long-lasting prophylactic. This second period of sustained decline, which started over 40 years ago in 1962—

and has every sign of continuing—has not been a time of hardship, rampant unemployment, poverty and wholesale loss of life. Quite the opposite. These past four decades have been times of boom, economic flourish, wealth creation, social liberation and sexual freedom. Yet such modern-day riches seem to have an even greater prophylactic effect than the hardship and adversity experienced by our grandmothers.

So how low is 'low'?

Now, half-way into a new decade in a new century, does it matter that we are not reproducing? Is our low total fertility rate (TFR) rate of 1.75 babies per woman really such a problem? After all, how low is low?

Back in the 1980s when some Western European countries dropped to where we are now—a fertility rate around 1.7—they panicked. Those nations, in particular France, the Netherlands and the Nordic countries, sharpened their pencils, did the sums and realised if they didn't arrest the fall an aging population and a shrinking workforce would mean a fiscal nightmare. The pressure on government coffers to cater for the elderly, while worker numbers diminished, tax revenue declined, and GDP developed irreversible anorexia, added to the economic forecasts of nightmarish proportions.

According to Professor McDonald, some of those countries got aggressive and 'enlightened' about introducing work and family policies that helped smooth the transition for women from the role of worker to mother, and back to worker again. For example France, often sighted as one of the most family-friendly regimes, has financial incentives and tax benefits for parents that Professor McDonald suggests 'are bigger than any country in the world'. Sweden, on the other hand, introduced a generous maternity leave scheme that pays women eighty per cent of their former wage for a full 90 weeks while they are home with their baby.[23] Eager to boost their numbers, the Swedes also introduced a 'speed bonus', giving women an extra financial advantage for having a second child rapidly after the first. But the Swedish Government knows better than to rely simply on policy to boost the numbers. It went full throttle on ramping up the PR: putting the sex back into . . . well, sex. After a healthy *incline* to fertility replacement levels of 2.1 around 1990, Sweden then slipped backwards over the next decade. By 2001 the fertility rate was a worrying 1.6.[24] So out came the billboards with a fertile looking Bjorn Borg screaming out to his fellow countrymen and women to 'Fuck for the Future!'.[25] Making John Howard's excited urge to 'come on, come on!' sound positively lame. It's also a little more overt than Singapore's campaign to 'Have Three or More if You Can Afford It'.[26] But then Sweden has never been known for subtlety when it comes to sex. And good luck to them.

Other Scandinavian countries such as Norway and the Nordic Iceland and Finland set about introducing a range of work and family policies to support women having children *and* maintaining a foothold in the workforce. With an eye to a more 'whole of family' long-term approach, places such as France and the Netherlands also enshrined in law the *right* to part-time work for parents of young children. Holland went even further and gave the same rights to *non-parents* as well—a sign of true modern-day enlightenment.

The end result of all these fertility-booster efforts over the following years (including Sweden's hard-core PR approach) has not been a continuous, or significant, rise in birth rates in any of these countries. Instead there has been stabilisation. In other words, a halt in the decline.[27] That, says Professor McDonald, is the crucial point:

> The effect has been that these countries continue to experience birth rates of about 1.7 children per woman, while the birth rate in the countries of southern Europe and the German-speaking countries have fallen to levels about or below 1.3 births per woman, that can only be described as precariously low.[28]

So parlous is the state of fertility around the globe, we can almost cluster countries into 'going, going, gone' baskets. Some cases are more likely to end up in the basket than others. Nations, such as Japan and Greece, with fertility rates around 1.3 babies per woman, are uncomfortably in the 'going' basket, whereas, Italy and Spain, with rates around 1.2, and more recently Korea sliding to 1.17, are perhaps already headed for the 'gone basket'.[29] About such nations, Professor McDonald says:

> Their child populations have already dropped by a large amount and they are facing big labour force crises. I think the word 'crisis' can be used in respect of some countries and their future labour supply.

> These are the countries which, despite seeing the early warning signs of a fertility slide almost two decades ago, did nothing about it; until the fall had reached below 1.5, at which time it would appear to be too late.

Not everyone is heading towards crisis. While Australia is one of more than 60 countries around the world with fertility rates below, or well below, replacement levels, it may come as a surprise to learn that two of our close friends and trading partners are bucking the trend. One is New Zealand and the other, more surprisingly, is the United States. For its part, by 2000 NZ had managed to hold its fertility rate at around a healthy 2.0 for about five years; and is perhaps only a spring wedding carnival off reaching a replacement level of 2.1. The United States has steadily defied the general trend and managed a very gentle incline in fertility since first arresting the decline in 1980, when birth rates dropped to 1.8. By 2004, the USA was sitting comfortably on a population replacement level of 2.1.[30] This is all the more extraordinary given the USA has one of the highest rates of workforce participation by women in the world (60 per cent), yet shares the infamous reputation of being one of only two OECD nations with no paid maternity scheme to speak of (the other being Australia). The United Kingdom, on the other hand, did join the downward trend as seen in almost all other developed nations. By 2002 the TFR in the UK hit a record low of 1.64; and it has continued to hover at or below 1.7 ever since.[31]

Is Australia, once fearful of a population explosion, now in jeopardy of a population implosion? Are we heading towards a crisis with fertility rates caught in the grip of an undertow, plummeting towards zero population growth? Well if we are, Professor McDonald is surprisingly calm about it. He's been crunching fertility rates for governments around the world for years. While he says Australia's downward trend is bad, he's seen worse. For Australia, 'The important thing is to try to halt the decline. It is to stop the fall that has been going on over the last decade or so.' McDonald believes Australia can sustain a fertility rate of 1.7—or even 1.6—so long as we balance such low fertility with immigration, which he optimistically suggests shouldn't be painful for a nation that is a 'migrant country'. 'So the situation is all right, so long as the fertility rate does not fall down below the 1.5 level', he adds. Which it would seem is the cut-off mark, as no country has managed to raise its birth rate above 1.5 once it falls that low. And there is the crunch.

Like many others, Professor McDonald is not confident the fall from 1.75 babies per woman won't continue—at least in the short term. One of the key reasons is marriage. Or rather the lack of it.

A hitch in the stats . . .

A growing body of research in Australia has highlighted marriage— or a stable, committed de facto relationship—as pivotal to a woman's decision to have a child. Professor McDonald says it doesn't matter if the actual marriage takes place before or after having a child; the fact remains for demographers that the curve and dips on the marriage graph are a key indicator of likely movement in the fertility stakes. While Australia has experienced a steady decline in marriage over the past four decades, the leap into the twenty-first century seemed to really take the wind out of cupid's wings more than ever; and blow apart a few theories on demographic trends.

A lousy year for romance, 2001 saw Australia's marriage rate plummet to an all-time low, with only 103 130 marriages registered.[32] Theoretically, this wasn't meant to be. The year 2001 was *supposed* to be something of a boom year for the wedding industry. To understand why, it is necessary to hark back to the grand old days of the post-war baby boom, when fertility rates were over three per cent. The peak of the baby boom happened in 1947, when 182 384 babies were born. It was a good year to be in the nappy business. By 1971, around the time the baby girls of that first boom were almost 25 years old, snappy pants (the modernised nappy) were doing a roaring trade. In that year, when the median age of mothers was 25, Australia's biggest crop of babies ever was born: a grand total of 276 361 little Australians.

By virtue of their record number, the 1971 babies were considered the first 'echo' of the baby boom.

If we project forward 30 years to 2001, when the median age of a bridegroom is around 30 and the median age of a mother is also around 30, we could expect a mini explosion in both industries—nappies and wedding cakes. We got neither. In fact, quite the reverse occurred. In 2001, we saw not only the lowest marriage rate ever, but also the lowest birth rate on record.[33] So much for following in our mothers' footsteps.

On the margin of the would-be-but-wasn't 'second echo', the following year, 2002 to 2003, saw a slight increase in the fertility rate to 1.75; up just 0.02 per cent. Not enough to get excited about, but enough for the Australian Bureau of Statistics to allude to a whiff of improvement in the baby stakes: 'While it is too soon to be definitive, this plateau effect may represent a faint second echo, to be followed by a continuation in the downward trend in births and the total fertility rate.'[34] While the official demographers expect things to worsen, so too do the scientists. In its 'Future Dilemmas' report to the government, outlining options to the year 2050, the CSIRO worked with a declining fertility rate as low as 1.65 children per woman.[35]

By now the writing is on the wall. Clearly Australia is going to get older, faster. Naturally, no-one is happy about it. Currently, the median age of our population is 36 years old. But by 2051, half the population will be 50 or older![36] We will be surrounded by a sea of grey or greying heads, where children will be a delightful luxury and a spoilt minority. The social, economic and political implications of such a demographic shift will be far-reaching and, frankly, frightening.

Not even fear—be it fiscal, financial or downright fearsome—can stop this revolution. Women are responding to the world around them, and the circumstances in which they find themselves, by voting with their trump card—their fertility. This movement shows no sign of abating. Yet, the war by women to win some personal ground in their lives—before their body, mind and spirit are claimed by others—is an oddly silent one. It's a war where the foot-soldiers are not in collaboration with each other and there is no collective game plan. Instead each individual makes her choice, and takes the appropriate action privately, in isolation from her fellow warrior. No-one called for this revolution. It just gradually happened. Some people, despite being right in the midst of it, don't even know it's going on. For those women taking part—those who have delayed or are in the process of delaying child-bearing—the call to revolt may have come in many different forms. Perhaps some of us simply tuned into a subconscious *global* message: that this is the way it has to be, this is the revolution we had to have.

The childless revolution

For god's sake, people are entitled to make a choice about their lives. So what are they getting at? Am I supposed to not be a real woman because I haven't had children?

Helen Clark, prime minister of New Zealand, June 2002

The woman who does not have motherhood as a positive adult female identity has been, and is, a complication in our theories of female development.

Mardy S. Ireland, *Reconceiving Women*, 1993

Nicole is wide-eyed as she slaps a pile of scripts down on the studio news desk. 'Have you heard that?' she announces with incredulity. 'Have you heard what they're saying about how many Australian women are childless?'

'Yes,' I had. 'Why?'

'Well can you imagine what that means?' she says as if trying to come to grips with the incomprehensible. A small group of us stop for a moment, to consider it.

The 'official' rate of childlessness has bounced around demographic circles and become mired in academic debate for years. The Australian Bureau of Statistics seems to have settled the score with a figure so astonishing, it's got everyone talking. 'About a quarter of women in their reproductive years (15–44 years old) are likely never to have children' they announced.[1] Just when a one in four ratio seemed bad, the longer term forecast was even worse. Given current trends, the ABS warned, Australia's 25 per cent rate of childlessness 'is expected to reach 28 per cent'.[2] Nicole announces the figure in horror.

'Can you imagine the implications of that? I mean, what sort of future are we going to live in, with so many women childless?' Everyone nods, with solemn acceptance that this is indeed a terrible thing. We're silenced by the potency of it. But . . . hang on! What on earth are we imagining? A cold, heartless world, full of selfish, single-minded career woman? Workplaces full of embittered, barren broads? There are four of us leaning around my desk at the time as we absorb this dreadful news: three mothers, and me.

I'm certainly not the first woman to put a baby in my 'possibles' queue for too long. And I certainly won't be the last. When the American edition of *Time Magazine* ran a cover story in 2002 that screamed 'Babies vs. Career', you could be forgiven for thinking a whole new species of woman had been discovered. The cover, with its tantalisingly cute, naked baby, cheekily lying on top of an office in-tray, piled high with paper work, was a sidewalk stopper. The baby's bare bottom poked up from behind as he (or could it be a she?) laughed into the camera, teasing you to grin. The full-page photo inside was not so cute. Nor was it complimentary.

This new species of woman clearly has some sort of psychotic problem. Here she is, decked out in a designer power-suit, cradling a briefcase swaddled in a baby shawl, while she longingly caresses her palm pilot with the tip of a stylo. It's a ridiculous image, with a ridiculous message, but nevertheless it sounded a loud warning: women who pursue a career at the expense of early child-bearing will end up barren and miserable (and possibly take to hugging briefcases and rocking office chairs).

It wasn't just *Time Magazine* that leapt onto the 'new' childless career woman bandwagon. Around the same time in the US, the American *60 Minutes* program, the *Today* show, *Good Morning America*, *Oprah*, *Newsweek*, the *LA Times* and *New York Times* all hopped on board. The source for the new fascination—and post-feminist flagellation—was the release of the book *Baby Hunger: The New Battle for Motherhood*, by Sylvia Ann Hewlett, a respected American economist, author, and mother of four— including an IVF daughter she gave birth to at 51 years of age.

Hewlett sets out to document what she says is a 'painful well kept secret': the fact that career success for many 'high achieving' American women has come at the cost of having a baby; which for most of them is a source of great heartache and sorrow. Targeting the top ten per cent of earners in the United States, Hewlett found 33 per cent of high achievers—those earning US$55 000 to $65 000—are childless, and the figure rises to 42 per cent in corporate America. That proportion increases with income and status. Among the 'ultra high achievers'—those earning US$100 000 or more—Hewlett found 49 per cent were childless; compared to 25 per cent of similarly achieving men.[3] The core theme in *Baby Hunger* is *regret*. Only 14 per cent of the women say they never wanted children; with most arguing they are not childless by choice. One of her interviewees calls her childlessness a 'creeping non-choice'. 'What she meant,' explains Hewlett, 'was that during her thirties and early forties, career constraints and relationship difficulties gradually squeezed the possibility of having a child out of her life.'[4]

While it may be informative and somewhat comforting for women like me to know I'm not alone, and that I might be part of a bigger, broader trend, Hewlett's book, and America's obsession with it, nevertheless presents a conundrum. In fact, more than a conundrum. It presents a critical contradiction. On one hand, Hewlett would appear to applaud the smart, sassy success of the older women she interviewed: the so-called 'breakthrough generation' who were 'the first large cohort of women to deal with equal opportunity on a significant scale, the first to enter the world of work on—more or less—the same footing as men'.[5] On the other hand, Hewlett's solution to the growing rate of childlessness is somewhat alarming. She urges young women to set about finding a man and get procreating *before* focusing full throttle on their careers: 'You will make some compromises in your career. But you will catch up, re-invent yourself, when the time is right.'[6] In her final chapter on 'Having it all', Hewlett advises young women to have their first baby before 35, to choose a career 'that will give you the gift of time', and a company 'that will help you achieve work/life balance'.[7] Now if you think this is all sounding very nice, hang in there—it gets nicer.

While suggesting that women are happiest when they are able to have both a career and family, Hewlett also argues that, 'Mothers who work long-hour jobs tend to be significantly less happy than mothers who work reduced-hour jobs'.[8] And while extolling the value of children—'children help parents deal with the central questions of human existence—how to find purpose beyond the self'—Hewlett argues that, 'If employment is good for women, so are marriage and family'.

Now, I don't disagree with Hewlett's sentiment—I really don't. I have *no doubt* that children give meaning to one's life, and that they are 'enormously important in warding off loneliness, providing love and companionship'.[9] It's just that Hewlett seems to be living on another planet. I can just see some of the women you've already met in the earlier chapters of this book rolling their eyes upon hearing the American doyenne's suggestion to choose 'reduced-hour jobs'. As we know, many who *do,* do so at the cost of not just income and status, but their long-term career prospects.

We already know that the Australian workplace is neither forgiving nor flexible. We also know that many of those who 'opt out' of a corporate culture to raise children will often not find their way back. Remember Jenny in chapter 6. For her, the option of taking a reduced-hours job meant a 'lesser job'; and that was potentially more dispiriting and demoralising than no job at all. So she chose the latter.

For many women—certainly not all—work can be a tremendous source of fulfilment, empowerment, challenge and reward. For some, it can provide a singular and much needed sense of purpose and direction. For others, it may be just a job, but with the added bonus of social connection, stimulation and occasional gratification. Whichever way you view it, the personal satisfaction derived from meaningful contribution, and the value of an employer's appreciation, can be a powerful boost to the immune system; not to mention the ego. When it's not routine, boring and laborious, work can be fun. After years in television I still get a terrific buzz from a live broadcast, when we're flying by the seat of our pants. The whiff of adrenalin, the stink of sweat and the angst of expectation when big news is breaking can be sexy, exhilarating stuff. After a day of that—if you pull it off—a girl can be feeling pretty good about herself. But there is a flipside.

Career achievement takes time, effort, heartache, long nights, long days, lost weekends, before-dawn wake-up calls and forfeited playtime. Most of all, achievement takes energy: lots of it. For some of us, successful careers suck all the energy we have. While

Hewlett would appear to recognise this in her focus on childlessness, she fails to reconcile it. Her advice to young women to 'Give urgent priority to finding a partner' and focus on creating, building and nurturing a family first is all very well, but hardly practical. What about those careers, those paths to success, driven by the very women she has interviewed? Hewlett's 'achievers' clearly know how to focus—they wouldn't be where they are if they didn't. It's just that their highly trained focus hasn't been on their fertility. In all the empathy, pity and apparent compassion Hewlett gushes for her childless sisters, she has in fact re-cast such 'high achievers' as lowly failures: fertility flops and childless losers. In their place Hewlett wants to create winners. To that end she urges young women to lower their expectations. She suggests they water down career aspirations and put work plans and ambitions on hold. It's a message of: don't follow in the footsteps of these career hungry, ambitious women, because it doesn't work.

Here is the crippling—even painful—paradox. We *know* there is some truth in Hewlett's message that ignoring, postponing or delaying child-bearing is playing on the wrong side of fate. The 'leave it too late and you're stuffed' mantra is unequivocal. Her solution sells women dangerously short, though. A conclusion that encourages young women to lessen their expectations, rather than raise them by demanding more equity and support, is doomed. Such a conclusion simply isn't good enough. We can do better than this. We *must* do better than this!

Unfortunately, the stench of a feminist backlash has permeated much of the media fascination with this newly discovered species— the sad and sorry, childless career woman. The 'outing' of this miserable and barren being has played right into the hands of those wanting to turn back the clock. This is dangerous stuff. Those who begrudge women an equal place in our society, in our communities, in our parliaments and in our boardrooms, have latched onto the idea of an embittered-childless-career-woman with enthusiastic self-congratulations. 'I told you so!' they sneer. I was initially dumbfounded, then horrified, when my own 'outing' was lapped-up by various right-wing pockets of ardent anti-feminists, anti-abortionists, religious zealots and misogynistic nutters. Initially, though, I was touched by the care and compassion, even though I may have been confused by the politics underlying it. I was so focused on my own pain and my overwhelming need to express it, I didn't realise how dangerously polarised the issue of childlessness can become.

A *less than* identity . . .

Childlessness is an elusive thing. Unless a woman tells you straight out why she doesn't have children, you're left guessing. Since first broaching the subject of childlessness in a range of public forums, I've been frequently stumped by some of the forthright and unsubtle questions asked of childless women. The curiosity isn't just from other women. A male friend of mine leaned towards me over dinner and said in front of both our partners, 'I bet you're childless not just because you can't have kids'. Implying, I suppose, that there is more to the complications of childlessness than infertility. In that, he is right.

How does one respond to such a loaded question, masked as a provocative statement? Why does anyone care about another woman's childlessness anyway?

Fascination with childlessness is at fever pitch. Much of it is tied up with fear. We fear that the growing number of childless women in our society is spiralling out of control, and we're at a loss to know what to do about it. We sense a need to somehow arrest this growing trend because, frankly, it makes us uneasy. A female whose ovaries are aging yet who remains childless presents a serious challenge to our core sense of a woman's identity. It's the issue of identity that cuts deepest. What do we make of such creatures? Are they simply selfish 'hedonists' as one Australian study suggested back in 1994?[10] Barren, dried-up old prunes with taut skin, a heavy briefcase, a mournful lonely stare and a gaping hole in place of a womb, is an image that comes to mind (not surprisingly, given that was the pencil illustration one newspaper used to accompany an article I once wrote). In whatever guise we view childless women, it's negative. Even the terminology is negative: women are child*less*; the 'less' denoting an absence, a loss, something missing.

I was recently interviewed by a teenage girl for her year 12 project. She repeatedly interchanged the words 'feminism' and 'femininity', as if they were one and the same—an interesting, if not rather quaint, concept. It echoes a much more damaging and far-reaching integration, though: the failure to separate femininity from fertility. Female identity and the complex web of womanhood is so intrinsically enmeshed in motherhood that those who are non-mothers can be seen as nothing more than '*less*'. Harsh, but true—albeit unfair—as US psychologist Mardy Ireland argues when she says, 'A woman should not have to be left feeling that she has a hole in her identity, is unnatural, or is threatening to others simply because she is not a mother.'[11] Yet female identity would seem to demand that. The centrality of motherhood to women's identity has followed us throughout history. Despite the strenuous efforts of second-wave feminists, who reacted against that centrality by 'championing all other alternatives', as Ireland puts it, we are nevertheless stuck with motherhood and mothering as the most valued contribution a woman can make to society. Every mother I've ever spoken to about this confirms it: mothering, they all say, is the hardest and by far the most important thing they've ever done. However, where does that leave non-mothers and women who will never be mothers? Lurking somewhere in the shadows perhaps, forced to grasp at some sort of grown-up identity that isn't defined by its '*less*-ness'.

For the purists—some might call them extremists—in this revolution, being 'less' is in fact *more*. They are the ones who have embraced childlessness with such vigour that they intentionally and proudly define their life by it. These are the women who have denounced the 'less' in childless; instead they brand themselves 'childfree' in order to celebrate life in a world without children. So dedicated to the cause, some of the 'childfree' devotees will go to radical lengths to thwart their fertility in their twenties and thirties, as we'll discover later in chapter 11. While still a small minority, like most at the pointy end of a revolution, the 'childfree' are nevertheless vocal, and not without their political clout. Yet their noise and determination sit in stark contrast to the overwhelming majority, who are silent participants in the Childless Revolution. Although childless women continue to present a social 'complication', we urgently need to get over it. Because, as author Madelyn Cain puts it, 'Childlessness is about to come bursting out of the closet!'[12]

Show me the numbers!

Citing the numbers of women joining the Childless Revolution is as slippery an exercise as the revolution is silent. Often forgotten, or ignored, in the discussion is the fact that childlessness among Australian women was quite high a century ago. Back then about one in five women did not have children. Demographer Professor

Peter McDonald shrugs his shoulders and remains unalarmed by that figure, largely because back then the four out of every five women who *were* having babies, were having plenty of them. Unlike now. Also, as the Australian Bureau of Statistics points out, women born between 1910 and 1920 were at their fertile peak through some pretty tough and rotten times—when the Great Depression and war put a major economic impediment on courting, marriage and breeding.[13] The last several decades, and now well into a new century, these times—our times—are very different. We're richer, healthier and smarter. Indulged by a sense of economic prosperity and abundance, we've become complacent about soaring levels of personal and household debt and buoyed by a vague assumption that our future will remain forever fruitful. Yet we are even *more* prone to remain childless. The trend just continues, some would say, alarmingly—I say defiantly.

At its lowest, the childless rate dropped to around nine per cent among women born between 1930 and 1946, my mother's generation.[14] Women of this generation grew up to become the beneficiaries of the fruits of economic and social improvements post the Second World War. Then, the good times led to . . . well, good times. Not only was the childless rate at its lowest, but this generation took Australia's fertility rate to its highest level on record—peaking in 1961, when Australia produced on average 3.6 babies per woman.

Lifetime childlessness began to increase among women born after 1946. Since then, childlessness has steadily grown with each decade. Now, at 25 per cent, the rate of childlessness in Australia is higher than both the United States, estimated to be around 22 per cent, and the United Kingdom, at 20 per cent.[15] Like Australia, both the USA and UK have shown steady increases in these rates. *Time Magazine*'s seminal article, introducing the hapless-childless-career woman to the world (yes, the one who lovingly cradles her briefcase), reported that childlessness in America 'has doubled in the past 20 years'.[16] In Australia, it's taken just one generation to almost triple it.

The ABS is unequivocal about the trend; hence its forecast that 'for women born more recently', up to 28 per cent are expected to remain childless.[17] As we climb past the one in four women remaining childless figure, possibly towards one in every three, there is no doubt we are in the midst of a revolution. Women are making choices, both directly and indirectly, that delay, postpone, cancel or reduce their fertility outcomes. Call it what you like, but women are doing it. How much of this is conscious *choice,* how much is *chance* and how much is *circumstance*—or 'happenstance'—is open to vigorous debate and will be addressed in the coming chapters of this book. The fact is, women are continuing to do it, and it is changing the face and feel of our society. One of the more extraordinary things about this revolution is that the foot soldiers are largely unaware of the part they play, or the movement as a whole. Yet our numbers are growing and our demographic clout is strengthening. As Madelyn Cain so eloquently puts it:

> Childless women today are on the precipice of redefining womanhood in the most fundamental way ever . . . they feel they are alone; they do not know they are surrounded by a silent multitude.[18]

So who's signing up?

Who are these women? Obviously, some of them are women like me, but many of them aren't. There are some characteristics we all share, and plenty we don't. You may be relieved to know that some childless women don't even own a briefcase, much less aspire to big desks, leather chairs and a corner office with a view. The hapless, hungry, childless career woman is only part of the story, certainly not all of it.

The anxiety surrounding the need to define this new species has given birth to a range of academic studies over the past decade, all making a valiant attempt to understand and unearth the 'childless woman'. Some of those studies lend useful trend descriptors to the definition of 'childlessness'. We know, for example, that the more educated a woman is and the more she earns the more likely she is to be childless. Using data from one of the largest and most comprehensive social surveys ever conducted in Australia, The Household Income and Labour Dynamics in Australia (HILDA), in which 14 000 people were interviewed, Dr Nick Parr from Macquarie University found that 23 per cent of women with a bachelor degree remain childless.[19] He also found that one in five women who work in a 'professional occupation' are childless. After delving into women's upbringing, he concluded that childless women are most likely to have attended an independent, fee-paying school, have a father who worked in a profession and have been encouraged from an early age to obtain tertiary qualifications. Like many academic overviews, Dr Parr links childlessness to money.

'One third of women with a gross income of $50 000 or more are childless,' he says.

'Is that a lot?'

Parr is unequivocal. 'Yes. It is.'

Also using data from the HILDA survey, Professor David Charnock, from Curtin University delves even further into the issue of childless women and income. In examining the *expectations* of women he found those who earn between $50 000 and $90 000 were much more likely to 'expect to be childless'.[20] In stark contrast, women earning in excess of $90 000—those who Sylvia Ann Hewlitt would call the 'ultra high achievers'—were *less* likely to expect they would be childless. No doubt these are women who feel they can afford to have children. They can buy the support services they need—if they are to continue in their high-income careers. Or they have reached a career ceiling, glass ceiling, personal ceiling—call it what you like—but they're willing to let their career go on hold while they take time out for mothering. It's perhaps fair to also assume that such women feel they've established their career credentials solidly enough to enable them to 'opt-out' for a little while.

Perhaps most fascinating, if not obvious, is the number of inverse trends between men and women when it comes to childlessness. According to Professor Charnock's study, if women in a partnership are the main breadwinners, they are more likely to be childless. On the contrary, as a man's capacity to be the breadwinner increases, the likelihood of him remaining childless decreases. The higher a man's level of education, the lower his expectation of being childless, whereas the inverse is true for women. The more a man earns, the lower his expectations of being childless—again the flipside for women. Sadly, as Professor Charnock points out, across all groups of women, the desire to have children (or to have more children) is very often much stronger than the expectation that they will succeed in doing so. That is a miserable reality. Driven by what, for some of us, is a very natural, even fierce, longing to mother a child, and yet knowing that you probably won't, is painful. These depleted expectations aren't just about affordability, and the cost to one's career. Nor is childlessness necessarily a conscious or long-term plan.

After surveying over 1000 women across Australia—a third of whom were mothers and two-thirds non-mothers—academic

Rosangela Merlo believes that for most women childlessness is 'an unintended outcome, rather than a planned choice'. When I first met Rosangela in 2002 she was 36 years old and in the early phases of a PhD on childlessness. Back then, she was of the view that the so-called 'creeping *non*-choice' was perhaps more of a 'creeping *choice*'; in other words, the older a woman got, the more set and comfortable she was in her lifestyle, the more she would confirm her *choice* to remain childless. To her surprise, that is not what Rosangela found. 'I thought the ideal of motherhood had died for a lot of women, but it hasn't,' she now says.

Of the women interviewed for her survey—all between 25 and 39 years of age—only ten per cent said they didn't want children. Just one in ten! A shocking thought, when we already know that between 25 and 28 per cent of them will remain childless. Not surprisingly, Rosangela warns:

> You have to be very careful about the word 'choosing' not to have children. I don't think it's a conscious choice for the majority . . . Women want a lot of things in place before they would consider having children. It's very difficult to get the timing right, in terms of making sure that you're financially secure, that you have a partner that you want to have children with, and that your career is in place. It's all really difficult to manage.

This we know.

While it's all very well for Sylvia Ann Hewlett to urge women to think of breeding before career climbing, the reality is it's fiendishly difficult to get all the pieces in place, before many women feel ready to have children. Education takes time; establishing career credentials takes time; if you value the security of home ownership, then saving for a deposit takes time; getting the mortgage in place takes time; growing up, travelling, having fun and getting a handle on being an adult, all takes time. For some of us, even developing a maternal urge . . . takes time.

Despite the numerous demands pulling at young women during their most fertile years, the one overriding prerequisite for child-bearing is actually quite simple. It's not about career, money, owning a home or any other material acquisitions. What women want more than any other life detail, in order to have a child . . . is a secure, stable relationship. An increasing number of studies are beginning to unearth this, including Rosangela's survey, which found between 75 and 80 per cent of women nominated a stable, secure relationship, or ideal partner as the most important prerequisite to motherhood.[21] And as every woman reading this knows, partnership is not easy.

For some women, a secure, loving partnership remains the elusive holy-grail, as we will discover in the following chapter. Before we even begin to grapple with the problems of modern-day coupling, the problem of modern-day ignorance deserves a mention because, in the true spirit of revolution, how many revolutionaries have nailed their sail to the mast, blissfully ignorant of where the journey might take them? Among the Childless Revolutionaries, my hunch is . . . lots.

Putting your eggs on ice . . . and your head in a bag

The level of ignorance among women about our own fertility is astounding. In fact, mind-boggling. I'm no exception. As mentioned earlier, I had very little understanding of the rapid decline in women's fertility from the time we hit our late twenties.

I didn't know about the dramatic deterioration of our eggs from the age of 35.

When my GP curtly suggested I was leaving it 'a bit late' to consider pregnancy at 38 or older, I left his surgery dumbstruck and walked home in shock. Later, when it dawned on me that I might indeed have an infertility problem, like many women, I assumed medical technology and IVF would provide a miracle 'fix-it'. A view I clung to until I was given a list of IVF success rates and learnt that women aged 40 or over had around a six per cent chance of delivering a live baby at the end of the process (although that grim figure is gradually improving each year, as reproductive technology continues to advance). Nor did it occur to me, until the data was thrust in my face, that half the eggs in women aged over forty have a chromosomal abnormality. Little wonder most IVF publications insist on reminding women that while IVF may provide a pathway to conception, it can never 'reverse the effects of aging on fertility'.[22] It now seems ludicrous, even cruel, to think I spent so many years avoiding pregnancy by taking the pill, only to later learn that by the age of 35, a woman's chance of conception is only about fifteen per cent per cycle; by forty it is less than five per cent per cycle.[23]

Perhaps too, like many women who have never been pregnant, I had only a vague understanding of the role our fallopian tubes play in the fertilisation process. I do now—now that one of mine is in a hospital bin and the other is stuffed. But when first told I might lose my tubes, both Anne Marie and I had to scramble for our old copies of *Everywoman*, as we wondered what effect absent tubes might have on menstruation. Would it stop? (Unfortunately, no.) Only this week a 33-year-old work colleague, while telling me about her ovarian cysts, wondered out loud if fallopian tubes were like our appendices—basically unnecessary.

'Not really,' I explained. 'Not if you want to fall pregnant naturally.'

'Oh,' she said looking at me a little unsure. 'So you need them then?'

'Yep. You do.'

Perhaps the greatest misconception among the misconceived is the notion of freezing our eggs. Just wack 'em on ice! On hearing me equivocate about the possibility of having a baby 'at some stage', a friend of mine once suggested I simply 'freeze some eggs' before they got any older. At the time it sounded like a reasonable suggestion, if a little fiddly. Little did I know that no-one in Australia has ever achieved a pregnancy from a frozen egg. The technology is still in its infancy. Only two centres in the world have managed to succeed in creating a frozen egg pregnancy—one in Bologna, Italy, the other in Spain. Even then, less than a handful of pregnancies have resulted. Professor Gab Kovacs, Medical Director at Monash IVF, laughs gently when he explains all this.

'Unfortunately, I think the public information has been misleading,' he says. Although not wanting to be a complete kill-joy, he offers, 'What looks a more promising option is to freeze ovarian tissue—slices of ovary—but even that is at the very early stages.' While trying to be helpful, Professor Kovacs is also blunt. He says half the new patients he sees each week are women over the age of forty, all desperately wanting to fall pregnant.

'It's depressing,' he says. He's been in the infertility business for 25 years, over which time he's watched a dramatic change in women's expectations.

'Everyone expects to succeed these days,' he says. 'The community expectation is that everything can be fixed and everyone can fall pregnant.' Quite clearly they can't. Sadly, many of us find out too late.

Not all those who inadvertently sign up to the Childless Revolution are struck by the shock of failed fertility. For some women, their fractured fertility is little more than an interesting occurrence. A blip. A by-product of a deeper ambiguity. For them, life is rich as it is—with or without children. For such women, unplanned childlessness is met with gentle ambivalence; perhaps even relief.

Oh dear! Weren't we going to get pregnant in Paris?

We were a good few gin and tonics down and several rollies into a summer afternoon's yak, when Kate stumped me by revealing the Paris Plan. At the time, we were lazing on a couple of old, threadbare chairs in Kate's little, inner-city courtyard. I think I must have gazed past her, looking up at the high-rise housing commission flats towering over us, and held my pause for a little too long. I wanted to laugh, but wasn't sure if I should. Kate saved me, laughing raucously. I joined her. It wasn't that the Paris Plan was all that funny. It was just funny that it didn't work out. Or so it seemed at the time of telling.

If you live in Melbourne, you've no doubt seen Kate in the newspapers, or on TV, debating the merits and failings of Victoria's planning policies. Kate is a rare breed: an academic who can make urban planning sound enthralling, even sexy. She's a dynamic media talent, and unfailingly committed to notions of equity and humanity in the built environment.

For a decade or so, during the late 1980s and 90s, Kate Shaw was a key activist in and around the Melbourne bayside suburb of St Kilda; once home to a bohemian, counterculture of artists, actors, musicians, writers and film-makers. Before gentrification reshaped the place, Kate was one of St Kilda's local darlings. She was a celebrity agitator with high ideals, a wild child with laughter in her eyes. On a number of occasions she managed to hold major developments at bay with her sassy wit, intelligence, and all the legal and statutory muscle she could bring to the bargaining table.

Now, as she closes the last chapter on her Phd thesis, soon to be awarded her doctorate, Kate is ready for a long, long life of . . . thinking. Hers is an intellectual life. The less lofty practicalities of conception, birth and child rearing have eluded her. Both of us roll another cigarette, and contemplate why.

The Paris Plan wasn't all that radical; it's just that it came out of the blue. I have known Kate almost twenty years and, until now, I have never known her to seriously contemplate motherhood. She had always been whimsically 'ambivalent'. Sure we had talked about babies, our little circle of three: Kate, myself and Suzanne. Our tight-knit group met as undergraduates at Melbourne University. As we got older, married, staked out careers, bought houses and travelled the world; all three of us were a little surprised to find ourselves edging towards our late thirties . . . and childless.

The lobbying for a baby began in earnest when Kate was working on her Masters thesis. She was at a pivotal point in her academic career, when success would open the way to a lifetime of academic work—something she craved. Failure would send her scurrying for another career stream. Kate had already dipped in and out of various degrees, and was getting too old to start again. This time she was deadly serious. But Royce wanted a baby.

Kate and Royce married in one of the most romantic country weddings I've witnessed. She was 34, wore a short white dress and looked ethereal. He was 37, wore something hip and turned up in an old Chevrolet. Royce began the gentle process of lobbying for a baby almost straight away. Distraction, diversion and both their needs for career consolidation helped put a baby on the backburner—until Kate was almost forty.

At the time she was engrossed in her research and the absorption was making her bleak. 'I actually started becoming quite dark about my perspective on the world, and doubtful of our ability to change it in a way that would make it a world that I would feel comfortable bringing a child into,' she says. She smiles at the memory of it now—all that 'heavy', cumbersome worry— and laughs as I roll my eyes when she explains the 'theoretical despair' she felt about the inability of a post-modern society to improve things. At the time this was real, and Kate became increasingly miserable.

> Royce and I had quite a difficult time of it. So when he was talking about babies, I was just thinking, 'I can't. I haven't got the emotional space to even consider this.' We argued about whether or not to have a baby, with me saying in the end, 'I really just don't want to have one and I wish you would stop pressuring me.' Eventually, what he did was interesting. He just accepted it and didn't raise it again. He was disappointed. I think that was probably the lowest patch in our relationship.

For a couple of years a kind of truce was struck on the baby issue—albeit clouded by a lingering lack of resolution. However, by the time she enrolled to do her PhD, Kate's spirits had lifted and the world seemed brighter. Kate says she felt 'lighter'. She also felt she was in a stronger career position—a critical barometer. Around that time, with renewed emotional space in which to move, Kate found herself musing over thoughts of a child. Soon the musings became a full-blown preoccupation. Eventually the baby issue had to be revisited: 'It felt very cruel in a way, having already said no, putting Royce through that, and then opening it up again. It was very difficult for him.'

Now at 44, Royce felt he was getting old. After plenty of talk, they decided to give it a go. That's when Kate cooked up the Paris Plan. She was due to go to Europe for a couple of months to do field work. Her arrival in France would coincide with their wedding anniversary. Hey presto! Here was a conception date made in the stars! So that was it. Royce would fly over and find the perfect little Parisian corner of the Latin Quarter. Kate would arrive on cue, and their baby would be conceived in a few glorious days of French-inspired passion.

Now if it's sounding all a bit far fetched, you've got to know Kate to understand she was deadly serious. In fact so serious, that she even set about planning the birth:

> I went to the Royal Women's Hospital and wandered into the birthing centre and said, 'I'm thinking about having a baby and I just need to know that my body is up for it. I'm 40 and my husband is 44.' And they were like, 'Oh, gosh, well . . . older women make such great mothers'. And then I got the guided tour. I certainly didn't expect them to be encouraging, but they really were. They like women who plan.

As Kate and I laugh over the midwives' enthusiasm and Kate's cockiness at the time, I struggle to find that line about 'even the best laid plans . . .' By now, you've no doubt guessed—the Paris Plan fell through. Kate was there, ready and waiting on their anniversary day, sitting in a chic, Parisian café with wine glass in hand. But the chair opposite was empty. Royce didn't show. A dedicated journalist with an important career opportunity on the table, Royce stayed back in Melbourne to sign off on the deal. Kate spent their anniversary alone. And their Parisian conception remained . . . but a romantic idea.

Months later, when Kate returned to Australia, the baby idea had subsided for both of them. And life got busy. Now aged 43, with Royce 47, Kate says they're still giving it a go, but they're not holding their breath.

> We've just agreed to stop trying *not* to have kids. We've just thrown it open and put it in the lap of the gods. It's up to fate. If it happens, it happens. If it doesn't, it doesn't.

Kate knows that at her age a pregnancy is unlikely. And so do I. Which gets us both wondering aloud about 'why?'—why did she leave her run so late? Kate considers this for a moment:

> I think it's about denying the passage of time and feeling like I have forever. I just can't, won't grow up . . . I was a wild girl in my twenties. It was a difficult time to be a young woman in the 1970s and 80s. It was difficult to work out where to land. It was only in my thirties that I started making decisions about what I wanted to do. There's just a sequence of events in my life that have occurred, none of which I regret. That's just how my life panned out. A lot of it was not about conscious choices at the time.

Kate's childlessness isn't only about timing. It's also about ambivalence: ambivalence back then and a lingering ambivalence even now. Various factors have fed into that. One of them, Kate believes, is her upbringing in a household where both parents were academics:

> My mother says she didn't do a PhD because she had three kids. She's always been very clear that while it's not a position of regret, she wouldn't have done it that way if she had her time again. She has actually been a lobbyist against my having children in the most subtle way for a long time.

Considering that point, Kate later adds, 'Okay, I am a very grateful but complicated result of feminism and that doesn't escape me for a moment.'

Another contributor that has played into her ambivalence is what Kate describes as a fear of being 'trapped':

> It was a sense of closing off choices. That was kind of terrifying. Having a child is not a choice you can go back on. It's so irrevocable. It was a fear of commitment maybe . . . a fear of being constrained.

Does such a fear subside with age, with time? Like many of us at this stage in our lives, Kate has found her work—although passionately engaging—is no longer enough. The single focus of an intellectual life, while stimulating, is limited. She feels it's time to reorient:

> Of course, given my timing, I've reached that decision too late. Had I reached this point when I was 35, I would be in no doubt whatsoever that the thing to do now is to have kids, and I would do it. The fact that I'm almost certainly not going to be able to raises a very interesting question for me, because I think, 'What is there? What do I do?'

For a moment we're both stumped. I don't know the answer to that frighteningly hollow question from childless women, 'So now what?' I sense Kate is not struggling for an answer. In fact she's not struggling at all:

> I'm kind of excited about the possibility of working through that and moving into a whole new kind of era in my life. Who knows? Royce and I are free—we can travel, move as often as we like. Maybe we'll live and work in different cities. Maybe I'm going to end up in Borneo as a member of Greenpeace.

I really don't know. But it will be something that creates and maintains meaning in my life, in *our* lives. I find that openness exciting, enticing and full of potential.

Is this *relief* I hear? It's certainly the word that comes to mind. After all the talk—about the Paris Plan, the disappointment, the baby lobbying and the 'leave it in the lap of the gods'—what I'm hearing now is simple, unadorned relief. Kate has been spared the anxiety of child-rearing and all its attendant struggles with identity, constraint and compromise. For that she is glad. She looks at me flashing one of her famous smiles, and kind of shrugs.

Wanted: a way out of the unbearable lightness of modern-day coupling

In our world of rampant 'individualisation' relationships are mixed blessings. They vacillate between a sweet dream and a nightmare, and there is no telling when one turns into the other . . . As long as it lives, love hovers on the brink of defeat.

Zygmunt Bauman, sociologist and philosopher,
Liquid Love, 2003

Genevieve cuts me off before I finish speaking, 'But it's not through choice,' she says. 'It's not through *choice* that I don't have a husband and children. I'd love to be married. I didn't *choose* this,' she says lowering her voice. Genevieve stares at me. No, not just stares, she eyeballs me. She's scanning my face now, as if looking for a reaction, a clue that might help explain why at 39 years of age she is single, childless and desperately lonely. I have no idea. I just stare back. We both look down at the breakfast crumbs on the table and ignore the waiter who is asking if we'd like more coffee. Then she says very quietly, in a way that almost breaks my heart, 'I don't know why this has happened to me.'

Genevieve is extraordinary. She is the sort of woman that other women envy, albeit from a distance. She is smart, attractive, immaculately groomed, has a runner's figure, a great job, a spectacular CV, owns her own home, and travels overseas regularly. Yet, right now, it's pretty clear she feels empty. To look at her few would guess it. In her frantically busy job, in which she is the boss, Genevieve gives the appearance of a woman driven by work. In reality the long hours are a blessing—they fill the void.

Genevieve tells me about a school reunion she attended where she was fawned over by old school mates, impressed by her career success. Gee, they'd even seen her on TV. When asked if she was married and had any kids, she simply replied, 'No.' 'Oh, of course not,' was the quick response. 'You wouldn't have time for any of that. Not with your life!' Genevieve rolls her eyes as she recounts the story:

> And you know what? When people hear me say, 'Well actually
> I'd really love to be married. I'd love to have kids', they just
> don't believe me. It's not like I'm saying that just to make them
> feel good. It's the truth.

A few days after our conversation over breakfast Genevieve rings me, sounding awful. She says she doesn't want to go ahead with the interview. She says she doesn't know where she is right now. She says she can't bring herself to think about the choices she's made in her life just now. She says she is going to turn forty this year and the questions I'm asking are too hard, too confronting. 'Sorry Virginia,' she whispers before hanging up. 'It's just making me too sad. Bye.'

Searching for a clue . . .

Recently I was asked to participate in a radio forum, along with the Medical Director of an IVF clinic, to discuss fertility choices. Very quickly the discussion turned to examining why women are delaying childbirth; which inevitably led to the issue of men, partnership and commitment. It was a robust, frank exchange, supplemented by some insightful and intimate stories from talkback callers. When it was over and we finished our post-program debrief, I headed for a coffee at a local café. There I ran into a work colleague, who was having lunch with a friend of hers.

I recognised the young woman sitting opposite my colleague as Sue, one of an exceptional group of women I had met recently at a Sunday afternoon soiree. It was one of those lazy, laidback days. A journalist friend had invited a group of women over for an afternoon tea of homemade cupcakes, cigarettes and endless bottles of wine. I didn't know the host very well, and knew nothing about her guests, but I immediately warmed to them. Sitting around the table were half a dozen or so young women in their late twenties, perhaps early thirties; all of them bright, attractive, funny, successful, well-travelled, well-educated and simply enchanting. Yet, most of them were single. Hours later I wandered home wondering—yet again—why is it that women like this are alone. Well . . . not alone; there are plenty of them. But why are they alone in the relationship stakes?

Right now, in this crowded café, Sue is looking at me as if I might tell her a secret. Twisting her back around to block the people behind her from hearing our conversation, she says in a low, almost conspiratorial voice, 'I heard you on radio, but I missed the end of the program. Did you get around to talking about, um, you know . . . the blokes?' She shot me an embarrassed, almost apologetic smile. I immediately knew why. The real question, buried in this somewhat timid inquiry, was: 'So what about *men*? Where the hell *are* they? How am I supposed to find one? Why is it *so damn hard* to have a relationship?'

My current home city, Canberra, is a rotten place to be in if you're female, young, smart, successful and looking for romance. Chances are every other woman around the dinner table is too. It may be Australia's national capital, but it's also Australia's demographic nightmare. Everything here is out of wack, nothing more so than romance. This is a career town brimming with smart, young things, drawn by the scent of power and opportunity; or lured by some of the best academic facilities and resources in the nation. Here work rolls into leisure, and leisure into work: everyone is on the make. It is little wonder then that Canberra has Australia's highest income per capita, more doctorates per square mile, the nation's lowest fertility rate and . . . the highest proportion of childless women in the country. No wonder Sue might harbour a secret hope that a local radio program can give a few clues about unearthing love in a place that's so stiffly suited, middle class, politically preoccupied and loveless. Sadly for her, we didn't.

On the hunt . . .

Much has been said about why more and more women are remaining single through their twenties, thirties and into their forties. Most of it is crap, but we listen anyway. Some of us are scratching for clues; others bask in a smug glee that the 'have-it-all woman' isn't *getting* it all. So prominent is the new, hapless, single woman in-search-of-a-man, a media genre has been built around her. She's glorified for all her shortcomings in *Sex and the City*; celebrated for being a drop-kick in *Ally McBeal*, patronised in *Bridget Jone's Diary*; and held up as a one-dimensional, mostly selfish, sex starved, neurotic and chaotic broad in the countless chick-lit spin-offs. Still, we read them, watch them and, in Carrie Bradshaw's case, even try and dress like them. We identify with these desperate, single women hankering for a soul-mate, a committed partner, a husband—or, in Carrie's case, just a bloke who can utter the words 'I love you'. We identify with them because, despite their makers' creative exaggerations and moments of farcical parody, we *know* these women. Some of us *are* these women; even though most of us have never owned a pair of Manolo Blahniks.

When the four stars of *Sex and the City* appeared on the front cover of *Time* magazine back in 2002, single women everywhere could identify with various traits of at least one of these archetypical women. There was the independent, free-spirited Carrie; the nurturing, maternal Charlotte; the corporate, career hungry, anxious and somewhat humourless Miranda; and the glamorous, in-your-face, sex-loving Samantha. Along with the whiff of recognition felt by women eyeing the magazine, all of us—single or not—knew that *Time* had got it wrong. The foursome was deliberately depicted looking powerful, strong, sexy—a female force to be reckoned with. Fine, no problem with that. The problem was the cover's headline: 'Who needs a husband?' That's where we smelt a fat rat—albeit one gorged on misunderstanding or perhaps just a diet of *missing the point*.

Women everywhere instantly knew the headline's underlining premise was way off the mark. Of course these women—the gorgeous epitome of singledom—don't *need* a husband, a long-lasting mate or a committed love—call it what you like. Do they *want* one? You bet! And *we* know it. After all, that's what the whole show is about. That's the dramatic current that ran through each and every episode: the eternal quest to score a bloke. Not just a bloke to bonk—that's the entrée stuff, fodder for amusement—but a bloke who stays around for the full meal, and the dishes; the type that hangs in there longer than just breakfast. Carrie set the scene for bloke-hunting and husband-shopping right at the beginning when she said:

> There are thousands, maybe tens of thousands of women like this in the city. We all know them and we all agree they're great. They travel. They pay taxes. They'll spend $400 on a pair of Manolo Blahnik strappy sandals. And they're alone. It's like the riddle of the Sphinx: why are there so many great, unmarried women, and no great, unmarried men?[1]

To suggest the fictional, tough, smart, independent, single heroines of modern-day fables don't want a deep and lasting love in their lives—be it a marriage or a commitment to long-term partnership—is like suggesting they live on meat pies and milk shakes and never put on weight. It's crap and we know it.

Single girl smarty pants . . .

In 2004, a landmark report on partnering in Australia slapped another problem on the desk of policy-makers. We were all aware of the national 'fertility crisis'; the 'Childless Revolution' was beginning to gain media momentum. Now there was another prawn to throw on the barbie; *another* looming national crisis with women at the epicentre of blame. Australia, we were told, is in the grip of a collapse in coupling—we're just not mating like we used to. To most of us this was stating the bleeding obvious. At least now it's official.

The report, 'Men and Women Apart: The Decline of Partnering in Australia', was produced by Dr Bob Birrell along with a team from the Centre for Population and Urban Research at Monash University. In it Dr Birrell, a passionate and highly regarded sociologist, warned that since the mid-1980s, 'The marriage rate among young adults in Australia has plummeted and the overall level of partnering has significantly declined'.[2] By the report's end, partnering in Australia is not just in 'decline', it's in '*striking* decline'. The finger seemed to be waging in the direction of women; specifically *educated* women:

> Marriage and parenthood (whether in the context of marriage or not) is becoming a rarity amongst young degree-qualified women in Australia.[3]

> It is true that one third of degree-qualified women aged 30-34 are not partnered. It is also true that there are now many more single women with university education qualifications than single males with these qualifications.[4]

The situation, according to the Birrell report, is set to worsen. By 2001, among 25- to 29-year-olds, there were 40 per cent more women with degrees than men.[5] In fact, across every age group, women are now more academically qualified than men. That 'gap' is continuing to grow.

If we put educational qualifications aside, the situation still remains miserable. On total population figures, 47 per cent of women aged 25 to 29 are single; as are 30 per cent of women aged 35 to 39: a percentage that remains more or less constant for women right through their forties. Sadly, all of these rates have steadily increased over the past couple of decades.[6]

It's not that there is a shortage of men. There isn't. They *are* out there—in numbers at least. The 2001 Census figures showed, there were 287 000 *more* 'never married' men than women, aged 25 to 44.[7] Of course, being 'never married' doesn't mean the bloke might not have a partner. He could well be happily shacked up, even with kids. Perhaps it's more instructive to examine how many men admitted to having *no* partner. Those figures are . . . well, surprising. A whopping 41 per cent of men aged 30 to 34 declared themselves single in 2001.[8] By way of comparison, if we wind the clock back to 1976, we find 84 per cent of men in the same age group (30 to 34) were not just partnered, but *married*.[9]

So what's going on?

Dr Bob Birrell lays much of the blame for our declining partnership rates on the great 'economic divide', the so-called 'winners and losers' created by the social and economic policies of years of conservative, market-driven governments. Certainly at the bottom end that's true. There is no doubt the biggest drop in partnership rates is among the lower income, poorly educated sector (which should be a major policy concern, given this is usually the most fertile social class). However, that doesn't account for the ballooning proportion of educated, independent, financially secure women who can't find a mate. For that social class, Birrell and others blame the so-called 'marriage gap', a spinster-like term that nods to the women-have-out-educated-themselves chorus— a chorus repeatedly sung by those who'd rather see women back in the kitchen and blokes back in charge of the boardroom. Lamentably, it's a chorus getting an increasing amount of air play. 'Mr Right is no longer good enough for uptown girl', is the sort of headline to which we've become accustomed,[10] with another suggesting that women should learn to lower their standards and settle for 'Mr Not So Right'.

The belief that intelligent, educated women, who have managed to forge a career and economic self-sufficiency, are somehow to blame for the mismatch in the mating stakes is not only simplistic, it's offensive. 'Too fussy' is the frequently smirked remark about the countless single women I know. Popular demographer, Bernard Salt, who enjoyed almost cult status with the publication of his book, *The Big Shift*, in 2004, bought into and, perhaps unwittingly, fed the 'too fussy' theory. In pointing out the glut of unmarried men available in Australia, he told the *Sydney Morning Herald*, 'There is enough product on the shelves . . . It's just that many [men] are not meeting quality control standards.'[11] Is the inference here that educated women are simply too up-themselves to see past a bloke's university qualification—or lack thereof? Not only is such nonsense highly offensive, it's simply not true. Salt tries to explain the 'too fussy' problem by pointing to 'hypergamy'; the custom for women to marry or mate with a man of higher social status—'higher' by virtue of his income, education, gene pool or job. A throwback to yesteryear, 'hypergamy' no doubt still exists within certain mating circles, but there is plenty of evidence to suggest that women (and men) have moved on.

Back in 2003, a study by Dr Mark Western from the University of Queensland found that among childless couples, where both worked full-time, more women than men held bachelor degrees.[12] Dr Western also noted that many of those women were earning more than their male partners. He reluctantly admitted to the *Australian* newspaper, 'I don't like describing it as a market but . . . it appears men are "marrying up" in these relationships.'[13] Of course the flipside then must be true: women are clearly prepared to 'marry down'. This is no passing fad. Dr Western says he suspects the trend for women with higher education, and possibly higher income, to marry down is only going to grow.

Published the following year, Dr Bob Birrell's report goes even further. It noted that one in three degree-qualified women under the age of 45 have chosen to hook up with a bloke who holds a lesser qualification—either a diploma, or trade certificate.[14] If all levels of education are taken into account, the picture is even clearer. Dr Birrell suggests, 'Almost 50 per cent of women have married down, at least in educational terms.'[15]

Paula times one

Paula could be called a 'total package' kind of girl. On first impressions—she seems to have it all sewn up. She's good fun, well-accomplished, has a winning smile, loving friends and owns an immaculate, trendy townhouse that's great for entertaining. She's also carved out an exceptional career in one of the most male-dominated industries in Australia: the police force. When she joined up, almost twenty years ago, there appeared to be no such thing as a female sergeant. Paula never met one, never worked with one. Now she is one, heading up a team specialising in sexual assault. It's tough work but it is a supervisory role in which Paula thrives. 'I can confidently say I'm very good at it and I enjoy it,' she tells me, quickly adding, 'The police force has been very good to me.' Needless to say she's won numerous accolades. On top of all that . . . Paula is free and unencumbered.

With no kids and no partner, she seems to live a pretty breezy kind of life. I've known her since we were teenagers, although never very well. On the few occasions we meet at the weddings or parties of mutual friends, Paula is one of those women whose warmth and laughter are an instant magnet. It comes as quite a shock to learn that privately Paula's 'perfect' life is not what it seems.

I had never been to her house before. As soon as I arrive in the street I can pick the place. It's smart, gleaming new, with every white garden pebble and sleek, tall plant harmonised in perfect symmetry. Canvas sails, providing shade from a blistering afternoon sun, sweep across the upstairs terrace. Paula greets me barefoot, all smiles, cradling her pet dog, and we sit in her cool dining room, at a table big enough to seat twelve. The room, like most of this house, looks as if it's just been photographed for a David Jones' catalogue. She says she's getting over a dinner party she hosted last night and I marvel at the lack of dirty dishes (trying to suppress a mental flash of me lying on the couch on a Sunday afternoon, post-dinner party, surrounded by bottles, glasses, stale food and over-flowing ashtrays).

We talk of families. Paula has four siblings, all of whom married young and have families of their own. 'Most of the girls I went to school with were married in their twenties and early on I just had this expectation that I'd meet someone, be married at 25 and have children.' That didn't happen. And it still hasn't happened. Having just turned forty, Paula is privately agonising over why. 'I hate Christmas,' she suddenly spits out:

> I hate Christmas mornings because I'm going off as the single
> relative *again*. I've been single so long—maybe ten years—
> that some of my in-laws have never known me to have anyone
> sit at the Christmas table with me.

We're both a little shocked by the outburst, so uncharacteristic of Paula. Now that she's poked at a wound, exposing a little of the pain beneath, she peels back her cover:

> People often say 'Oh, but you're such a nice person, blah, blah,
> blah', as if to say, 'Well what's wrong with you?'. I know they
> don't mean to be offensive. Sometimes I think, 'Well, I don't
> know. I don't know why I'm single'. I would love to have
> someone in my life. I truly don't believe that I have been not
> open to meeting someone, I don't believe I've closed myself

off, or put up a wall. I don't believe I'm fussy. I've not been unrealistic or picky. I'm not a gold digger looking for a rich man. I really just want someone to complement my life not complete it, because I've got on with my life.

Paula stops, looks away, then quietly says, 'Look, I'm not a bad person.'

I'm speechless. I had no idea she felt so strongly about the lack of a partner in her life. Staring now at the ceiling, and desperately holding back tears, she tells me she is so, *so* sick of being 'Paula times one'. Having spent years proving herself in a tough work environment, accepting every challenge, excelling in every exam, Paula says her hard-won independence and success has in fact become a 'turn-off' in the mating business—a relationship hindrance:

> I just get the sense that because you have gone on and achieved and you've got a roof over your head and a good job, men don't have that sense that you need them. You're a strong woman and men are needy too. I think they need to feel they can provide.

Not surprisingly, being long-term single and working in the police force, many people assume Paula is a lesbian. Which wouldn't bother her—except she's not. As a police Sergeant she has avoided mixing work and intimacy. Her only long term relationship was for three years, back in her twenties, with a fellow junior police officer. It ended lovingly, but sadly, when she rejected his marriage proposal. 'He was terrific,' she says. 'But I just couldn't commit. I was doing a lot of travelling overseas. He was not interested in that whatsoever. I was happy just going out. I don't think I was ready for marriage in my twenties, I really don't.'

Now? As she's watched most of her friends settle into relationships, renovate homes together, marry, have children and become 'family units', the pain of what she's missing has taken a firm grip. 'In some respect,' she says, so quietly now I can barely hear her, 'in some respect, I feel cheated.' At this point Paula has given up trying to stop the tears streaming down her face. 'It's not my choice not to have children,' she says firmly as if that's a point that must be understood. 'My life has taken me in a direction that has chosen for me that I'm without a child.'

Just as I'm absorbing all this and realising how very different the public Paula is from the private, she floors me again by revealing she is contemplating having a baby. It turns out this is no recent consideration. She's been toying seriously with the idea of using donor sperm for the last year and a half. 'I don't think a day goes past without me thinking about it . . . mentally picturing what my life would be like with a child and doing it on my own.' Paula has met women who've done this, sourced the resources and studied up on what's involved. The biggest obstacle is proving to be a very deep and personal battle with the ethics of such a choice, and her fear that choosing to be a single mother may be a selfish act. 'I'd be bringing a child into the world who will never know a father. Something I have to deal with is: have I got the right to make that choice?' We both ponder that for a moment then Paula says:

> I've got so much love to give and I know that I would be a good mother. To bring a child into the world and love them and provide for them, to me that's just human nature. That's what we're here for. It's the circle of life.

While not rushing the baby decision, I can't help wondering aloud if perhaps Paula is still waiting in hope that a man, a potential partner, might appear in her life. After all, she's finally given in and dipped her toe into the world of internet dating. Okay, so all four dates so far have been contrived and unsuccessful, but at least it's a start. 'To be honest,' she says, 'my gut feeling is that it is not going to happen. Deep down my gut feeling is that I will forever be single.' Around this point every effort she has made to try and appear optimistic, even practical, collapses and dissolves. Paula tells me she feels she is a failure. Her reasoning is heartbreaking:

> Marriage is about publicly saying, 'I have chosen you. I love you. I want to spend the rest of my life with you'. That's a huge thing. I've failed because I've not been good enough [such] that someone wants to make that commitment to me. So many other people have been chosen by someone . . . but I'm not important enough for someone to do that. No-one has seen me in that light. That's where I see I'm a failure.

I ask Paula if she fears being lonely. Her answer is quietly matter of fact. 'I don't fear it because there are many days that I am lonely now. So it's not something that I fear because I'm there now.'

The loneliness of living alone is a wretched thing. For many women it's both a gift and a curse. There are times I would celebrate my peace and my space; when living in Sydney as a single woman I'd close my apartment door at the end of the day, relieved that I was finally alone. I loved that home, and I loved the sense of sanctuary I felt there. The rollercoaster emotions of loneliness meant there were also times I used that solitary place to bunker down and hide. At those times the cocoon could morph easily into an oppressive enclosure, where the rigid sameness, neatness and quietness of it all would set the black dogs howling.

No doubt, some of the growing number of single women in Australia would argue they are neither lonely, nor in need of a permanent partner. For them that may be true. Somewhere, at some stage, most of us are going to ache for something more. A place deep within someone else's heart, where we rate as 'important'; perhaps even 'most important'. Maybe it's a need to turn the free flowing, fast moving, liquid love of modern-day coupling into something solid.

Available now: brain, brawn and balls

Jen doesn't get lonely. She knows what she needs and purposefully sets boundaries around it. 'I need about three hours a day of company. I like people for about that. I don't like to eat dinner alone. I like to eat with someone.' So she does. Jen lives in a share house with like-minded friends, people who are also her intellectual peers. She couldn't live with them otherwise, as this is a girl who just can't brook dullards or dummies. Jen is 29, single, gorgeous and, according to a number of men I know, drop-dead sexy. She oozes fascination, and is a knock-out headturner when she's decked out in her favourite bustier, sipping martinis and ready to party. But a warning: if you choose to linger long, you'll need to be a member of Mensa in order to keep up with her. 'Either I'm really difficult and a little bit intimidating, or I'm meeting or looking for the wrong kind of people,' she says by way of explanation of her singledom.

Voila! Yet again, the hapless single woman blames *herself* for the unbearable lightness of modern-day coupling. It is true Jen's style is full on. Her rapid-fire American accent can make her an immediate draw-card; an object of curiosity. It's the speed and diversity of intellectual stimulation that gets you hooked—be it a discourse on world affairs; the ethics of immigration, the war in Iraq or her fascination with violent cinema . . . and that's just entrée. So why does she think she might be intimidating? 'Largely because I'm a lot of person. It's like a lot of thoughts, a lot of talking, a lot of thinking. I don't sleep much. I've been accused of exhausting people.'

Now I'm hooting with laughter as there is no doubt Jen would give anyone's brain *and* body more than a good work out. But this is serious. Jen is serious. She starts digging around for a few of her more conventional attributes, because as you may have guessed, there is nothing conventional about this girl, born in California, but a gypsy of the world, having lived in Europe, India, Japan, Britain, Scotland—in a tee-pee—and now in Australia. 'I'm a fantastic cook!' she offers, as if I'm taking notes for an introduction agency profile.

'I cook for my partners. And I like to do a lot of traditionally womanly things. I'm very into that kind of stuff.'

'Really?'

'I make pickles.'

'Pickles?'

'Yes.'

'I've never met anyone who makes pickles,' I respond, struggling to keep a straight face, but I can see Jen is on a mission to make a point. She is not just all global-sized brain and breast. She can also 'do stuff'. We push on.

'And jam,' she adds. 'And bread and all this kind of stuff. I like that stuff. I'm really diverse.' She pauses—most uncharacteristically—for a moment, then adds, 'I think a lot of people either find that a little bit disturbing or they find it interesting for a while and exhausting after a while.'

Like most single women Jen has sat with her closest girlfriend for hours mulling over the perennial, 'Why can't I find a bloke?' puzzle. Naturally, none of the concocted answers are satisfactory, or even true. That doesn't stop any of us devoting countless evenings, gallons of alcohol and three-hour phone calls to the, 'What's wrong with me?' question. There *is* no satisfactory answer, because we're all asking the wrong question, starting from the wrong premise. There is in fact nothing *wrong* with any of us. Right now Jen isn't hearing that. Like Paula, Jen suspects she perhaps doesn't project enough neediness; enough feminine vulnerability:

> I don't give off a sense of security that most men want from women. I think in my presentation of myself I focus on the independence because that's what I'm proud of and that's largely what defines me.

Jen is a woman who thrives on freedom, mobility and adventure. 'I love extremes,' she says by way of explaining her nomadic tendencies. 'I go to outer Mongolia so I can stand on top of a mountain and feel like the first woman on earth.' She is also probably the only woman who, as a ten-year-old, told her teacher she wanted to be a 'mercenary' when she grew up. Given her speedy yanky accent, I have to double-check with her that she doesn't mean 'missionary'.

'No!'

Of course not; silly me.

Born the only child of academic parents and into a circle of writers, editors and intellectuals, Jen's prime focus has always been education and life experience. Needless to say, she has bucketloads of both.

Her handful of long-term relationships have always been with men who live in another country—the kind of romance my own father used to politely describe as 'geographically unsuitable'; only Dad meant it with reference to one of my sisters dating a boy from Geelong. Jen's geographic complexity involves meeting in Tibet as he lived in Berlin and she lived somewhere between Australia and the USA. As Jen says 'I think about the whole world, the way that everybody else thinks about their city, like moving suburbs.' Yet, while she's never stayed too long in any one spot, Jen now says she's content to sit reasonably still for a few years while she works on her PhD at the Australian National University.

Maybe it's this new-found stillness, or maybe it's the fact that she's soon to turn thirty, but something has shifted inside this woman born of wanderlust. While not exactly looking for a life partner with whom to start a family—just yet—she nevertheless craves something 'solid' in her life. With an echo of Paula's description of wanting to be 'important enough' for someone to 'choose' her, Jen also hankers for that 'chosen' state. 'I miss that there's not someone who goes, "Your life is important and I'm looking out for you",' she says.

In the absence of that someone, Jen has filled the void with a passing parade of partners whose staying power can be counted in hours, rather than days—forget about months. For the most part, that's been okay with Jen, who is upfront and frank about her love of casual sex:

> It's that immediacy of knowing the newness, the strangeness of it; I find that totally intoxicating. I've pushed a lot of boundaries. I've had a lot of casual sex. [Then the lingering *but* . . .] At this point I'm just kind of bored with it.

When pressed, Jen admits it's a combination of boredom and disappointment that has rendered the continual stream of casual encounters empty, and perhaps nullifying. For her it's the lack of intellectual and emotional content that leaves the exercise, little more than that: a bit of exercise.

> The sex can be satisfying on some levels—like on a physical level—but it's no longer whole I suppose. I've explored the limits of my sexuality that I can with any casual-sex scenario. To move on with some of the things that I might like to enjoy and explore emotionally, there has to be more trust. I think that trust, and willingness, is something that's formed inside a longer-term relationship where you feel that it goes both ways and it's not just an act.

Then almost as an afterthought she adds, 'I'd really like someone to just give me a chance.'

Now the really hard stuff: how and where to find a willing mate? If she does, how tightly would Jen and he be prepared to tighten the bonds between them, before the tug of adventure, or the call to freedom, demand they loosen them again?

When free-flowing love leaves a stain . . .

British-based sociologist Zgymunt Bauman calls it 'Liquid Love', the stuff of ill-defined substance that flows freely in the fast, competitive and selfish world in which we live.[16] The stuff of modern-day love is so liquid it's increasingly difficult to try and structure something solid out of it. For a good part of our young adulthood, we just don't. Instead we let it flow: occasionally to the point of effervescent overflow or accidental spill. Later we wish we'd been more careful. 'Welcome to the age of semi-detached couples,' says Bauman. 'In Modern "liquid" society, relationships are, like high-tech toys, upgradable. We want the ties that bind us to be just as easy to cut.'[17] Bauman's is a bleak and pessimistic view of the world of modern-day romance and love. Sadly, it resonates with many of us; perhaps *most* of us?

Anyone born post baby boom into the world of generations X and Y, who has struggled to find lasting love, knows well the world of contradictory connections that confuse and confound modern-day coupling. Bauman argues that while we yearn 'to relate', we nevertheless remain fearful of going in too deep; of losing ourselves and surrendering to commitment. In an age where rampant individuality is not only tolerated, but actively encouraged, our primary focus is ourselves and the preservation of 'me'.

We are the daughters and sons born into a world of flagrant consumerism, where most things are measured by their productivity value, and all things have a use-by date. We toss aside anything that breaks, leaks, stalls or doesn't perform as we hoped it would. Disposability marks our generation. As does speed and turnover. Little wonder then that our approach to coupling is fraught with doubt, ambiguity, and little faith in durability.

Confounding our tepid trust in the longevity of partnership is the lack of structure and certainty that increasingly characterises modern-day coupling. While the timetable for wanting to settle down—if we can call it that—has crept past our twenties, well into our thirties, even forties, so too have the rules surrounding mating changed and elasticised. We are largely doing away with 'Marriage'.

By 2001, the rate of marriage in Australia had reached the lowest on record, and the number of divorces granted was higher than any other year in the previous quarter of a century.[18] For those who do sign the official register, we know that more than a third, and close to a half, will cut and run well before 'till death do us part'—the median duration of marriage is just 8.3 years.

While the ritual of engagements, weddings and old-fashioned vows of commitment might be considered limp and passé, we haven't really replaced the old fashioned stuff with anything better. Instead now we simply 'live together' until further notice, or until we're ready to move on. Cohabiting—once a sign of being wild and willful—is now recognised by even the Australian Bureau of Statistics as a norm. Given the loose and unspecific nature of the deal, it's impossible to track and trace the duration of such arrangements, so the ABS doesn't bother. In the USA it's been suggested only about ten per cent of cohabiting couples last more than five years.[19] In Australia it's anyone's guess. In fact, so blurred are the ambiguous terms of 'living together' many of us can remain a bit vague about when it began, and whose idea it was anyway. Often, it just seemed like a good idea at the time. Living with a lover can be as simple as shifting a bit of furniture. Leaving can be just a matter of shifting it out again. As Bauman puts it, 'You ask for less, you settle for less'.

Do we really want *less*? I doubt it. Yet we agree to merge aspects of our daily living (only *aspects* mind you; we keep much in reserve) without asking, or clarifying, where the relationship is heading or what the desired outcome is. In the world of corporate mergers, such uncertainty and ambiguity would be nothing short of laughable around the boardroom table. I can hear it now:

'So, what have both parties agreed to?'

'Nothing, Ms Chairwoman. They just want to see how it goes.'

'For how long?'

'Well, no-one is sure.'

'What sort of merger are they hoping to achieve?'

'Um . . . not clear. That hasn't really been discussed.'

'Well, does this merger fit in with each party's long-term plans and goals?'

'Don't know Madame Chair. That hasn't been stated . . . as such.'

'Given both parties seem to be edging towards their mid-thirties, have they considered the possibility of long term production, such as children—maybe a family?'

'Not exactly. They don't want to . . . push things. They're just going to see how things pan out.'

'In order to do what?'

'Well, nothing in particular . . . But there are a few economic savings with the sharing of household resources, etc.'

'I see. Is there to be an announcement to celebrate the beginning of this partnership, this merger?'

'Oh no, nothing like that. It's not that big a deal. But don't worry, we'll know when it's over. One of them will hand back their keys.'

Pity is, each time we do return the keys, both parties are that bit more battle scarred and weary. Necessarily, the armour against further love-bruising gets thicker and tougher with each failed match. For some it eventually proves impenetrable. For them, even a glimpse of unguarded intimacy becomes too much to risk.

'Relationships for me had become so threatening, a state to be cautious of, to protect myself against', wrote a male correspondent to *The Good Weekend* magazine, who at 44 was languishing in his love-battle fatigues. 'I was sick of repeating myself with women.'[20]

As we all toughen against the wounds inflicted by failed love, we resolve to take more care of ourselves and less risk. And why not? Born into a world of such liquid love, where the ground beneath us is forever shifting, we are a generation that favours being risk adverse. We carry on, perhaps eventually taking up with another lover, but making no pronouncements, no promises, but with an eye to keeping our options open. All of which is fine, if we want to remain in the transit lounge of commitment. But we don't. Some of us just get stuck. The simple fact of female biology—with its finite window of fertility—means that in the end it is women who lose out most.

'Look, I got in just under the wire,' says Anne Marie, all wide eyed and thumping the table to drive home the point (or is this a percussive way of thanking St Jude?). For most of her 20s and into her mid-thirties, Anne Marie lived with a bloke who was never going to be a long-term bet. In truth, he wasn't even a short one. But Anne Marie hung in there. In her defence he *was* very handsome, had the body of Zeus, and could cook a mean curry. That, however, didn't forgive his copious other failings. Anne Marie talked vaguely of marriage, 'One day'. But they never did. He talked vaguely of getting his shit together, 'One day'. But he never could. Thankfully, Anne Marie eventually saw the light and managed to extricate herself, with just enough time to meet David. The pair fell in love and within a few years produced two exquisite daughters, shortly before she turned forty. She did indeed get in 'just under the wire'. Not all women are so lucky.

Some women who find themselves suddenly single *and* childless in their late-thirties and early-forties, will privately admit to wasting vital—fertile—years in relationships that were never going to consolidate. As the window of fertility begins to close, for some it's then that a painful urgency kicks in. It is an urgency that is perhaps not possible for many men to fully comprehend, much less embrace. An urgency that may serve to skew the view from where each party sits. Men of course have no such timetable and no need to fret. Why would they? For the aging lad, uninterested in lasting love (just yet) the pickings are far from slim, as US author Barbara Dafoe Whitehead notes:

> Today, single guys . . . can count on a pool of attractive peer women who are willing to sleep with them, compete with them, take care of them, spend money on them, and make no big demands of them. And many men now believe that they have no reciprocal responsibilities to her beyond her orgasm, if that.[21]

Not surprisingly, it takes an Aussie bloke to reduce such an issue to its bare bones—or balls. Angus Fontaine, the former editor of *Ralph* magazine, does this when he bluntly explains: 'We want from women what we want in underwear: freedom and support.'[22] Ah, what a wag.

Going it alone: a jam jar of seed . . .

The decline in fertility over the past decade or so would have been much greater if it had not been for the increasing number of births to women who were unpartnered as of 2001.

Dr Bob Birrell, 'Men and Women Apart: The Decline of Partnering in Australia', Monash University, 2004

It's not about Jack

'It's quite a modern statement,' Catherine says as a matter of fact, 'to say that you want to have a child and you don't really care who the guy is, because you're not going to stay with him.' She pauses a moment. 'But I was never like that.' Instead Catherine did it the organised, methodical way. In an effort to reduce the element of 'chance' in her choice to have a baby, she opted for medical intervention and a sperm bank.

'At my age, Sydney is not a very friendly place to meet people. It's such a "me" generation. You do get battle hardened. I guess

I have withdrawn,' says Catherine. 'It's funny isn't it?' We both muse over that for a moment, because we know it's not funny at all. If she wasn't slumped back in her chair right now, Catherine, who is a youthful looking 43-year-old, could pass as a principal ballerina. Draped in a light summer dress, she is all beauty, long limbs, grace and serenity. Or so it seems. The serenity is in fact masking a troubled perplexity.

The idea of a baby, just like the idea of marriage, had always existed in Catherine's mind as an assumption—she just expected it would all happen.

'I assumed that there would be a house somewhere, a two-storey house, and all of that kind of thing.' But she didn't sit around waiting for it. After leaving university in her twenties, with a couple of degrees in sociology under her belt, Catherine turned her hand to journalism and landed a plum job on one of the nation's most respected newspapers. From the outset it was a tough, competitive and hungry environment, which was fine by her. With a flair for finance, Catherine eventually found her niche in the male-dominated business sector, specialising as an investment writer. Along the way there were several, unsuccessful relationships; mostly, she laments, with male colleagues.

'I didn't really have a plan. All I knew was that I wanted to have an equal relationship with a man. I wanted it to be a good, strong relationship and then I wanted to have a child.' As is the way with relationships, some hit the wall, others fizzled. Each time, Catherine did what most driven women do: she just got on with it:

> I was a career girl up until my late thirties . . . but by then I was feeling that this was just not enough. I had bought all these great suits and I really like all that stuff. But there was something obviously missing; although, I didn't really formulate

it in those terms. I didn't have much of a pop psychology insight into myself. You can be driven without knowing what is going on.

Eventually that 'thing' that was missing became an unavoidable presence in Catherine's life. 'I was just taken over, I suppose, by this sense of regret,' she says. The baby she had never had began to develop a life and persona of its own. Catherine was swept up in a furious mind battle: was this maternal 'urge' biological and primal? Or was it social conditioning—part of a middle-class wish list? Catherine wasn't sure. She desperately searched for some sort of intellectual rationale to explain what was going on, but found none. Eventually, several years of anguish won over and by the time she turned forty Catherine made getting pregnant her priority.

'There was just so much tied up for me in the sense that this was it, and I just had to give it my last shot,' she tells me.

As every women who has considered going it alone—choosing to have a child as a sole parent in her thirties or forties—will tell you, the journey is fraught with anxiety and moments of great doubt. The consequences of their choice are raked over and *over.* Can I do it? Will I cope? Can I provide financially? Can I deny this child a father? Will those around me support me? Will my child be stigmatised? Will it suffer? Have I got the strength, the stamina? Who will comfort me in the black of night when my baby won't settle and I'm exhausted? All these fears, and pages more, I've heard expressed by women contemplating single motherhood. How can I, we, any of us appease these fears? We can't. It is impossible not to be touched by the power of these women's desire, and empathise with the force of their urge. The courage of those women who, after examining every aspect of parenthood as an older, single mother, still choose to go ahead with it, is nothing short of remarkable. Catherine is one such woman. Although she is quick to admit she often felt less than courageous.

'It was awful. It was really awful to be a single woman and go through that program.' The 'program' was the DI, or donor insemination program, run by a Sydney fertility clinic. At the time Catherine was grateful she was a resident of New South Wales. Had she lived in Melbourne, Adelaide or Perth, she would not have qualified for the program as legislation in those states prohibited fertile, single women from accessing donor sperm. A challenge to the law on grounds of discrimination has since changed the rules, but the testing waters remain murky and new legislation is on the way. Under state laws in Victoria and South Australia women must still be 'medically infertile' not just 'socially infertile', to access fertility treatments. By mid-2004, one of the major Melbourne clinics had found a way around the prohibition by offering a self-insemination facility for single or lesbian women. If it fails after a set number of attempts, the women qualify as 'medically infertile' and are therefore eligible for reproductive assistance. Fortunately for Catherine, however, she wasn't put through the humiliating rigours of arguing her case.

The major question she had to face was the issue of the donor's identity and whether or not the male donor was willing to be identified in the future, should any offspring from his sperm wish to make contact. Naturally, for many women planning single motherhood, identity is a key consideration. Is the sperm provider a parent, with the right to be acknowledged as biological father? Or is he but a donor, anonymously handing over a tube or two of easily produced body fluid? While some women are very clear about the level of anonymity or acknowledgment they want from the sperm donor, Catherine wasn't.

She was given a file containing male 'profiles' and asked to select someone with traits similar to her own. It was a sort of introduction agency 'shopping list'—without the prospect of a date. She examined eye and hair colour, height, skin type, body build as well as brief biographical details about hobbies, interests and levels of education. The man she eventually chose said he liked bike riding and worked as an engineer. He also specified he was 'open to contact'.

After supplying details of her income, 'because they asked me whether I had the wherewithal to bring up a child on my own', she was engaged in a round of counselling sessions. Seven months after beginning the process, Catherine felt she was finally ready for her first insemination. 'From there,' she says, 'it gets pretty grizzly.'

The insemination itself was quite straightforward: you lie on your back and the sperm is inserted via a catheter, with little more discomfort than a pap smear. The whole procedure takes less than twenty minutes. To get the timing right, Catherine carefully monitored her cycle. Around the time of ovulation she did a daily dash out of work and down to the clinic for blood tests. At forty, her fertile 'window of opportunity' was slim and the business of getting pregnant was all about seizing the ripe moment. Given the sperm used in clinical donor insemination is initially frozen, its lifespan is shorter than the ready-made stuff—all the more reason to pin-point the ripest of right moments.

Quick success, of course, is never guaranteed. As is often the way when women deliberate and agonise over the decision to conceive a baby, Catherine assumed the hardest bit—the decision—was over.

'I was sure that I would get pregnant. In fact that was one of the reasons I quit my job. It was a kind of pre-emptive strike.' Around the time she first began considering donor insemination, Catherine had taken on a major career challenge, accepting a job as editor of a new magazine. Intent on not squandering a moment of down time, she also took up studying law part-time. Now, in preparation for a fulsome preoccupation with pregnancy, she knew she couldn't keep up the pace. The option to work from home as a freelance journalist seemed a perfect solution.

Set with a maternity mentality, Catherine was surprised, and perhaps a bit dumbfounded, that the first couple of attempts of DI didn't work. Yet, for a woman accustomed to success, failure only gave rise to increased determination:

> Medical technology is basically endless if you've got tons of money to pour into it. So I said, 'I'm just going to go for the basic treatment'. If you're a healthy person and the sperm is healthy, then it should work. But you get more and more committed as you go through. By about the fourth go, I couldn't believe it. I couldn't believe that I couldn't conceive. I suppose I should have checked the statistics, but I just thought surely I would get pregnant.

Although Catherine can't recall what she was told at the time, most clinics now are frank and upfront in telling donor recipients that between fifty and sixty per cent of women will fall pregnant after between six and nine cycles, which can mean up to nine months of regular inseminations. Most will stress that it is a 'process', rather than a one-off attempt. Many will also shy away from offering the service to women in their early forties.

Catherine had placed great faith in success, but even fierce faith can wilt. Eventually, after more than a year of treatment and eight attempts at donor insemination, the waiting, hoping and failing took its toll. Catherine was wrung out.

'I'm quite business-like. I made the decision to stop and thought, "That's enough. There's just no point in throwing any more money at this".' The business of women's business doesn't always obey businesslike rules. The truth was Catherine was shattered:

I was incredibly unhappy. You're rendered completely inarticulate by the misery. But I don't think I realised for about a year afterwards that it had kind of paralysed my life.

What does a woman do when she's restructured her life and mind around having a child and it all falls over? There is not much to do . . . but work—and perhaps study. Catherine has done both furiously. In the last couple of years she has completed a masters degree, bought herself a dog and begun a PhD. But the going has been far from smooth: when her new puppy, Jack, was recently found to have a rare disease and the prognosis looked grim, Catherine was inconsolable. The flood of tears and heartbreak were very real, but Catherine says she knew it wasn't all about Jack:

> It was this wound that had just not healed. I could not believe that it was still that strong. There is something so terrible about crying that goes on for hours and hours and hours.

Catherine told only three people about her dream of having a baby but she has not raked over the collapse of that dream with anyone. Now, rubbing her heart as if rubbing a wound, she says quietly, 'Somehow you have to find a way to let people who know you really well, know how deep it is.'

Since she closed the book on donor insemination and ended her baby-making journey, Catherine has remained in awe of the power of these emotions. It's not just the aching urge to have a child, and the consequent failure that has rattled her; it's also the shock of realising how little she understood herself during those busy career-building years:

> I got to the end of my thirties and I'd just kind of been scrambling around, and that's when it all came down on me. Even more so after the failure of the DI program. I really felt, 'How could I have not known myself?' It's just astonishing

that you can live with a set of assumptions and not know what you really fundamentally want.

We both pondered that for a moment; then she adds:

It is such a gamble isn't it? I do look back now and it feels like I made this huge gamble. It's kind of like a high stakes game I didn't even know I was playing.

A dearth of donors . . .

Maybe we are a generation of 'gamblers'. Hordes of thirty-something women playing a 'high stakes game', with only half-an-eye on our biological clock and a winking eye on lady luck. Perhaps it's an inherent optimism fed to us in the 'having it all' gruel we consumed when young. Or maybe it's just flimsy naivety. Whatever it is, it's causing more and more single women to front up at infertility clinics in the hope of making a baby. Many more will leave empty handed than those who flip an ace.

Few are aware of it, and even fewer talk about it, but Australia is tinkering on the verge of a sperm drought. Fertility clinic fridges are low on stock. Supplies are running dry. For a nation that prides itself on macho virility, this would be funny if it weren't so serious. Just as an increasing number of women are requesting access to donor sperm, fewer and fewer men are prepared to give it up. And for good reason.

Around the country state and territory laws governing sperm donation are becoming increasingly tough on the issue of a donor's identity. Once a sperm donor could nominate whether or not he wanted his identity revealed but now various jurisdictions are taking that choice away. When Victoria passed *retrospective* legislation allowing a sperm donor's identity to be revealed to his offspring at the age of eighteen—however many offspring there may be—many fertility clinics went into a panic. They knew most donors would not want the complication of their identity revealed.

'We just don't hear from them again,' says Dr Chris Copeland, the Scientific Director of the Canberra Fertility Centre. While the ACT does *not* have legislation that exposes a donor's identity, Dr Copeland says his clinic warns potential donors that the law could well change. He expects it probably will. His clinic is therefore up-front in telling would-be-donors that they could have a biological 'son' or 'daughter' knocking on their door in eighteen years' time. It's perhaps not surprising then that sperm donors are quickly becoming a dying breed.

In January 2005 one of Australia's most active fertility clinics, Victoria's Monash IVF, revealed it had only thirteen sperm donors on its books. In desperation, and with a keen eye for wicked irony, Monash's Professor Gab Kovacs wrote to every male Member of the Victorian Parliament, aged forty-five and under, with an earnest request: 'Have you ever thought of becoming a sperm donor?' He went on to press the case for urgently needed 'suitable' sperm, while highlighting the new legislative requirement in Victoria for a donor to agree to be identified. Not surprisingly, there were no takers (or givers). While political wanking—metaphorically speaking—may be acceptable in public, apparently not in private, albeit for the public good.

If Monash IVF's donor list looks slim, Canberra's is positively anorexic. In 2004 there was a grand total of just eight sperm donors for the whole of the ACT region. Over a twelve-month period their sperm was used for around 110 treatment cycles to try and impregnate around thirty women. To supplement their meager supply, Dr Copeland says the clinic also buys sperm from Denmark. Canberra has another fertility clinic that offers a full range of reproductive services to women, but they don't bother with donor insemination.

'They won't touch it with a barge pole,' says Dr Copeland, 'And to be perfectly honest, I can't blame them. It is a minefield.' He says a number of Sydney clinics have stopped offering donor sperm services for the same reasons. In fact, he's been wondering if his own clinic should continue the service: 'We've talked about this and we've taken the view that perhaps we're a bit mad doing it. Perhaps we should be a bit more realistic about it, but we've decided to stick to it.'

Nevertheless, by April of 2004, Dr Copeland's clinic had stopped offering direct donor insemination. Instead the clinic provides single and lesbian women access to donor sperm through IVF. The very low success rate of donor insemination, and the scarcity of available sperm, made straight insemination too wasteful. Dr Copeland says DI could take up to sixteen 'straws' of sperm to achieve one pregnancy, whereas the more efficient IVF process could achieve success with an average of less than one and a half 'straws'. While donor sperm is quickly becoming a rare commodity, it was a matter of rationing the resources.

The downside for single and lesbian women seeking sperm is that they now have to go through a much more invasive and costly process, even though they may not be medically infertile. Dr Copeland says he has resisted pressure to stop providing the service altogether.

'The other option is that people just go out and have one night stands,' he says, 'And we're not really sure that's the right way to do things.' Despite being costly in resources, time and money, Dr Copeland says he believes his clinic is providing a much needed service by trying to meet the needs of women in search of sperm. If they go through the clinic he says, 'At least there's a set of rules, people know where they stand before they start. These other "open-ended" arrangements are just fraught with danger.'

Difficult as they are, *some* of those 'open-ended arrangements' prove to be far from dangerous—just dangerously fraught.

Close the bathroom door, I'm basting!

What's not to love in Heather's house? It's sunny and light, a chocolate cake is cooking, Mozart is playing and several little people wearing no clothes, other than multi-coloured undies, are squealing with laughter, running in circles around the loungeroom. At the centre of all this energy sits Heather, relaxed and laughing as one child tumbles over another. Today is her 41st birthday. The kids are helping decorate the house for tonight's party, but paint and paper have given way to catch-me-if-you-can. One little dot throws herself at Heather and wriggles into her lap, as the bigger two take off up the stairs, a trail of giggles left in their wake.

I wonder if Heather's staff ever see her as I see her now— basking in motherly love and radiating calm. As senior executive and divisional head of a Commonwealth department, Heather manages a staff of seventy, and oversees a department of 5000. It's a huge job that sometimes has her wondering if she should try and restructure her life to give more time to parenting.

'At various times I think I want to do something else. I don't want to live like this. My work is too all-encompassing,' she says. Only one of the squealing children is hers, the others are playmates. Her beautiful, lanky little boy, Zac, has just started kindergarten, and Heather is feeling the tug between his need for playtime and her need to work. 'At the beginning of this year, I went through a whole, "I can't keep doing this. I can't work like this and manage him at school. This is ridiculous".' Not surprisingly, Heather *is* managing it all exceptionally well. But then, she's an exceptional sort of woman.

Heather insists she was never particularly career orientated. Born in the 1960s and one of the first wave of women given full and free access to tertiary education, she wandered into university, and wandered out with an honours degree in history and a job in the public service. The times were good and life was long—or so it seemed:

> It wasn't until I got to about thirty that I noticed there was a lot of relationship mucking around with a lot of my friends. We had relationships that would last about four years; then we would meet someone else and move on. We never actually thought, 'This is the person I'm going to be with for my life'. It became a real issue for me. I just felt that life was very self-absorbed and had a fair degree of vacuousness to it. There was lots of money, lots of disposable income, but I started to think 'What am I doing? Where am I going?'

Heather says she developed a fear of waking up later in life and wondering where and when it all passed her by: a fear of never 'kicking into adulthood'. So she got serious about the thing most central to her sense of being grown-up—having a child.

At the time Heather was in a lesbian relationship, which, she wryly points out, meant there was no chance of an accidental, 'Oops, I've just found myself pregnant' kind of pregnancy. 'It wasn't going to happen for me without doing some thinking and planning about it,' she acknowledges. There were clearly a number of practical and emotional hurdles to tackle before she could even begin to ponder a method of conception. There were also more immediate issues: the very same issues any woman considering motherhood can face, regardless of the gender of her mate. Firstly, and most painfully, Heather's partner responded with only lukewarm enthusiasm to the idea of parenthood. Secondly, Heather's years of battling with endometriosis placed doubts over her ability to get pregnant at all. It was with this cloudy and uncertain backdrop that she began the journey towards motherhood—a journey that took several years, numerous attempts, agonising set-backs, loss and plenty of grief.

From the outset, the baby-pull was an emotional one for Heather; a 'driving force' in which she invested an enormous amount of painstaking consideration. 'It became a project and it took up more and more of my time. And I became more and more insistent that that was what I was going to do,' she tells me. As the idea took shape, and the search for a father began, Heather's partner showed signs of withdrawing from the project. Ironically, that only served to help clarify Heather's commitment to motherhood. She realised what she was prepared to lose.

'I knew that if I had to make a choice,' she says, 'between having the child and the relationship, I would have the child.'

Initially the women agreed that together they would try and choose a male friend to supply the sperm. Their quest ground to a halt, after months of deliberation. Heather then made a unilateral decision and put the delicate question to one of her oldest and dearest friends, Colin.

'I chose the person I thought I could talk best with. I thought if we ever got into any confusing conflict I would be able to negotiate a path through it with him,' says Heather. Colin was neither surprised nor shocked by the request. He knew Heather intimately—they had been childhood sweethearts. Now he was in his early-thirties, single and hopeful of one day becoming a parent himself. 'There was a lot of talking,' Heather adds. 'I think it was a very difficult decision for him.'

Eventually Colin agreed to help Heather conceive a child, so that she and her partner could become parents, but there were some clear parameters to be drawn up first. Colin explained he wanted to have a child of his own and he wanted to live with that child, and therefore he did not want this arrangement to be his only experience of fatherhood. To that end, he said he would take no financial responsibility for Heather's baby. Instead he wanted to be nothing more than a good family friend, 'an uncle' of sorts. In explaining the deal to me, Heather is still clearly moved by the profound generosity and integrity of her friend. After struggling for words befitting the gesture, she says simply, 'He is a very, very generous man and it was a really enormous gift.' The love evident here is palpable.

At the time, Heather had a supportive local GP and got a referral to a fertility clinic in the ACT. Already into her early thirties, and fearing her endometriosis could slow down the conception process, Heather just wanted to get going the moment Colin said yes. Nevertheless, she visited the clinic and began a round of consultations. She was told Colin, her chosen sperm donor, was required to undergo tests for HIV and hepatitis C, and then wait six months before taking the tests again. In the meantime his sperm would be frozen and available for use once the second round of tests proved he was clear of any transmittable disease. Additionally, Heather was told she must undertake a course of clomid, a fertility drug used to help induce and enhance ovulation. For Heather, it all seemed too slow and too cumbersome. Colin had already arranged his own HIV test and they were satisfied with the results. Heather had been carefully monitoring her cycle for some time, and was confident she knew when she was ovulating. Eventually she decided she could manage the conception herself.

The equipment was simple: the privacy of a bathroom, a jam jar of seed and the modern-day version of a 'turkey baster': the needle-less syringe. Heather discussed the process with her doctor:

We talked about technique and how to keep things sterile. I had very comprehensive temperature charts in the morning. When I was ovulating, Colin would come over and he would ejaculate into a jar and then I would inseminate using the syringe. I did it straightaway so it was fresh semen.

After two failed attempts, Heather got lucky on her third cycle. Then she got unlucky.

The reality of this long discussed pregnancy suddenly hit home to her partner of four years and it was too much. 'The relationship broke up as soon as I was pregnant. It just fell apart that very minute,' Alison says, still sounding a little bewildered by the finality of it. There was more loss to come. At ten and a half weeks Heather miscarried. 'It was horrible. I lost the relationship and the baby. Also, I didn't know whether the miscarriage was going to be the first of a long stream of miscarriages.' Heather was almost 34 years old and was feeling desperate. She knew Colin's 'gift' of sperm had always been in the context of a lesbian partnership, but now she was alone. The boundaries were blurred. None of that crushed her sense of entitlement to motherhood, though:

> I certainly felt I had a right and I could decide to have a child on my own if I wanted to. It didn't feel like it wasn't okay for me to be a parent if I didn't find a partner. I didn't feel that at all, which is sort of astonishing really. In retrospect a lot of that was blind optimism which was not very realistic.

Heather returned to the fertility clinic to consider trying again, but this time with an anonymous donor. 'In some ways that would have been much easier,' she says now. 'It's all set up. I wouldn't have had to take any extra responsibility. There is no legal confusion. It is all controlled.' But there was a hitch. While donors are now told that their identity may one day be revealed to the child, at the time Heather sought treatment the legal case against donor anonymity was in its infancy. Back then, in the late 1990s, many donors and donor recipients felt they could only participate in an insemination program *if* anonymity was guaranteed. Heather felt the opposite: 'It wasn't that I wanted to sheet home any responsibility for the child; I wanted to take responsibility myself. I just didn't think anonymity would be fair to a child.'

Heather decided to sit down with Colin and asked for his help, again. Again he agreed, but, as Heather explains, there was some 'reclarification' of the terms and conditions:

> For him that meant, 'I want to do it on exactly the same basis. I still don't want to be financially responsible. I don't want to be legally responsible. I don't want to be on the birth certificate'.

All of which Heather accepted, albeit with disappointment:

> I would have liked him to have more involvement. It would have been good for me if he had said, 'We'll co-parent this child'. I was terrified of doing it on my own. But he was always very clear about where his boundaries were.

Colin and Heather agreed that the child born of this 'gift' would know that Colin was the biological father; and they also agreed to be open about the paternity with their friends and families. With these boundaries drawn-up, the basting device was put into action . . . and Zac was conceived.

Then . . . along came Phil.

If you hadn't guessed by now, Heather's story is as complicated as it is unusual. Just when you think you've got a handle on the deal, another man turns up. Phil met Heather when she was three months pregnant. A veteran of two marriages and father of three children, he began wooing Heather immediately. At this stage she had moved from Canberra to Tasmania for a job promotion and to be closer to her family. Phil moved too. Four weeks before her baby was born, Phil moved in with Heather. He was by her side throughout the labour and helped deliver the baby, from the outset calling himself 'Dad'. For a while the happy couple were very happy parents.

'He was fabulous,' says Heather, smiling at the memory. 'He was just fantastic.'

After the birth of her beloved Zac, an interesting thing happened to Heather—the woman who said she had no strong career ambitions. Suddenly everything was possible and her confidence in her own capabilities surged. She applied for, and won, bigger, better and tougher employment positions. The new family returned to Canberra and soon Phil was a stay-at-home dad, while Heather hit executive level in the public service big time. But it was short-lived. After about two-and-half years Phil left and Heather was alone again.

He didn't go far. Love and care for his son drew Phil back on a regular basis. Now, three years down the track, Zac continues to have a dad of sorts, who lives in another house and has him around for sleep-overs two nights a week. The truth about this complex little family unit is there for the asking, but rarely does Heather get the opportunity—or feel the need—to explain: 'For many people in my broader life, they still think that Phil is Zac's biological father. They just assume that it is a normal separation.' As for Zac? Well he still calls Phil 'Dad'. But at five years old, he's been told the difference:

> Whilst Zac doesn't understand reproduction in any depth, what he knows is that I was on my own and wanted to have a baby, and Colin helped me make a baby; and that was a really big

gift. Then when I was pregnant Phil came along and wanted to be his dad; and that was another sort of gift.

Where is the biological father in this scenario? Perhaps unsurprisingly, he has remained gracious about the whole deal.

'He handled it in exactly the way that he said he would,' says Heather. As for any future twists and turns in arrangements or unforeseen requests from Zac as he grows up? According to Heather, Colin has promised to help provide however he can.

'He said he would be open to dealing with Zac's needs as he got older in whatever way we thought made sense. So it was a big offering,' Heather admits. Colin continues to spend time with Zac, but has no input into his parenting, and treats him just like the son of any close friend. In the interim, Colin's own circumstances have changed. Having finally realised his dream of partnership, he has fallen deeply in love with a woman who is now expecting their first child.

Perhaps the saddest and most difficult aspect of women going it alone is the lack of a shared responsibility.

'There is really nobody who has the same emotional investment in Zac's life as I do,' says Heather, struggling a little to maintain what has been up until now an optimistic composure. She adds gently, 'And sometimes that is really, really lonely.' In a loving move, Colin has offered to take full custody and care of Zac should anything happen to Heather, which clearly gives her an enormous amount of comfort. In the meantime, Zac has a father figure in Phil, and for that Heather is grateful:

One of the things that lesbian women I know who have had children with anonymous donors say to me is that at least Zac has *someone*. They describe a real 'dad hunger' among their children; which may be more symbolic than actual.

Just as the children of donor arrangements might demonstrate a dad hunger, so too does the broader community express a 'partner hunger' attitude to women who go it alone. When Heather first managed to get pregnant with Zac, and announced her intentions to go-it-alone, many family and friends remained uncomfortable about the path she was travelling. Little wonder a man who suddenly tuned up on the scene was greeted as a gift from the gods.

'I think people were obscenely happy—I actually found this a bit sickening,' she says. 'But people were very pleased that Phil had turned up out of the blue, on his great stallion, to rescue me from this life.' It's an image that makes us both laugh out loud. Yes, she couldn't have done it without Colin, and with much gratitude to Phil, it is clearly obvious that Heather is fine on her own; and her life is blessed.

At that point Zac emerges from upstairs, decked out in long pants, ready for a play in the park. He tells me he is wearing his 'wedding pants'.

'Oh, did you get married?' I enquire.

'No. Not me. I just went to a wedding, and these are my wedding pants.'

'But we got married,' pipes up his exquisite strawberry-blonde friend, Halle.

'Yes, Halle and I got married,' he tells me earnestly. 'And we might get married again.'

Those deviant women

Heather's story is one of a loving home, a beautiful, happy child and supportive caring adults, but it is nevertheless an unusual one. Unusual in that we rarely get to glimpse over this side of the fence. Instead, much of the public discourse and political debate surrounding lesbian and single women choosing to become mothers is fed by a stereotype, a figment of the conservative imagination, that suggests such women are selfish, undeserving and self-serving. Possibly even deviant.

While the position of single or lesbian women who want children has long been maligned and their status demeaned, the demonising has been ratcheted up of recent times as more and more of these women come forward. Ever since the rights of such women to receive access to reproductive technologies in Victoria was battled out in the federal court back in July 2000, the issue has raged around the *morality* of a woman's choice. In the mainstream media, and throughout our houses of parliament, lesbian and single women have been dumped at the extreme bottom end of the 'good' mother versus 'bad' mother slippery pole. It would seem there is no let up.

'I cannot believe the selfishness of some women', bellows a Melbourne man, so incensed he penned his objection to the *Herald Sun* newspaper. 'This is madness', he adds. 'First they put themselves in relationships where they cannot have children, then they have the cheek to claim they have been discriminated against'.[1] Mr Madness is not alone in his opinion. There is also the outrage from Mr Taxpayer.

'It's scandalous that single women and lesbians are able to access IVF treatment and my taxes have to pay for it', he rails.[2] 'God forbid taxpayers foot the bill for lesbians and single women . . .' chimes in another.[3]

In case you might think this is selective quoting, consider the *Herald Sun* newspaper's poll of readers, just after a Melbourne IVF clinic announced that it would circumvent the law aimed at banning single and lesbian women from accessing reproductive technologies. The poll of over 1200 readers asked 'Should single women and lesbians be given access to IVF?' A tiny 6.3 per cent of readers said 'Yes'; a whopping 93.7 per cent said 'No'.[4] Mr Taxpayer displays an insight into the *real* rage:

> They [lesbians and single women] have made a lifestyle choice to reject the companionship of men. Yet they still believe they are entitled to the natural fruits that come from a union between a man and a woman.[5]

That is the nub of their problem—'natural' means man *and* woman. By implication, a woman seeking to have a child alone is considered 'unnatural'. The debate is grounded in emotive and at times self-righteous beliefs about what is considered 'normal' and what, or *who* is 'abnormal'. No wonder Alison found people around her became 'obscenely happy' when a man entered her pregnant life. Not only would the shining knight help carry the load but he would bring 'normality' to her situation.

In arguing her case in federal parliament in 2001, against single or lesbian women gaining access to reproductive technologies, National Party MP DeAnne Kelly went out of her way to exempt from her criticism single mothers who didn't *start out* as single mothers: 'Let me say quite clearly this is not a judgment on those sole parents who through divorce, death or other unforeseen circumstances, find themselves raising children alone.'[6] It was all about distinguishing the 'valid' from the 'non-valid' single mothers. A point not lost on Queensland University academic Dr Jennifer Lynne Smith, who says:

> The single mothers to which Kelly refers are seen as valid because they have not *chosen* to raise children in this manner. It is a woman's ability to choose this life and to make that

choice on her own or without a valid partner that is deemed problematic. In government arguments, it seems that *any* man, no matter how long he is in a woman's life for, is necessary for valid conception.[7]

Smith's PhD thesis rakes over the language and stereotypes used to depict single and lesbian women in IVF policy debates. She says recent parliamentary debates are riddled with references to such women as immoral and sub-normal:

There is this idea that these women are having children on a whim, or that they are treating children as commodities, or having children for all sorts of frivolous reasons.

As Smith points out, such impressions could not be further from the truth:

The women usually have to go through years of very intrusive procedures, often at an enormous personal, financial and psychological cost in order to have a child. There is absolutely no way that this could be considered as having a child on 'a whim'.

Nevertheless, Smith maintains single and lesbian women continue to be 'demonised for desiring an "antisocial" form of motherhood'.[8] Thanks to conservative Prime Minster John Howard's love of the 'traditional family'—mum, dad, and a couple of kids—we are all well-versed in what is considered socially right, proper and morally correct. 'A child who is brought up in a traditional family', DeAnne Kelly reminds us, is 'happier, healthier and more well-adjusted to deal with life as they grow up'.[9]

Just in case you are wondering about the plight of children in not such happy or healthy 'traditional' families, fear not. Liberal

MP Alan Cadman has a solution: just change the law. Cadman told federal parliament in 2001, 'I believe it is possible to legislate against unhappy families'.[10] And the extraordinary bit is ... he wasn't kidding.

11 The child-free zone

Disliking children is one of the strongest social taboos in existence. Not bearing a child is blasphemous enough, *not liking* them is tantamount to infanticide. Admitting it out loud takes either a foolish woman or a brave one.

Madelyn Cain, *The Childless Revolution*, 2002

'Is it possible there are women with no maternal instincts?' asks American author Madelyn Cain.[1] An earnest question, no doubt proffered with genuine concern, but a daft one. Of course there are. What's more, some of them are increasingly willing for you to know about it. If you haven't already spotted them, you will. They are the ones sporting car stickers that read, 'Bored with Baby', or proudly wearing t-shirts with a child-free zone logo emblazoned across their breast, or writing to the Australian prime minster and treasurer complaining about their taxes being used to fund maternity schemes—among other things. If you haven't yet witnessed any of this public activity, just scan the various childless women you know (which shouldn't be hard, as there are plenty) and among them you'll find one or two who, when pressed, might admit to a maternal gene deficiency. Although in the company of strangers some choose to remain coy, some don't.

'I don't find babies cute. In fact I find them repulsive,' squeals Sandra, loud enough for her neighbours to hear. Not that that would bother her. I have no doubt everyone who comes into contact with this petite but fiery, wide-eyed beauty knows exactly how she feels about the 'kid-thing'. 'No-one ever stops and says, "Maybe women aren't having children for reasons other than economic reasons",' she says as we sit at her kitchen table while she slap red hair colouring onto her head. 'Maybe women just don't want to have children,' she bellows, whipping the colour into a lather.

Such is Sandra's own horror at the thought of ever conceiving a baby she has been shopping around for a doctor who would agree to sterilise this healthy, happy, single woman:

> It's not like I woke up one morning and said, 'I need milk, eggs and I might get a tubal ligation'. I've thought about my decision carefully. Most people assume that my decision is temporary and that I will change my mind. And that makes a lot of us who are child-free really mad. It insinuates that you don't know your own mind. I'm 33. I have a good education, an honours degree. I'm not ignorant or naive.

Nor will Sandra be silenced.

Up to this point I've roamed through the lives, hearts and pain of women who want children: some desperately; some not so. I've shared the stories of women who are feeling crippled, frustrated and guilty about the conflicting pull between children and career. There is yet another group of women who are also feeling confounded by the pressure to have it all. Their issue is they *don't* want 'it all'. They are the women who actively choose *not* to have children. A choice which, if publicly stated, can cop a lash of moral abuse. The tirade usually starts with loud debate over what is and isn't 'natural'. Then it ranges over issues of 'normality', 'selfishness', perhaps even strays into the area of 'deviants'—ironically the very same slap in the face used for single and lesbian women who *choose motherhood.*

I know these barbs and know how they can sting, having been on the receiving end of them myself. As you will recall, as a young journalist in my early twenties, I once asserted a lack of interest in ever having children to a group of work colleagues, including my boss, and I copped what my mother would call 'the rounds of the kitchen'. That was back in the late 1980s. I had hoped—naively it would seem—that now in the twenty-first century we would be well past a social hang-up with *chosen* childlessness. But we're not. Instead, our current day preoccupation with defining women by their fertile output, and their prowess as career juggling mothers, is giving rise to a whole new militant breed of women . . . who'll have none of it. These are not women who easily bruise, but the hard-edged tone of their message is almost certain to leave a mark on the rest of us.

They call themselves 'child-free', proudly celebrating their 'child-freedom'. They are willing participants in the ever-growing childless revolution, but they come at it from a very different angle. Unlike the other foot-soldiers who may be childless due to a 'creeping non-choice', delay, ambiguity or infertility, the child-free have chosen to be that way from the outset. Now, the more vocal and political among them are rising up against the notion of being 'less'. Instead, what the wider community may see as less, they see as 'more'. In choosing a life without children they believe they are missing nothing, but gaining everything: adult autonomy, independence and most importantly—freedom.

The term 'child-free' and the child-free movement's modus operandi is, perhaps not surprisingly, an American import.

The concept is still in its infancy here in Australia but child-free groups are increasing in number and clout. Emboldened by finding other like-minded women (and men), the child-free are organising themselves into lobby groups which, according to the Sydney-based founder of the World Childfree Association, Marije Feddema, is all about making them stronger in the fight for their cause.

'Our aim is to make the choice between having or not having children equally valued by society, which it isn't at the moment,' says Marije. 'At the moment society favours women who have chosen to have children.' Marije and women like her are sick of it, understandably, but the targets of their anger and the focus of their campaigns is what sets the child-free apart from the childless, and has some of the latter wincing with discomfort.

Following the release of the Australian federal 'breeder' Budget in 2004, which dangled various maternity, childcare and family-focused schemes before the (pre-election) electorate, child-free groups lobbied the federal government in protest. At the time Marije wrote on her website:

> I don't see why I have to subsidise other people's hobbies/ lifestyle (having children is a hobby). Plus I think the government doesn't respect my 'belief system', I'm forced to pay taxes for something that I think is totally wrong, which is adding more people to an already overcrowded world.[2]

Others lobbied the ACTU in protest against its landmark 'Family/ Work Balance' test case before the Australian Industrial Relations Commission.

'The bar is being pushed further in the favour of breeders', complained the author of another child-free website.[3] 'If you need to give that flexibility to the parents,' says Sandra, 'someone (in the workplace) has to take up the slack. Who is it going to be?' she says, pointing at herself. 'That is my concern.'

The child-free have plenty of other concerns. What about tax expenditure towards childcare facilities, family tax allowances, support for stay-at-home-mothers, the disturbance children cause in public places, environmental sustainability, the effect of a growing population on our diminishing resources etc? With these and other matters blasting a wind in their sails, some within the proudly declared child-free fraternity are hoping to establish a political party in Australia, to further publicise their cause. Marije is at the helm.

'People see me as the leader,' she says. 'They like what I do and I get a lot of positive feedback.' Her website, established mid-2003, attracted around 54 000 visitors within its first year. Now, despite its Australian focus, the site is translated into thirteen languages. She is also establishing a central register of Australian doctors who are willing to sterilise young and single women. For those who *do* get sterilised, the World Childfree Association will mail out 'tubal ligation announcements' to friends and family. For Marije and the women hearing the bugle call to action, it's all forward from here.

No doubt most non-parents and childless women at times get fed up with hearing a gushing media bang on about the bliss of motherhood and the virtues of parenthood. Even those of us who love children and embrace families can get sick of hearing about them. At times the preoccupation with the 'family' in Australian politics is nauseating, and infuriating in its exclusion of people like me. That said, it doesn't mean I want to wipe the place clean of children, mothers or families. Nor do I want them to stay out of my way. Nor would I ever stop arguing for the right of mothers and families to get a better deal. Maybe this is what separates the childless from the child-free.

In truth, the strength of child-free women's dislike for children and all things maternal left me a little cold. This was before I met with women who proudly flaunt their child-free status; women like Sandra, Marije and Kirsten. I'm struck by the strength of their convictions and the clarity of their choice.

Marije

Perhaps it's the Dutch in her, or perhaps beneath the soft, creamy skin of this 28-year-old is a leathery thickness. Whatever it is— Marije Feddema has proven she has a hide. She has always refused to dodge pesky inquisitions about her choice to be child-free. Proffering a blunt and honest response, she'll tell anyone who asks that she doesn't like children, doesn't want any and thinks there are too many being born anyway. Not surprisingly, many an inquisitor turns judge and juror. Despite her youth, Marije has already copped more than her fair share of abuse.

It's the usual stuff, she admits, 'too self-centred', 'too materialistic', 'don't know what I'm missing', 'irresponsible, immature' and the rest. It's the 'you're not natural' barbs that annoy her most. She says she has lost friendships because of her child-free stance. Little wonder then that she felt alone and ostracised until the ever-reaching tentacles of the world wide web helped her find like-minded women—and relief.

'I found out that my "condition" was called "child-free". Then I felt I recognised myself,' she says. Marije quickly tapped into this new world of women, creating an internet discussion board to ask other women how they felt. 'As soon as we started talking to each other, I didn't feel so strange anymore,' she says. For

Marije it was a life-changing discovery. It is a place where new bonds are forged—albeit as part of an exclusive club. 'The only child-free friends that I have exist in the virtual world,' she tells me.

Marije is now on a mission to expand that world and bring it out in the open. 'Child-free women still want to remain anonymous, as they feel embarrassed or they want to avoid the hurtful questions,' she explains. 'Most of them don't speak openly about their child-freedom. Women supporting each other could change this.' With her help, it already has.

Marije met her husband Michael in Holland when she was twenty. Almost instantly their shared dislike of children clinched a bond between them. Within three days they had discussed marriage, leaving the Netherlands, and their desire for a child-free kind of lifestyle. Within another two years, at the age of 22, Marije was sterilised.

'It was really hard to get it past the doctors,' she says, explaining that there was a lot of talking, a lot of justifying her decision, and a lot of discussion about possible regrets. If there was any chink in her young, brave armour, no doctor found it.

'I have always felt very confident about it,' says Marije, now six years after making her decision and sounding every bit as confident. The operation was carried out in Holland before the couple immigrated to Australia. There was a little discomfort, a slight nausea and minimal pain.

Nevertheless, for the squeamish, sterilisation may seem a drastic step for a women in her early twenties. On learning that Marije's husband had *already* undergone a vasectomy, one can't help but wonder aloud, 'What is the point?' Marije says she loves Michael and has every intention of staying married to him. He was her first boyfriend and only lover. So isn't the double-barrel contraceptive precaution going a bit far? Apparently not. Marije argues it's all about 'fairness' and equity within the relationship. It's also about her independence.

'I sort of felt that it's given me a bit more freedom for some reason,' she says, struggling to explain what some might view as an extreme measure: 'It's my decision and I wanted to take the action. I wanted to take responsibility for me not becoming pregnant.'

What drives a young woman to take such finite action: a life of radicalism, a history of wilful determination, perhaps an abhorrence of breeding, and an entrenched hatred of children? It's none of those. To meet Marije is quite a surprise. All peaches-and-cream complexion with a schoolgirl ponytail, a pretty smile and conservative dress, she looks more like your average earth-mother than a child-free political agitator. So serene is her presentation, you could expect to see her at a craft expo giving quilting demos . . . but you won't. Where you will see her is at a bank of computer terminals, trouble-shooting for blue-chip corporations. She's a successful IT consultant, with her own business that can operate anywhere, at anytime—the benefit of being child-free.

'People are expected to work 24/7,' she says, 'And I can hardly keep up with that myself. But it seems a worker has to be available day and night.' Knowing that such 'ready now' flexibility gives her an edge, Marije even includes mention of her child-free status on her CV. 'I put it on my resume so people can see, "She's never going to have children and she's therefore going to be a reliable employee".'

Why such pride in disliking children, and why dislike them at all? Marije tells me it's not about 'hate', it's just 'dislike'. She has never liked children. Nor does she like the idea of anyone being dependent on her. She says it's difficult to explain but she knew from the age of three she didn't ever want to have children. As we talk further about Marije's own life as a kid, a possible key to her fierce distaste for anything resembling a family unit begins to emerge. Her childhood, she explains, was fraught with disappointment and a struggle for attention.

'I don't think my father has ever wanted me,' she says, throwing our conversation a little off guard with a sudden and unexpected vehemence:

> I'd rather die before I pass on such useless genes as his to my own daughter—or son for that matter. What I mostly hate about my father is that he puts a child in this world and doesn't look after it. It would be really hard to see my father mirrored in my child. I don't think it would make a good human being.

While this is awfully sad to hear, and seems somehow out of place, Marije nevertheless goes on. We talk about intimacy, and her father's lack of it, which appears to be what hurts most.

'He's cold and insensitive. He really has problems showing his emotions to other people,' she says flatly, with no perceptible trace of bitterness. While she feels her dad's genes are unfavourable for procreation, apparently so too are her mother's, but not for the same reasons. Marije explains that her mother is quite sickly and may have 'hereditary diseases'. Just when this is all sounding too bleak and I'm a bit lost for words, Marije perks up.

'I think I'm kind of a perfectionist,' she says. 'If I have a child, I want it to be perfect, to be just like me or my husband and do the same things we do.' I sort of feel I should remind her that it's never going to happen anyway, so she can forget about fretting over her progeny's level of perfection. I chose to shut up instead.

Sandra

'There is a lot of invective aimed at child-free people,' says Sandra, whose mother believed she 'was taking feminism too far' when she first announced her intention to never have children. Now at 33 years old, and happily single, her resolve to remain child-free has only strengthened.

'A superior form of morality is always assigned to parents . . . it's always assumed that someone who is a parent is somehow more responsible,' she says, clearly pissed off that her stated choice to be child-free means she has copped a regular blast of negative judgment. She says the worst of it is the assumption that she is some sort of morally inferior, sexual predator.

'It isn't hard for me to find casual relationships,' she says, as she pats the last blobs of hair colouring into place and begins wrapping plastic wrap around her head. 'I'm a good option: no children, doesn't ever want children, professional, independent, has money—all those things. Ideal mistress, I guess.' But it seems such attributes can cause a girl grief when seen in the context of a woman who flaunts her child-free status. Sandra says she is viewed as a threat to 'women who have procreational sex', and has been accused of being a 'wretched Jezebel':

> Being child-free still . . . carries the same baggage as homosexuality [for a lot of people], in that it insinuates recreational sex as opposed to procreational sex. So a woman who even so much as hints that she has sex for pleasure and not for procreation is still considered a Jezebel. That's why I think a lot of people still find being child-free a social taboo.

While the moral finger-wagging may be annoying, Sandra clearly has no intention of being shut down. We already know that she finds babies 'repulsive'. 'Funnily enough,' she says, 'children like me. They'll gravitate towards me. But I'm just not interested.' What *is* interesting is Sandra's own view of the morality of parenthood. Having spent time working for Legal Aid as an undergraduate, she says she saw some shocking examples of poor and careless parenting. These examples serve to prove, 'parents aren't necessarily morally superior beings at all,' she says.

Would she be a 'good parent'? On that Sandra is unequivocal: 'I know I wouldn't be.' For her this is the *real* issue of moral responsibility: 'I can't deal with high maintenance people. So, isn't it better that someone like me recognises that and doesn't have a child?' Having finished with the hair colour, she pushes the paraphernalia to one side, leans forward and says, 'We're not monsters.' Nor is she a relentless, hard-nosed, step-on-toes, career bitch.

'It's a stereotype,' she says of the image of child-free women peddled by the finger-waggers. 'I am career-focused now,' she says, 'But for the last few years I don't think you could call me career-focused. I was working as a waitress for crying out loud.' Today, as a smart, fast, talented recruit to the Commonwealth Department of Defence, who also happens to speak Mandarin, it is highly likely Sandra will go places—places that may be out of reach for her female colleagues with children.

'I must admit that it is certainly easier for a woman to get ahead in her career if she is child-free,' she says. Knowing she may have a leg up—so to speak—doesn't stop Sandra from insisting all workers, mothers and non-mothers, play by the same daily rules:

> I was once involved in enterprise bargaining negotiations at a workplace where one of the union delegates said that she wanted to have Christmas Day off. She wanted the day off

for all people with small children. I said, 'That is outrageous. What, do you think I came from a Petri dish? I have family too!'

Entitlements in the workplace are perhaps fast becoming one of the more vexing issues between mothers and non-mothers. I was rendered momentarily speechless back in the mid-1990s, when my boss at the ABC's *7.30 Report* told me I was rostered to work over the Christmas period because I didn't have 'a family'. Those with children would be given holiday priority. I wish now I'd thought of Sandra's 'Petri dish' line. Instead I simply corrected her—yes, it was a 'her' who happened to also be a mother—explaining I actually had quite a large family: five siblings and two parents. Nevertheless I relented, no doubt feeling I had little choice in the matter. Sandra is not so willing. Nor is she willing to watch quietly as her colleagues in the public service receive maternity leave—something Sandra views as an unfair advantage.

'It's twelve weeks' paid leave for doing nothing,' she says, adding 'sorry! [the 'sorry!', 'excuse me!' kind of sorry]. Why should someone be paid to do something that isn't part of the workplace? Why can't I get a year off to do something I've chosen?' Sandra knows the response. She's heard it all before:

> 'You're just bitter', they say. Or, 'you're just jealous'. I'm just waiting for someone to throw something new at me. And the argument that [women on maternity leave] are raising the next generation. Well, okay, so were Martin Bryant's parents. I don't think throwing money at people will make them better parents.

To that end, Sandra wants her taxes diverted away from maternity payments and into educational programs for young people, to help them understand the responsibilities of becoming a parent and raising a child. She is lobbying on that front but her greater preoccupation these days is ensuring she never becomes a parent herself.

Like many proudly declared child-free women, Sandra is a walking encyclopaedia on contraception and methods of sterilisation. Tired of juggling the former, she's dead keen on the latter and is considering a number of options.

'One of them,' she explains enthusiastically 'is a device inserted into the fallopian tubes, thereby irritating the lining and causing permanent scarring and sealing off the entire length of the fallopian tube.' She is also looking at an 'intrauterine device which contains progesterone, which while not permanent, acts on the endometrium thereby reducing menstrual bleeding'. Or, she could opt for 'endometrial ablation', which destroys the lining of the uterus. Whichever the choice, Sandra hopes to get the procedure done this year and believes the increase in lobbying from child-free women will make it easier to find a willing doctor:

> To some people it seems extreme, but it means that I no longer have to play hormonal roulette. And if I end up in a long-term relationship with a partner, he's not going to be waiting and waiting in the hope that I'll change my mind. Once I'm sterilised, there is no way it can be reversed.

Kirsten

Kirsten is a 31-year-old single lawyer, living on Sydney's North Shore. After months on a hospital waiting list in order to get a publicly funded tubal ligation, she is thrilled that she's finally 'had it done':

> I feel like a real weight has been lifted off me. I feel free and that I can put the whole kid issue behind me and get on with

the rest of my life without having to worry about accidentally getting pregnant or taking hormonal contraception.

For Kirsten, there has been an added bonus to sterilisation: 'I feel a lot better now I'm not taking the pill or getting periods. I don't retain fluid, and I've lost about five to six kilograms since the operation!' The whole ordeal has been well worth it, and she would 'strongly encourage other women to get it done'.

But why? Why take such a drastic step in the first place? Like Sandra and Marije, Kirsten says she knew from a young age that she never wanted to have children. In year 11 at school, when other girls put marriage and two or three children on their ten-year plan, Kirsten was painfully aware hers was a very different dream.

'I'd written things like owning a horse, pets, a farm, having a good job and driving a Mercedes.' Indeed, in less than ten years she had more or less achieved those things—although the 'farm' is still just a rural property awaiting development. Given her grown-up wish list was so at odds from those of her school friends, Kirsten, like so many similar-minded young women, was beset by—you guessed it—a fear of being 'abnormal'.

'I just assumed that boys wouldn't like me or wouldn't want to be with me because I wasn't a normal woman,' she says, laughing at the memory. In fact, quite the opposite was true. From the moment she hit university, Kirsten has rarely been without a serious man in her life. The problem is, they've always wanted children, including the man to whom she was engaged.

'Six months away from marriage, he said "I've been rethinking this and I don't want to shut the door on having children. Don't you think you'll change your mind? You're still young . . ."' Kirsten knew her mind so she called the engagement off. She says at the time it was devastating for both of them, but on her part there was no equivocating:

> It's a non-negotiable issue. We were going to end up making each other miserable. One of us was going to feel that we'd lost out, and it wasn't going to be me, because I've got control of my biology. So it was going to be him.

There are no unhappy skeletons in her childhood closet. In fact, Kirsten's experience of family life as she grew up with a younger sister and two loving parents was nothing but positive and supportive. Her father was a mathematician and, once she and her sister were well settled at school, her mother bought and ran a childcare centre.

'I remember seeing women pushing their prams,' she says, 'having children and giving up their careers and thinking at the time, "I don't ever want to be like that". I was really worried about it.' Although, Kirsten secretly expected that maybe she was just immature, and that as she got older a 'light bulb' would go on and 'presto!' she'd have the maternal urge. 'But the opposite happened,' she says. 'The more independent I've become with my career and my life, the more I've realised that I really don't want this.' In fact the real moment of illumination came just a couple of years ago, when she first read the term 'child-free' in an internet chat room discussion.

'This woman explained that she had made a conscious choice not to have children and suddenly a light bulb went on in my head and I went, "Oh, my God. There is someone else like me!"' Thus, just like Marije, Kirsten's connection with other child-free women began in the virtual world.

While single now, Kirsten is clearly content. 'I'm very happy with my life as it is at the moment.' She works ten to twelve hours a day in a law firm that poached her from a top job in another state. It is there, within the career realm, that her child-free choice starts to make real sense.

'My career gives me a lot of fulfilment. I really, really love it and I can't imagine not working. I can't imagine giving up everything I've achieved so far and then falling behind. I'm a competitive person.' According to Kirsten, that's what happens to smart women who do the un-smart thing of opting off the career ladder to have a baby—they 'fall behind':

> The feminist in me really objects to the fact that I see men in my firm whose careers are advancing when they have children. Fatherhood means they're seen as responsible. Meanwhile their wives have given up professional careers, to sit at home and wipe noses. That to me is a complete waste of education. It really angers me that in this day of '*equality*', there really is none; even in a professional organisation like a law firm. It's expected that a woman will give up her career and that a man will advance. I don't want to perpetuate that.

Clearly she won't.

Reflecting the strident and increasingly vocal argument used by child-free women, Kirsten has no patience for female colleagues who try to 'have it all' *and* expect some sisterhood support. Those women who put their careers on hold, while they leave to have a baby, can expect a very cold shoulder from Kirsten and her mates:

> For women to say, 'I'm going to opt out for a few years', that's fine. If they want to do that, that's great. But then to expect to be paid to sit at home and look after children, then come back to work and have their job waiting for them, *and* have the same salary as a man who's slogged himself out for the time she's been away—that's wrong.

You get the strong sense that she will have none of it. Kirsten is just 31 and a partner in a law firm, but when she is senior partner, managing director, then CEO, watch out women who *want it all*!

Held to ransom by hope in a test tube

... as long as you are in the program, your life is in limbo.
Jenny Sinclair, *The Sunday Age*, 20 July 2003

This scenario is hypothetical: purely hypothetical. Imagine a woman—perhaps a close friend of yours—so desperate for a child she eyeballs her lover and agrees to make a promise that she knows she can never keep. With his hands on both her shoulders he asks her again, slowly and deliberately, 'Are you sure?' 'Yes,' she says, repeating, 'I *promise*.' Knowing it's a lie.

She is in her early forties. Let's say, forty-two. She and her partner have been trying to conceive a child through IVF for a couple of years. In the early stages, this friend of ours—yours and mine—got lucky; or so she thought. A healthy harvest of her eggs had resulted in half a dozen embryos—a good score. A couple were used immediately. The rest were frozen. Given our friend and her partner are not flush with money, they had decided from the outset that they could only afford to do this once. After that first implantation our friend waited, desperate with anticipation, for signs of pregnancy. None came. She was devastated when the clinic called to confirm the embryo implantation had failed. For weeks and weeks we, her friends, couldn't console her as she grieved. For a while it seemed we lost her altogether as she wallowed in sadness and sorrow. Then a breakthrough. She lightened up. They had four more embryos on ice: they would try again. They did. And failed. And again. And failed.

By the time there was just one lone frozen embryo left, our friend was a wreck. That's when she agreed to the promise: a promise to not get upset, to not grieve with despair and spiral into depression, if this latest attempt should fail. Our friend knew she couldn't keep such a promise, but she'd do and say anything for one last go; one last chance at becoming a mother.

It was early on a Tuesday morning when our friend got the call from the clinic. They were 'very sorry' they said. 'Unfortunately, not this time,' they said. 'They would like to see her again.' Our friend knew that wasn't going to happen. When she turned to tell her partner the news, he looked her in the eye, held her by the shoulders, and said, 'Remember what you promised?'

Because this is a fictional story, it's anyone's guess as to how our friend responded. My guess is that given she is a professional woman—hypothetically—she nodded, agreed she'd made a promise, resolved to stand by it, and then got on with her day's work. Later that evening, our friend's partner went looking for her in the garden. He found her out the back with scissors in hand and surrounded by cuttings. She'd cut the head off every flower, every rose, daisy and every camellia in their garden. That's when she told her partner her promise had been a lie.

Carolyn

There is nothing hypothetical about Carolyn's story. Nor anything hypothetical about Carolyn. She has devoted eleven years of her life to getting pregnant and she's happy for everyone to know all about it. Carolyn was born with an insuppressible maternal urge. From girlhood, whenever a baby was in sight, Carolyn was the first to covet it: 'I knew when I was really young that I desperately wanted children,' she says. She wanted lots of them. Born into a family of ten kids, Carolyn knew all about the sacrifice involved in having a big brood, but she also knew about the enormous pool of love that's shared among those bonds.

Given all of this, it's heartbreaking to hear her now say there have been times over the past couple of years when her hardened heart meant she couldn't even look at children.

'I stopped being clucky. My sister had a child and I couldn't . . . I didn't want to pick up her child,' she says quietly, still embarrassed by the memory of it. There have been times when the bitterness born of an inability to conceive wore her down, and drove her nearly mad.

'We never tried not to have children,' she explains. Married at 31, Carolyn already thought she was leaving it late. She and her husband, Frank, planned to start a family immediately. Frank was almost forty and, although he had children from a previous marriage, he and Carolyn wanted to have kids together. That's how they saw their future—as a family. The method was simple: just don't use any contraception.

'I just expected I would eventually fall pregnant,' she says. Everything was in place. They had an inner-city house in Sydney's cosmopolitan Leichhardt. Frank had a good job and Carolyn's work as a special education teacher in a secondary school meant she would get reasonable maternity support and enjoy family-friendly work hours. So they waited in anticipation. It took over a year, but finally she fell pregnant, only to miscarry nine weeks later.

'At the time, I was sad about it,' she says, 'But I was very pragmatic. I just thought, "Oh well. It will happen again. We'll just wait".' And they did. Soon after, she was pregnant again. This time she lost it at eleven weeks. By the time she fell pregnant a third time, understandably Carolyn was taking extra care of herself and keeping her 'condition' a secret between herself and Frank. On Christmas day, as she sat down for lunch with her parents and hordes of siblings, nieces and nephews, Carolyn felt out of sorts and unwell, then rotten. She miscarried later that day.

'I was terribly upset,' she whispers. The drama on that bleak and awful day had a darker, murky undercurrent, though. Carolyn began to suspect there may be something seriously wrong: 'It started to hit me that maybe this isn't going to happen easily.' Despite the repeated disappointment and mounting suspicion over her fertility, Carolyn's view of herself as a mother remained unshakable.

'I still believed that I would have children,' she says.

At the time Carolyn submitted to a round of medical tests but there was no explanation as to why she couldn't carry a pregnancy. She was still in her early thirties, a picture of health, and she lived a gentle, conservative life. Not only was her mother a textbook breeder, so too were her nine siblings. All her brothers and sisters had children, and lots of them. No-one could fathom why Carolyn was having such trouble. However, this was only the beginning.

Born and raised a Catholic, Carolyn says she considers herself a 'spiritual person'. She also has strong faith in mother nature.

Despite the trauma of a third consecutive miscarriage she says, 'At that stage I could never do something like IVF.' Instead, she addressed her own health through complementary medicines. She and Frank visited a natural fertility clinic and agreed to undertake a long-term program of herbs, vitamins, homeopathic remedies and an alcohol-free organic diet. It wasn't cheap or quick. Over the next six months Carolyn spent around $4000 in potions and pills and an unmeasurable sum on sourcing and cooking organic foods.

'It had a huge impact on us,' she says. They both felt well and healthy during the course of the program but it was nevertheless draining and all-consuming in its whole-body focus. After half a year of dedicated adherence to the rules they'd had enough.

Another six months passed and still no conception. By now Carolyn was nursing a low-level desperation. By the time of her 37th birthday, she had already spent six years trying to have a baby. 'That is when we approached a specialist about IVF,' she says admitting this was both a desperate measure and a major turnaround, coming from someone who firmly believed she would never need any sort of medical intervention in order to conceive. It just didn't seem right. Not for her. Not coming from a family like hers—a family seemingly born to breed.

With all this in mind, Carolyn's first foray into IVF was with the attitude of someone finally handing herself over and giving in to the 'fix-it' men:

> I thought, 'I'll do it the first time and it'll work for me'. It was a positive meeting. I remember sitting in front of the doctor, who was a lovely man, and I just felt confident that, 'Okay, that sounds pretty straightforward. We'll do this, we'll do that, and then we'll be successful'.

Few people understand just how intrusive a procedure IVF can be and how unpredictable the emotional roller-coaster ride. First Carolyn took a cocktail of fertility drugs to control her ovaries. It was a matter of shutting down her system chemically, then stimulating it again through medication. In order to compress up to one year's worth of ovulation into one cycle, to maximise the number of available eggs, Carolyn was put on a rigorous routine of daily injections. Some women will go to the clinic each morning for this or learn to self-inject. Carolyn could face neither, so she delegated the task to Frank. Each morning he would rise just after 6.30 a.m. and prepare the needle, then pad back down the corridor to wake Carolyn.

'As time went on, I'd hear him come down the corridor,' she says. I imagine her body awake, alert and ready to tense. Along with the medication began a series of blood tests and ultrasounds to monitor the ovaries and map the time for egg harvesting. In Carolyn's case, she was slow to react to the initial medication and required daily injections for up to three weeks. Once her follicles (which contain the eggs) were deemed to be of the right size, she was given a trigger injection to release them at a precise time. She was then booked into a hospital at that given time for the eggs to be collected.

The harvesting is done via a surgical procedure, where a needle is inserted through the wall of the vagina into the ovaries and the contents of each follicle are extracted. The contents are then inspected by an embryologist, who locates the eggs inside the translucent material and isolates them. The actual fertilisation process then happens externally, after Frank has supplied a fresh semen specimen.

For Carolyn, her first experience of the procedure was 'miraculous':

It can hurt when they actually pierce through into your ovaries, but it is fascinating. You watch on the screen and you can see your eggs. I had a very matter-of-fact attitude towards it. As they drew the needle out, I think I was more fascinated by the process than aware of the pain.

A day later Carolyn called the clinic, as instructed, and was told she had four fertilised embryos—not a high strike rate, but enough to encourage a good dose of hope. However, as is often the way between the period of harvest and implantation, a number of embryos die off or prove too weak for transfer. In Carolyn's case, by the time she returned to the clinic for the transfer process three days later, only two embryos had survived. But two is better than nothing.

Carolyn was now flushed with hope. Still a little sore from the harvesting procedure, she was nevertheless optimistic, even excited as she watched on the TV monitor as each embryo was delicately and meticulously placed inside her uterus via a catheter. Afterwards she didn't want to get up off the surgery bed for fear one of the little specs might come sliding out. However, doctors are quick to reassure all women at this stage that it's impossible for the embryo to 'slip out'. Of course, smart women know this but it doesn't stop them from lying prone, or doing a slow moonwalk out of the place, desperately trying not to jerk suddenly and praying that the little blob of cells will implant itself in their womb—and stay there. So, begins another period of waiting. Hoping and waiting.

Two weeks later, Carolyn returned to the clinic for another blood test; this time to determine whether or not the embryo transfer had worked.

'They phoned me later and told me I was not pregnant.' The news was a shock. Carolyn in all her pragmatism and optimism hadn't counted on this result.

'I felt really sad. I cried a little, and I just felt it wasn't fair. I couldn't understand why I had failed.' She rang Frank, told him the news, and 'just got on with the day'. There wasn't much more to be said. She had 'failed' and that was that.

About three months later Carolyn experienced a delayed reaction. After pushing the whole experience to the back of her mind, she now began to obsess over it. Fixated on the failure— *her* failure—she couldn't concentrate on anything much else. Each day, surrounded by her young pupils, became more and more difficult to navigate as she moved slowly through a fog of sadness. Eventually, fully convinced this state of childlessness was her fault, she determined to return to the medical wizards and somehow try harder.

Already out of pocket by about $6000, she and Frank took another year before they were ready to do it again. As well as the cost imperative, Carolyn says it was also a matter of getting organised. She wanted to make sure she had the psychological and emotional strength, as well as plenty of time to give over to the process. In between making the decision and beginning the course of injections, both Carolyn and Frank renewed their sense of optimism. They spent endless hours on the internet reading other women's testimonials and revelling in the success stories, Carolyn became quite mesmerised by 'hope'. Hope and optimism became something of a mental chant—after all, the language of IVF is peppered with the stuff. Surely it would work. It was just a matter of time. In fact, in an odd twist, now that she had failed once, she was encouraged to believe that she had a much better chance of succeeding next time. Carolyn believed it and this stiffened her resolve: 'I was coming from the place of "Well it's going to work. I might just have to do it two or three times, but it's going to work".'

The second attempt didn't work. And neither did the third. By the time she had her fourth go at IVF the procedure was becoming increasingly traumatic. The energetic mind games used to build a scaffold of hope—propped up by increasingly flimsy supports—was taking its toll. With each failure the nervous structure would come crashing down. With each collapse, Carolyn took a full body blow. Again, *she* was failing.

Carolyn felt her own body was fighting against her, trying to ward off the medical wizards. Her experience with the regular blood tests was getting worse.

'On one occasion I had to have nine injections, from three different people, just to get a small blood sample.' During the fourth IVF attempt, the procedure was cancelled just as Carolyn was preparing for another egg harvesting session. She hadn't reacted to the fertility drugs well enough and this time hadn't produced a worthwhile batch of eggs. Things were rapidly going down hill and Carolyn was now edging towards forty years old.

As the number of IVF failures increased, Carolyn says she began to lengthen the delay in reacting. Try as she might to push it away, eventually the painful sadness caught up with her, with depression riding hard on its tail. A pervasive sense of hopelessness would take hold; then she'd have a sudden mood swing and she would be back in the grip of hope. It was an emotional see-saw and it was making her sick.

'I think each year it got worse. I got worse. It had started to impact on my whole life.'

Having spent more than $20 000 dollars on IVF at a private clinic, the couple decided to switch to the public system, and keep trying. At around this time a close and dear friend who had watched Carolyn slide into a pit of despair and a self-absorbed preoccupation with pregnancy, called it as she saw it:

She said straight out to me, 'It's holding you to ransom'. And that summed it up. She gave a word to what was happening. It was 'ransom', because I felt there were so many things in my life I was putting on hold. It was all about, 'When I get pregnant; when we have a child'. It has a huge impact on the decisions you make long term.

Being held to ransom by 'hope' also has an impact on the decisions you *don't* make long term. For Carolyn, *waiting* was the only decision she could manage. It was a foggy routine of waiting, hoping, trying and waiting some more.

Now under a new doctor in a different hospital, Carolyn undertook her fifth attempt at IVF. It failed. She immediately agreed to try again:

By then I was really getting more and more depressed, and more conscious of the depression. It was like I was walking around in a haze. It was the hopelessness of it. You think there is nothing you can do, so you feel really powerless. By the time I got to the sixth and seventh go at IVF, I was just going through the motions. At that stage I didn't think it would work, but I felt I had to do it.

Around this time, in what would seem to be an extraordinary manifestation of the depths of her depression, Carolyn began to question whether in fact she wanted children at all. 'The IVF became all about falling pregnant,' she explains. 'By then it wasn't about having children. That's the strange thing about it; it became almost disconnected.'

Was she failing at IVF because in fact she didn't really want children after all? It was a time of shocking confusion and doubt:

On the one hand, I couldn't face up to the fact that I wouldn't have children. But on the other hand, there was no longer a real passion for it. It was more just a need to get pregnant. I was in denial I think, as part of a coping mechanism.

After the failure of her seventh attempt at IVF, Carolyn knew her pregnancy obsession was unhealthy, unnatural and verging on being out of control. She knew she should start to think about letting it go. But not yet.

'Somehow I had come to the point where I thought, "If I'm 60, 70, 80 years old and I look back, can I live with myself if I didn't try?"' Having already tried and tried, it seems trying was not enough. Carolyn was prepared to thrash herself in order to give 'trying' more of a fighting chance. In the happy IVF hymn of 'hope' it seems there is no end to trying.

Carolyn set her mind on yet *another* go at IVF. By now the financial impost had bitten hard. Carolyn and Frank, although not tallying the cost, knew they had spent well over $35 000. Carolyn was now also 41 and 'running out of time'. The cash had run dry but there was equity tied up in their house, so they sold it.

'To free up the money,' explains Carolyn, 'So that we could continue to do a couple more IVFs.' They packed up their home, said goodbye to their life in Sydney and moved to Melbourne, where they thought they could live more cheaply and continue their quest for a baby.

'Within the first week I had made an appointment at a hospital and we were booked in for our eighth attempt.' This time she told her new doctor, 'We haven't got time to muck around. And he was very good at short cutting the process,' she says. Little good it did. She failed . . . again. By now there was no worry of a delayed reaction and a cloud of depression descending after months. She was already depressed.

As she approached her 42nd birthday, Carolyn was counselled to consider opting for a donor embryo, given her own fertilised embryos just didn't seem to have the staying power. What's more, she was producing fewer and fewer eggs. A donor egg was an option but Carolyn was deemed too old as the waiting list for donor eggs can be several years.

'They said I could advertise for one and try and get one myself,' Caroline tells me, 'But somehow that didn't feel right, and could involve a long waiting period anyway.' There was also an offshore option. Caroline could follow in the path of some other Australian women who have sought donor eggs in the USA. There egg and sperm banks are slick, well-oiled enterprises, with pages and pages of donor information available to would-be recipients. In fact it's as simple as shopping online, and the delivery is almost instant. On the downside, it requires a trip to the United States for the implantation and could involve several return trips if an embryo doesn't hold. Instead, Carolyn chose to sign up for a home-grown donor embryo, knowing it could take at least a couple of years to receive one. The cut-off age was 45 and she convinced herself she might just make it.

Carolyn had by now been waiting for eleven years and found she could not stand waiting anymore. She faced the confronting task of convincing herself that she and Frank could live with the idea of a donor embryo—genetically the offspring of another man and woman. It wasn't ideal. In fact, in Caroline's mind, it wasn't even right. At this stage she was dreadfully desperate and depressed. 'There was just complete hopelessness,' she says, 'And a bit of bitterness too.' While waiting for the donor embryo— someone else's baby—she had to keep trying for her own. So Carolyn signed up for her ninth attempt at IVF.

By now the repeated failure and self-flagellation about 'Why me?', had more than eaten away at Carolyn, it was rotting her—rotting her sense of self and rotting her soul:

I went through painful questioning about my life. It was sort of like 'What am I even here for?' There was a real sense of not knowing what my purpose was anymore, because I grew up believing I would be a mother. Even spiritually I felt betrayed, I felt really cheated. I have a very strong spiritual identity and belief about the way the world works. But I found myself saying, 'I just cannot make sense of this'.

Not surprisingly, Carolyn turned her anger and frustration on her faith. 'It's not that I stopped believing in God, but . . . I guess I just questioned his intent.' Central to this angst was a foreboding sense of loneliness, what Carolyn calls, 'A real sense of being alone in this. And the loneliness becomes bigger than it is.'

By January 2004, when everyone around her was cheering in the New Year, Caroline was numb with failure and wallowing in depression. This year she would turn 43 in the knowledge that the last dozen years of her life had been focused on having a baby—the last six with a single-minded obsession that at times rendered her angry, bitter and empty. She had lost sight of her true self, the happy, cheerful and bubbly person everyone knew Carolyn to be—once. She knew she had to get it back. She had to get herself back. Her ninth attempt at IVF would be her last. When that didn't work (by now she believed it never would) she would remain on the donor embryo waiting list but invest little hope in it. She would try and forget about it. The daily waiting, hoping and waiting *had* to stop. And it did.

She wasn't due to begin the next and last round of IVF treatment for awhile, so Carolyn had stopped monitoring her cycle. She missed a period and ignored it. She felt the pangs of pregnancy and put it down to 'phantom' fantasy. By now she had a steely resolve against indulging in hope. There would be none. Even when a home pregnancy test proved positive, she didn't believe it. Eventually, it took the calm patience of her GP to convince Carolyn in her steely haze of disbelief that yes . . . she was pregnant. There had been no IVF involved, this was the real thing. A natural, un-meditated, unexpected and, in many respects, unplanned pregnancy. In shock and terrified of more failure, Carolyn kept the news secret, even from Frank.

'I had to keep it to myself because I felt "If I let anybody know, it won't work".' She was so bruised and hurt by the cruelty of false hope, Carolyn found she could not invest joy in this pregnancy. She had to brace herself against the trauma of another miscarriage—more loss, more failure. She resolved to just get on with her life. While she did, the life within her got on with it too: growing stronger and bigger, until it was a secret no more.

Today, as Carolyn shares this part of her story with me, tears of relief roll down her face, splashing over her smile. She looks down at the beautiful baby she is cradling in her arms. His name is William.

Carrie

Carolyn was exceptionally lucky. And she knows it. Carrie wasn't so lucky. She knows it too. 'Why not me?' she says, staring with those big, beautiful green eyes that demand attention when spoken to. 'I would have been a bloody good mother, and the world needs good mothers,' she insists. Don't for a moment think my arresting friend with her rapid-fire New York accent is about to launch into a mournful tale of woe. She isn't. Carrie doesn't 'do regret'. She knocks me over with a verbal steamroller when I even mention the word:

> Regret? I *can't* do regret. Regret becomes victim stuff. But sadness? Well, yeah, sadness definitely. And there's a little bit of fear in there too. I think about the future—not about now, because my life is quite full. On a daily basis, I don't feel the loss, or yearning, but there are those moments when . . . it strikes me.

Then, just when she is on a roll, Carrie slows right down. She hurts me with the raw sadness of what she says next.

'When my husband Charles dies—which he probably will do first, according to the statistics—I'm going to be more profoundly alone than I can possibly imagine right now.'

Carrie is a dear friend and a lifeline of support for the people who lean on her. And plenty do. Carrie is many things to many people. She is a writer of beautiful and vivid prose, an actor, a screenwriter, theatre director and an acting teacher. Her very grounding and compassionate presence means her acting students have always expressed and revealed themselves at profoundly deep levels. Carrie is just like that—people open up to her. She has a gift for caring and nurturing. She is right, she would have been a bloody good mother.

Everything about Carrie is exotic. Even her name is exotic, Carrie Zivetz. She is American and Jewish, born in the United States to a father who joined the diplomatic corps. She was educated in California and later at various posts around the world. As a child of the 1960s, life was always bursting with opportunity and new freedoms. For Carrie it was intoxicating:

> We grew up in a time of extreme affluence in America. The world was open to us. We believed ourselves to be privileged

and deserving of privilege. Particularly as women, the door had been absolutely flung open. We could do and have everything: there was no question that you couldn't, or shouldn't, or indeed wouldn't.

She didn't—question it that is. Carrie chased it all; living and loving her way across continents. What she knew she certainly did *not* want was the 1950s style of conventional marriage and family that she saw back home:

> When feminism came to the fore, it was the generation just in front of me—so women maybe ten years older than me were saying, 'I don't want to be like my mother'. That whole concept of mother and motherhood and being a little fifties' wife waiting for her husband, was like this awful, awful, despicable thing.

By the 1970s, the women heralding women's liberation were well-versed in the horrors of *The Feminine Mystique*. Betty Friedan's book had been around since 1963 and the fight against the oppression of wifedom, and the chains of motherhood, was well and truly firing in the United States. Carrie lapped it up.

'I understand now that, in order to find another way of being, women had to invent that as a sort of demon, so that they could move towards something else,' she says. Understanding in hindsight, though, doesn't undo the effect such social influence had at the time. Consequently, Carrie resolved to live life to the full; demand her place in the world as an independent woman; and to never get snared in the patriarchal enslavements of wifedom and motherhood. They were high and lofty notions held firm. Until . . . along came Charles.

Rarely does one meet a man for whom life holds such joy, excitement and pleasure. Rarely do any of us witness a love and adoration as strong as that which is shared between Carrie and Charles. Together they are incurable romantics.

'Suddenly marriage put me in a very different frame of mind about children,' explains Carrie. 'But I was 38 and I thought there was plenty of time—fate would take its hand.' And fate did. After two years of 'vaguely' trying to conceive, nothing happened. By the time she was forty, Carrie had become very serious about wanting a child. She knew her body was capable of a pregnancy, having had an abortion seven years earlier. Charles' sperm, they were told, were 'swimming like a 25-year-old's', despite being in his early forties. Being practical and doggedly determined once her mind is set, Carrie's solution was quite simple:

> I just decided 'Never mind. We'll go with the high-tech'. I was under the impression that IVF was this miracle cure. More to the point, the Australian government helped you pay for it. I had a friend in America who could only do it once because it cost US$30 000 for one go.

Carrie went through two attempts at AIH: artificial insemination using husband's sperm (although more progressive clinics substitute 'partner' for 'husband', but no-one likes to call it AIP). Perhaps the simplest form of artificial reproductive technology, AIH involves fresh semen being placed directly into the woman's cervix. It is a straightforward and relatively non-invasive way of trying to assist the chances of pregnancy. But for Carrie it didn't work.

Next, she underwent a procedure called GIFT—gamete intra-fallopian transfer—a 'modification of the classic IVF technique'. GIFT is similar to IVF in that a woman's eggs are still harvested in the same way, but instead of fertilization occurring in a Petri dish, the eggs and sperm are placed directly into the fallopian tube in order for fertilisation to occur naturally.[1] This didn't work either. Carrie had another go at it—again . . . failure.

Eventually, Carrie opted for the full force of IVF, which was not an easy decision, given her fundamental dislike of doctors and mistrust of the wizardry of conventional medicine. She relented as, 'I understood time was running out and I believed them.'

After meticulously following every instruction she was given—monitoring her cycle, nurturing her body, carefully selecting her diet and ensuring she was well-rested and physically fit—the IVF failed. Then it got ugly. Unlike Carolyn, who was more than ready to accept IVF failure as *her* fault and *her* responsibility, Carrie would have none of it:

> They were discussing my body—this body that I depend on and has always served me so well—as if bits of it were no good any more. It was turned on me: 'Well, you know, your eggs are old'. I was so angry. I felt like shouting at them, 'How dare you not produce? You have all these expensive bits of equipment and knowledge that you laud over us, and what do you mean it didn't work? I did everything exactly as you instructed me to do.'

Once she cooled down and again faced the thought of a childless future, Carrie was overwhelmed with the need to try again. She begrudgingly returned to medical technology and expertise and the place with all the 'expensive bits of equipment' to prepare for another crack at IVF. Very quickly it all became too much. The process of preparation, taking medication, driving to the clinic for daily injections and regular blood tests wore Carrie down. But worse still was her body's reaction to the cocktail of chemicals she was having to ingest.

I was having heart palpitations in the middle of the day. I imagine it was to do with the level of stress of the whole thing. I rang Charles and said 'I can't do this anymore. It's freaking me out', and he said, 'Then that's enough'.

That was the end of it. The quest for a baby was over.

There was a vague and fleeting discussion about the possibility of adoption, but they were now both in their early and mid-forties and deemed too old. Besides, Charles didn't warm to the idea of raising someone else's child. Unceremoniously, Carrie closed the book on children and turned her mind to getting on with the rest of her life.

Today, at fifty, she is true to her word when she says she doesn't have any regrets. Instead, Carrie will tell you she lives a life that is 'blessed'. These days her childlessness is something about which she is philosophical:

> Each one of us is saddled with some challenge in life: those painful challenges from which you either learn or don't learn. This particular one was mine. If I didn't reckon with it, then it would become my life and who I was. I would become the victim of being childless and bitter and resentful; and I desperately didn't want that.

There are several different ways women respond to involuntary childlessness, as we'll see in the following chapter. Carrie's way was to use the depth of her disappointment, and sense of loss, to gain greater insight into herself. She didn't put a lid on it.

Instead, she examined it—plumbing the pain for meaning, in a quest to find a place of peace. She has mostly succeeded.

'What it has done is open my heart to a deeper level of compassion for others,' she says. 'And that is a gift, an invaluable gift.' Carries ability to deeply nurture her students over many years, helping them to know themselves and develop the confidence to forge careers, is undoubtedly an expression of that gift. The effort she pours into friendship is another such expression.

Perhaps it's the American in her, but her practicality—and her Californian inclination towards self-development—has meant Carrie set out early in her disappointment to *fill* 'the gap' rather than just *feel* it:

> Women without children don't understand this. Society doesn't understand this, but we understand it. We understand where we're sitting now in our lives and how we're filling the gap that might have been filled with our own children.

Along with Carrie's personal growth is a growing confidence to be frank about *other* people's children. Sometimes she enjoys them, even loves them. Sometimes she doesn't. After many years of childlessness now, Carrie's world is understandably an adult's world, and often children don't fit in. Nevertheless, like childless women everywhere, Carrie too has been forced to silently endure the dismissive treatment occasionally doled out by women who seem to believe motherhood confers some sort of moral superiority.

A recent trip back to the United States and a visit with an old school friend turned miserable when her friend snapped at her, 'You obviously don't have children.' Carrie had failed to properly entertain her friend's toddler while the woman prepared lunch. Fed up with the somewhat disinterested antics of a stranger, the young boy howled, demanding his mother's arms and attention. Carrie was hurt by the exchange, and left speechless by these words still hanging between the two women. Was it an accusation? The inference Carrie took from the unkind jab was that she was somehow deficient, unable to relate to and care for another being.

The afternoon visit went downhill from there. Now, well after the event, Carrie is still bruised. As she relates the story to me, her gentle, compassionate persona does a sudden and unexpected somersault:

> I don't want to see her ever again. I just find it insensitive and tedious—this attitude of, 'You'll never know the things I know because I am a mother'. It makes me want to vomit. I just want to say, 'You'll never know the things that I've been through and the suffering that I've done, so shut up and get out of my face. And by the way . . . your son is obnoxious.'

I'm gobsmacked. This is not Carrie. This is not how she talks. The revelation is shocking in its brutality. The worst part of it is, I understand exactly what she means. It makes me want to vomit too.

And I'm ashamed to admit it.

Negotiating the divide: mother vs non-mother

A woman should not have to be left feeling that she has a hole in her identity, is unnatural, or is threatening to others simply because she is not a mother.

Mardy S. Ireland, *Reconceiving Women*, 1993

What is it about the maternal gene that makes the desire to have a baby course through the veins of some women, lie dormant in others and bypass another group altogether?

'I think it's either in you or it's not and, for whatever reason, it wasn't in me,' federal Labor politician Julia Gillard told a journalist in her first major interview, after being elevated to the shadow health portfolio in 2003.[1] While hardly earth shattering, the comment was nevertheless telling. Here was an aspiring woman leader and powerbroker, baldly stating her lack of maternal desire or interest. A rare thing in Australian public life; and quite possibly a first. For some women, Gillard's frankness would have been met with an 'Ah!' moment—'At last!' At last, a high-profile example of someone to represent that growing demographic of women who just don't want kids. That said, describing Labor's pin-up girl as 'child-free' is something she would baulk at, and 'childless' is something she rarely thought about—until the Labor leadership battle in early 2005.

'I've just never felt the kind of drive to do it,' she says, when curiosity gets the better of me and I press the point. She goes on to say:

> I sometimes stand back and say, 'Will there come a time when I get desperate about it, because I'm now 42, and there's not much time left?' But it hasn't descended on me yet. And I doubt that it will.

And so do I.

'Julia Gillard! She isn't the type!' a colleague roars at me when I relay this conversation I had with Gillard back before Mark Latham was hounded out of the office, and the gender dogs began barking.

'What type?' I ask.

'You know, the *baby* type,' he says, as if stating the bleeding obvious.

By January 2005, when the race to find a new leader of the Labor Party caused the media spot light to shine on Julia Gillard, suddenly everyone in Australia knew she wasn't 'the type'. Not the baby type; not the mothering type; not the wife type, and most importantly, not the cooking type. A photo in the *Sun-Herald* of Gillard in her tidy and 'eerily stark' kitchen had radio talk-back airwaves clogged for days. 'There was something terribly lonely about that room,' lamented the ABC's Sally Loane on Sydney radio. The lack of 'a flower or a picture', with no visible trace of food left-overs, kitchen gadgets, and not even 'bread in plastic or anything' was raked over as evidence that Gillard lived a weird life. What kind of woman was she? Goodness, there wasn't even any fruit in the fruit bowl! The domestic austerity was used to highlight the abnormality of a woman who is single and childless at the age of 43. While Gillard's kitchen 'became a biographical reference library' as journalist Kate Legge put it, her 'failure thus far to marry and produce offspring' was used to render her candidature for leadership inappropriate at best—invalid at worst.[2] 'The trouble is that no-one can accurately predict how the electorate might react to someone as unique as Gillard', wrote *The Australian* commentator, Cameron Stewart.[3] Being single and childless, it would seem, is not only abnormal for a woman, but 'unique'! Odd isn't it that South Australian Premier Mike Rann who is single is never referred to as 'unique'. Nor is the childless NSW Premier, Bob Carr. In fact, children, a spouse and a messy kitchen have never been prerequisites for political leadership—perhaps until now, when *women* are getting uncomfortably close to winning power.

Ironically, if Gillard did have a husband, a gaggle of children and a kitchen that looked like it had just served up home-made pies and sausage rolls to the local scout group, she would still be deemed unsuitable as leadership material. What political heavyweight has the time—or inclination—to play mum?

Back in 1990 when Betty Churcher became the first woman to head the National Gallery of Australia the headline was predictable: '58-year-old mother of four gets top job'.[4] Churcher must have disappointed when she failed to front wearing an apron and waving a feather duster. Her successor, Dr Brian Kennedy, got no such headline, and despite his six-year tenure at the Gallery I wouldn't have a clue how many children he has—if any.

Childlessness is not an impediment for men, nor is it used against them to suggest abnormality or inadequacy. Yet for a woman in her forties, being branded 'single and childless' points towards an unnerving deficiency, as Gillard has discovered. 'We can't even blame the media for this', argued former Labor Minister Susan Ryan on the ABC's *7.30 Report*, when she admitted the single-childless-must-be-a-weirdo attack had first come from within Gillard's own party. 'Now we're back in the dark ages, where a woman's marital status and whether she has children or not is being used against her by her own colleagues.'[5] The 'anonymous' ALP source that began muttering about Gillard's unsuitable status did so for good reason: he knew the story had legs, and the public would take fright.

As the Childless Revolution continues to gain momentum, and the Gillards of our world become increasingly visible, I fear the growing preoccupation of dividing women in 'normal' and 'abnormal' camps will only get worse. Pivotal to this division is the separation of those who are mothers, and those of us who are not.

Dr Sheryl de Lacey is a busy woman. She is a research fellow in the department of obstetrics and gynaecology at the University of Adelaide. Her CV is the size of a small novella. Threaded through her distinguished list of appointments, prizes and publications is evidence of a very personal passion for understanding and empowering women involved in fertility treatments. Her own fumbled experience as one of Australia's early IVF recipients started her on this path, and countless women have benefitted from the work she has done since, particularly in the areas of medical ethics, education and public awareness.

Her feminist credentials are unquestioned, therefore, the following little anecdote might surprise.

The occasion was a very busy period in which a group of seven of Sheryl's work colleagues—all women—needed to arrange a meeting at a time that was suitable for everyone. Schedules were tight and time was hectic, so it was decided an early morning breakfast meeting at 8 a.m. was the best option. Best, it turned out, for all but one. One of the women shot to her feet and objected saying, 'Look, I was told that this is a family-friendly organisation and I've got to get children to school. There's no way I can ever do a meeting at that time.' A few heads nodded understandingly and diary pages began to flick as a new date was sought. For Sheryl, it was an awkward moment that presented a conundrum:

> I took a look around the table and thought, 'It's interesting because out of the women here, there are only two out of seven who are actually mothers and the rest of us are not.' So I felt an 8 a.m. meeting would be very convenient for those of us without children. And yet the agenda was being driven by the mother's requirements.

And here is the tricky bit: Sheryl could see that the non-mothers were all about to capitulate to the parenting demand of one, even though there had been no negotiation around this, or discussion about what might work best for the group as a whole. At that point she decided to unfurl the conundrum and lay it on the table for consideration.

'And I said, "Well, actually, the majority of people here don't have the issue of getting children to school, so this is your issue".' Perhaps at that point you could have heard a lone pin drop. Women are supposed to support women in these situations, particularly women like Sheryl, who are at the top of the game.

She acknowledged that they all supported the organisation being 'family friendly', but Sheryl then threw another question into the circle for consideration: 'In what way is it friendly towards people who aren't mothers?' Having posed the prickly question and invited debate, a frank discussion followed. Eventually the mother with childcare issues offered to make other arrangements and collectively the group determined that 8 a.m. *was* most suitable. After the meeting broke up and everyone awkwardly filed out of the room, one of the women took Sheryl aside and said, 'It was very courageous of you to say that because often I sit there and think these things but I would never dare to actually come out and say it.'

This small example highlights a very difficult and vexing problem, which goes beyond simply accommodating parental needs, or more specifically *mothers'* needs, in the workplace. At its core, this scenario is about redefining women from a base position of being mothers—first and foremost—and reclaiming a fair and equal status for women who are non-mothers. While it's a battle that urgently needs to be addressed, it's nevertheless unfortunate that the battle field is increasingly in the workplace. The very fact that an issue such as this is highlighted in the office, and not around the kitchen table—or the bar for that matter—makes the separation between mothers and non-mothers all the more public, therefore seemingly all the more divisive.

I've retold the above anecdote to a number of people, men and women, only to watch with fascination the impassioned responses . . . every time. Those who are parents rail and tell me women like Sheryl are way out of line.

'Look you can't have it both ways,' one male friend said. 'You can't spend decades fighting to make workplaces more accessible for women with kids, and then tell them "family friendly" comes down to numbers, and how many around the boardroom table have prime childcare responsibilities.' In part he's right. Those who are non-parents, women in particular, applaud Sheryl's stance and cheer her questioning of how the workplace is friendly to 'people who aren't mothers'. Most then pour forth with their own anecdotes and tales of feeling pressured into capitulating to maternity and the maternal needs of their work colleagues—and resenting it. In each instance these anecdotes are just as troubling, and the feelings of discrimination just as valid, as those stories we've heard earlier in this book about women who pay an unfairly high price for trying to combine child-rearing with challenging careers.

In truth, we all know that Australian workplaces are not 'family friendly'. Nor are they 'people friendly'. They are just not very 'friendly' at all. If they were, we wouldn't have organisations, such as the Commonwealth's Comcare, forecasting a massive increase in worker's stress levels.[6] The real issue at the heart of Sheryl's story is not about the workplace—that's just the stage setting. Instead, it's about ensuring that the position of women as non-mothers is seen as valid—not just in a female-dominated workplace, but across all sectors of our community. Currently it is not.

It is not that being a non-mother is seen as *invalid*, it's just that it is not seen at all. That's the problem. Claiming status and validity—in a context where womanhood is subsumed by motherhood—is therefore becoming increasingly important to the ever growing demographic of women without children. That is why Sheryl's anecdote deserves consideration and some honest contemplation. Raising awareness of the need for non-mothers to share an equal middle ground is an approach she adopts broadly as a matter of heartfelt principle:

What you are doing when you're not a mother is operating within a societal context in which motherhood is dominant; it is seen as the majority. Being a non-mother is like you are a minority view point. I'm very supportive of women who have children . . . and I'm happy to accommodate where I can, but I want to have myself respected as well, so I want to have a presence.

Too often the non-mothers in *any* grouping, be it a social or work context, are the ones forced to silently acquiesce to the needs of the mothers in the group. Such actions, even when unconsciously imposed—as they often are—nevertheless have the potential to offend and divide. These divisions can only send us backwards. Therefore we are faced with a grave and pressing need to redefine what we consider to be the mark of an adult woman. Is it her status as mother? Of course not. But how can we afford equal validity to non-mothers, when we don't even notice them?

Invisible women

The invisibility of non-mothers has long been an issue for women who don't have children, and it is one of increasing agitation. Regardless of the reason for her childlessness—be it by choice or chance—every woman who is not a mother will at some stage of her life be made to feel not only invisible, but peripheral to the mainstream. In Australia, non-mothers not only lack visibility, they are almost rubbed out entirely by an overriding political conservatism that perpetuates the notion of women as breeders, and parenthood as the only valid position in society deserving of government support and encouragement.

Anyone observing the 2004 federal election campaign in Australia could have been forgiven for thinking that all the good citizens of this nation are families, and all adults are parents; such was the obsession of the leaders of both major political parties with championing the family on a daily basis. When Labor released its much heralded tax policy, I waded through the tens of thousands of words reporting the story looking for a reference to someone like me: a female, mid-career, tax paying non-mother. I found none. The political and media obsession with families—mum, dad and a couple of kids from the suburban heartlands—was all that was splashed through every newspaper and TV news story. The headlines championed the then opposition leader Mark Latham's pitch for middle Australia: 'the $11 billion battler pitch'; 'Latham to ease the squeeze'; 'Labor pitches to "the forgotten people"'. Apart from doing a hell of a lot of pitching and tossing for families, there was not a jot of reference—not one sentence—directed at adult women who are not mothers or part of a family. So who are the 'forgotten people' then?

Similarly, Prime Minister John Howard's near pathological obsession with 'traditional family values' as some sort of national goal of goodness, both alienates and isolates those of us who are not a family. Where do non-mothers fit in a society whose key aspiration is an outmoded, old-fashioned notion of family?

By the dawn of the twenty-first century it was reasonable to expect the political administration that governs our lives, and shapes our society, could expand its view to a multifaceted appreciation of the diverse ways in which we live. It hasn't. Not only was Labor's tax policy devoid of any specific mention of women who were not mothers, but *all* of its policies released during the campaign forgot childless women. Not a single Labor *or* Liberal policy was targeted at the growing demographic of non-mothers. Instead every voter pitch framed women only in a single context: that of motherhood. The daily dose of both Howard and Latham, blinded by family bifocals, had many of us wincing; not least of all, Anne Summers.

A year before the compaign Summers had reminded non-mothers of our miserable invisibility in her book, *The End of Equality*:

> In recent years, none of the major political parties seem able to talk or think about women in anything but a family context; this means that women's agency and choice is not taken into account, and is rarely reflected in policies . . . policy assumes that all women are mothers, or potential mothers.[7]

When social policy is transfixed on motherhood being 'intrinsic to adult female identity', as author Mardy Ireland puts it, it seems there is little hope of expecting any real cultural shift in recognising non-mothers as women in their own right.

The exclusion zone

For a woman past her mid-thirties it is usually the second, maybe the third question we get asked when meeting another woman socially: 'Do you have children?' If the answer is in the negative, the conversation can quickly fall flat, sending the inquisitor in search of some other woman with shared terrain. Just recently I stood in a little circle of elderly people at a wake, when one of the immaculately groomed and politely spoken gentlewomen turned to me, her face brightening, 'Didn't I read somewhere that you had a little one last year? Goodness it must be a toddler by now!' I appreciated her effort to jolly up the somber mood, but what could I say?

'Er, no. Not me,' I replied.

'Oh, I'm sure I read . . .' she persisted, looking skyward, trying to force the recollection. 'You remember,' she said nudging her husband, 'We read about it . . . and we were talking about it, "Virginia the newsreader and a baby".' I just shook my head and repeated, 'No. Not me.' A few of the others shifted their feet. Then as the gentle lady recalled what in fact she *had* probably read, her face clouded and her beaming smile slowly dropped. In fact, she sort of soured right before us; then shuffled away. It was an embarrassing moment for me, and I felt a need to apologise to those still standing there. But apologise for what? Because no, I didn't have a child?

I suspect I will always feel uncomfortable with that question. Okay, it might be just be a polite ice-breaker; one that works better than, 'So who 'ya tipping for the Grand Final?' Nevertheless, the fact that strangers will ask other women if they have children is a constant reminder of how integral motherhood remains to a woman's identity, and how pivotal a bond it is among women. We may have nothing at all in common, but once we connect on motherhood there is a world of shared experience and understanding. No wonder my younger sister Fiona said weeks after giving birth to her first child that she felt like she had entered 'a secret club'.

It is a 'club' that, as Sheryl de Lacey points out, girls are encouraged from a young age to assume they'll gain membership of:

> There is a lot of your life that you spend being a mother-to-be. We are programmed and socialised to believe that motherhood is our biological destiny and that we're going to reach it one day or another.

For Sheryl, like so many others, it didn't work. Her own repeated attempts at IVF ended in her withdrawing from the program by her mid-thirties. Then she began the long struggle against a sense of failure, misplacement and, most of all, exclusion:

> I had a period of time in which I felt like I didn't belong anywhere. I felt like I was really out on the margin. That was quite a philosophical time thinking about, 'How is my life going to be?' 'Who am I going to interact with?'

Sheryl's own experience led to her academic study about the issues surrounding fertility treatment, and eventually a PhD on women who fail in their attempts to achieve motherhood through reproductive technology. The snappy title of her thesis was 'All for Nothing'. It's the 'nothing' that, according to Sheryl, these non-mothers are forced to grapple with most:

> As women pull out of IVF treatment, they mostly withdraw because they want to save themselves or get something back. There is something of themselves that is lost in the process of repetitive failure.

Clawing back some kind of solid sense of self is complicated, and at times it is thwarted by the politics of motherhood. This is where the gaping divide between mothers and non-mothers is most evident and, for some, most painful.

That divide can take some tough work to transgress for those non-mothers who feel themselves to be invisible, peripheral and marginalised in a general social context. Sheryl sums it up this way:

> What women who are not mothers have to do is position themselves within every day conversation which is dominated by an idea that women will be mothers. So there is a constant, if you like, resistance going on in which you have to resist people's ideas that you will be a mother.

It almost requires a non-mother to appear selfish just to be heard, or claim a space, in situations where motherhood is held up as the only really valid position. Sheryl tells of spending months playing tennis with a similar aged group of women and she was the only non-mother. The post-game lunch continued a weekly tradition of conversation about each player's kids, their schooling, their highs, lows, natural aptitude—the usual. All of which was fine, even amusing, but not once was Sheryl asked to contribute. 'I often felt like I was not visible. I was there but I wasn't there, I didn't have a presence. I was really silenced.' There is only so much polite sitting on the sideline a girl can take. Eventually the time comes to claim back some ground.

These days Sheryl utilises each opportunity that presents itself to validate the position of non-mothers. While her tough stand over the issue of the 8 a.m. meeting may have seemed confronting to some, Sheryl refuses to buy into the guilt associated with such an action. Yet it is not easy. The guilt can be toxic, especially when the strident stand taken by a non-mother must be pursued in a context that *could* be viewed as an attack against motherhood—a tilt towards the so-called 'mother wars'. It is not. Yet fear of appearing heartless, unsupportive and anti-mother, or perhaps even embittered, is what stops most women speaking up. For Sheryl that frustration and associated guilt was, for a long while, crippling:

> I realised that I had to get over it. To really be a person who was fully present in my life as a person who isn't a mother, I had to get over that feeling that I was being selfish, because that is a deficit position and I don't want to be a victim any longer—a victim of that social expectation that all women are mothers.

The hole in a woman's identity

Author Mardy Ireland's opening quote to this chapter is indisputably correct. We know this. Of course, no woman should be left 'feeling that she has a hole in her identity, is unnatural, or is threatening to others simply because she is not a mother'. Why then does she?

We are a society in a state of great flux and transition, as evidenced by our declining fertility, our inclining childlessness, and our increasing separateness from one another. Yet publicly and politically we hark back to an outmoded sense of 'traditional family' as if it is the glue that is needed to bind us together: to give foundation to our lives and make sense of our purpose. We want to build a better, brighter future—for our kids. We want to clean up the environment and save old growth forests—for our kids. We want to build better cities, more friendly urban environments, safer communities—for our kids. We want to boost education, improve schools and save subsidised university places—for our kids, for *their* future. All of which is fine . . . if you have them. What if you don't? Where then do you fit in to public policy discussion, political banter or media chatter? How can you talk about caring for the future when your future ends with you? While you love and care about those old growth forests, and might even shed a tear for the homeless leadbeater possum—whose habitat is being logged to smithereens—at the end of the day, it's not about you. It's about what comes after you. Your offspring, progeny, children—your gift to the world; your eternal well of hope. And it is within that well of hope that all meaningful purpose is invested. Let's ask again why the childless woman might therefore feel a little hole in her identity?

While the non-mother remains invisible to the healthy ebb and flow of public discourse, she nevertheless remains highly visible in the negative. When the glare of public spotlight *is* shone on her, what is projected is not an image of 'woman' as a whole, but rather woman *with a hole*. The stereotype of the childless woman has become so highly pathologised it is a wonder the poor dear isn't made to wear a womb bandage and perhaps a neck brace to stiffen her spine. On one hand, the childless woman suspected of being childless *by choice*, is typecast as the selfish, materialistic, career hungry, predatory deviant. On the other, if she is perceived to be *involuntarily* childless, she is seen as one to be pitied—a half-woman who is grieving, unfulfilled and barren. Either way, the pathologisation of non-mothers keeps them separate and out of the way. As such, society can avoid dealing with the messy 'complication' non-mothers present to our old-fashioned notion of what a woman should be.

Is it any wonder then that some non-mothers feel the need to fight hard against the assumption that all women are mothers or potential mothers? Because if we accept that, we are also blithely accepting a socially imposed role of victim, or outcast, for those who are not and never will be mothers. Neither place is a good place to be.

Adapting to a childless identity . . .

Just as many women arrive at motherhood through various and diverse paths—some planned, some unplanned, some accidental, some even incidental—so too do women arrive at that status of non-mother by various means. There are those who firmly and clearly choose not to be mothers—the Marijes, Kirstens and Sandras of our times. There are the Julias, for whom 'it's either in you or it's not and, for whatever reason, it wasn't in me'. There are the Kates, whose dalliance with the idea of motherhood melt away into ambivalence, and eventually relief that they remain childless. Then there are the Carolyns and Carries for whom an expectation of motherhood was a given. And the Catherines and the Paulas whose failure to achieve motherhood triggered an emotional and spiritual battle of existential proportions. Given such diversity of attitude is there any sense in labelling all non-mothers as coming from the same base? Of course not. Just as it doesn't make sense to suggest *all* working mothers can be accommodated by a one-size-fits-all employment policy, it's similarly daft to suggest all non-mothers are suffering a shared pathological problem. Let's dump the pathology and instead work towards understanding that not all non-mothers stand in the same shoes.

Some women will never recover from the fact that they don't have children. Just as some women, I suspect, will never recover from the fact that they *do*. In between the two is a vast ocean of women. For some of us the tide may flow in and out and the current can change almost daily on how we feel about our childlessness. Nevertheless, for many of us adapting and accepting a childless identity can be a painfully difficult process. It can indeed be just that: a process. Working through it can, eventually, be one of the most important things we do as adult women.

Kate's story often comes to mind when I think of those women who are comfortable in their own skin and perfectly peaceful with the absence of mothering in their lives. Kate played with the idea of getting pregnant in Paris when she was forty. Up until then life had just sort of 'panned out', without any 'conscious choices' getting in the way of a charmed life. Despite years spent avoiding pregnancy, when she finally wanted a baby, Kate found she couldn't conceive. The failure did not invite an emotional crisis, instead she slid gently and easily into acceptance. Around that time, Kate told me about a dream she had:

> In my dream this little baby looked at me with what I can only describe as a look of complete and unconditional love and joy and I just recognised that that was the thing. This look surprised me, because it's not one that I'm used to. I have seen children look at their mothers like that. I can see what that look is about. I can understand it, even intellectualise it. But in the dream, it kind of got into my gut and I woke up thinking, 'Oh!' It had a really strong pull. But it's not so strong that I need it. I know it. But I don't need it.

For Kate this was a moment of vivid clarity. At once she 'recognised' and understood this baby's love—or potential love. She also knew it was separate from her, and not something she needed in order to be complete. She already was complete. She remains so.

Not all women who fail in their attempts to become a mother are quite so serene or philosophical about it. Nor do many feel the need to write to a newspaper and tell the whole world about it. For some it remains a very 'secret sorrow', as academic Christine Moulet puts it. Christine knows, she's been there herself. So how long does it take to overcome such secret sorrow? Christine smiles at this question. As a trained psychotherapist who worked as a counsellor at a fertility clinic, she has heard the question many, many times before. For her she says, 'It was a matter of years.' Then she pauses, adding:

> It is a gradual process—and I think it is still continuing. I don't know if you can actually put a timeframe on that. It's something I think that you travel with and keep with you for a very long time. For me it was a matter of gradually going

from quite a bad place to a good place, with several stages in between.

Christine is 44. Born in Paris, she and her husband have lived in Europe and parts of Asia before coming back to Australia. As she grappled with her own profound sorrow after several failed attempts at IVF, her attention turned to the study of infertility. Now, Christine is working on a PhD that tackles the difficult issue of adapting to involuntary childlessness. In her work as a counsellor to infertile couples Christine says she encouraged women to confront their sadness over their reproductive failure, in order to help them move towards a sense of closure rather than remain in an ill-defined, sorrowful limbo. She says men involved in the process generally handle their disappointment at failing to become a parent quite differently to women. 'The centrality of the issue is much greater for women than it is for men—there is no question about that.'

Fatherhood, while generally expected of men, is not enmeshed in a man's sense of self, his masculinity, or his identity as an adult; not in the same profound and complex way that it is for women. Adding to this burden is what Christine refers to—and we all know only too well—as the 'generation process':

As women, we were brought up to have pretty much anything we wanted out of life. Certainly in terms of career we were encouraged much more than any other generation before us. 'Yes, we could have it all!' we thought. We didn't have to sacrifice anything. We could work, have a career, get fulfilment and a sense of individuality and then leave the child-bearing to whenever we felt like it, whenever we felt ready.

Not all women born in the 1960s and 70s heard the bugle call quite as loudly as others. A few of course didn't hear it at all. For those of us that pricked up our ears and danced to the beat of it, coming a cropper over childlessness later in our lives demands a repositioning of ourselves.

Author Mardy Ireland calls us 'transitional women': women who are childless primarily due to delay. We are the ones who now find ourselves shifting back and forth, going with the flow of our lives, chasing new challenges and at the same time trying to understand and interpret our desire for motherhood, to make sense of this gnawing notion of a 'hole' in our identity. 'For some of these women,' Ireland says, 'There was a feeling that time was forever young.' While in that comment I hear echoes of many of the women interviewed in this book, most of all it's in Ireland's description of the 'transitional woman' that I see reflections of myself:

> Feminism provided the transitional women with an open field of possibilities to explore . . . The pursuit of education, careers, relationships and so forth are sometimes choices that represent much more of these women's identities than the part that desires motherhood.[8]

Ultimately, for many so-called 'transitional women' (and, again, I include myself in this) confronting the fact that we will never be mothers—ever—can come as a shock. A shock that Ireland also shoots home to feminism:

> The deflation of feminism's heroic posture, the realisation that women can't 'have it all', fell perhaps most heavily upon these women.[9]

How do you negotiate a way out of a 'hole' and learn instead to adapt to this unintended state of being? Christine suggests some women 'return to a position of ambivalence' about motherhood:

Many of these women recall a particular period of time when they weren't sure about children—when they were ambivalent: a time when they were already thinking about the sacrifices having children would require. If they experienced that, they can use it as an anchor to return to.

Simple in philosophy, Christine is the first to admit that such a process may take a great deal of work. For some of these women adapting to childlessness may require constructing something new. That could mean shedding an old identity—one linked to notions of being a mother—and creating a whole new sense of self.

Regardless of how women manage to travel the path towards adapting to involuntary childlessness, Christine is convinced the journey can have some wonderfully positive outcomes. One of them is a formidable resilience:

> Childless women in their thirties and forties are forced to confront the finality of their life. At the end of the day this is what it comes to. This is something most people deal with much later in their lives. But for childless women the enormity of the work they actually put in to really thinking about their life, and how they will construct it, is nothing short of admirable.

The end of the line . . .

For childless women it's about coming to grips with the fact that life stops with you. Knowing that you are the end of the line. Christine was recently confronted with this herself when her aging parents began to dispose of their material possessions, giving her various mementoes of their lives. 'They were things that really meant a lot to them, and they're passing them on to me and I'm thinking to myself, "It stops here".'

For me, being the end of the line—my line—has me wondering every now and then about the several neatly packed, labelled and sealed boxes I have in storage. For many years now as I've travelled the world and moved from city to city, job to job, I've documented just about every step of my journey by taking photographs and filling countless exercise books with thoughts, impressions and often incoherent ramblings. At times I've furiously added to this collection, as if leaving any episode of my life out might somehow distort the story. A while ago I realised I've slackened off. I don't shoot photos like I used to. I've stopped scribbling in exercise books. I guess I've subconsciously understood that in the absence of my own child or children there is no-one for whom any of my collected stuff would hold a particular or private fascination.

When I was very young I was entranced by the few old photos we had of my mother and father when they were young. I'd lay them out and stare at them for hours, willing the small black-and-white shots to reveal more information, wishing the smiling faces would talk to me. I desperately wanted to know what my mother was like when she was little—what she looked like, how she smiled, what she wore and how she related to others around her. The same with my dad. The fading photos gave some clues, as did the precious jewellery box my mother kept hidden away. In it were a few glistening and exotic things 'from when she was young'. Every piece held a story, every story I would demand to hear over and over again. Even now I occasionally take a nostalgic peak into that old box for a whiff of connection with my mother's earlier life. That connection between my mother and me is so delicious it bestows those treasured items with an immeasurable value.

Now at forty years old, I've built up a box of treasures of my own. I just don't know who to show them to.

Still wondering . . .

'What's the model? What's the *model* we need to use? In other words, I'm asking you what do you think the answer is?'

This somewhat agitated inquiry, barked down the telephone line, was from a young female reporter at one of the major metropolitan newspapers. I took a deep breath. Lowering my voice—given she'd caught me in the middle of a busy, open-plan newsroom, during the 'peak hour' rush before we go to air—I quietly began to explain that there was 'no single model'. I told her the very complex issue of why an increasing number of women my age were not having children was multifaceted.

'There are a litany of reasons,' I said, as a precursor to listing some of them. But 'Lois Lane' wanted, fire, fury and a few one-liners; not a bloody discourse. She didn't have time for this. Frankly, neither did I. But I was trying to be helpful. If there's one thing I've always hated as a journalist, it's being fobbed off.

'Look,' said Lois, cutting me off, 'It's just that, well, aren't you saying that women should have children much younger, and *then* go off and have a career? In other words, wouldn't everything just work better for women if we all delayed careers and had babies first?'

Bloody hell! 'No that is not what I'm saying. Not what I'm saying at all. I certainly don't advocate that for all . . .'

'But,' Lois cut in, ramping up the agitation, 'Don't you think that would work?'

'No. Well, yes. If that's what some women want to do. Fine. Let's support them. I certainly don't think that kind of "model", as you call it, is a solution for all women. As I said, it's more complex than that. We need a major shift. We need much greater flexibility . . .'

'Mmm. Yeah. It's just that young women having babies *before* their careers would kind of solve a lot of problems wouldn't it?'

I was getting nowhere. The clock was ticking fast towards on-air time and this interview was out of control. I paused, then had another stab at it: 'No, again, I think it's not as simple as that. The sort of shift I'm talking about is . . .'

'Mmm. Look, sorry, I'm going to have to go. You know— deadline. Is there anything else you'd like to say?'

'Er . . .'

'Well if there is anything more you'd like to add, just give me a call. Must go. Thanks. Oh, and how do I spell your name?'

The terrible thing here is that I'm not kidding. That conversation really happened, word for word. It was late 2003. Weeks later I sat down and began writing this book. Not to provide the answers—I don't have them—but to begin asking the questions; and in doing so, try to unearth the problem. Just like Betty Friedan's discovery back in 1963 when she wrote *The*

Feminine Mystique, I too have found 'a problem that has no name'. This time it's *our* problem.

What I've learnt during this long process of investigation is that there is a big noise brewing out there. A noise that urgently needs a voice and a forum in which to be heard. Which is why when *The Age* newspaper ran a feature edition to commemorate its 150 years, it cited the original article *'The sins of our feminist mothers'* as the opinion piece 'published in recent years that generated more response than all others'.[1] While some of that was targeted at me, the anger, pain and angst expressed by so many women really had nothing to do with me at all. By now I hope it's abundantly clear that the noise out there concerns each and every one of us. This noise is about the frustrations in the lives of all the women born to believe that 'having it all' was our birthright—and remains so. We set out to have it and still we continue to push forward, tripping, falling and wondering what the hell is wrong with us? Why can't we do it? Why can't we manage to 'have it all', 'juggle it all', 'be it all'? In our failure . . . there is anger.

I've long tried to suppress this, but in truth I can't. I was angry when, at 38 years old, I discovered I had probably missed out on any opportunity I may have had to have a baby. Now— a couple of years, tens of thousands of words, and hundreds of hours of talk later—I'm *still* angry. In fact I'm more angry than ever. Not about my childlessness, but about the raw deal women still have in a World that's supposed to be 'Wonderful for Women'. I'm angry about the sentiment expressed by Malcolm Turnbull, back in 2002:

> There is compelling evidence that while women are increasingly accepted into responsible and well-paid roles, their acceptance

is often, albeit tacitly, on the condition that they don't have any children.

I'm angry because it is still an undeniable truth. I'm angry that women still feel the heavy price they are made to pay for their so-called 'choices' is a private and personal debt, something they feel they must struggle with alone.

It horrifies me to think that young women, such as Lois Lane and her pals, might now respond to the irrefutable message that 'having it all' is a crock of crap by believing there is only one workable 'model' for womanhood. One that suggests women should first and foremost become mothers, and '*then* go off and have a career'. If a generation of women take this path, we'll be right back to where Betty Friedan began; we may have to pull *The Feminine Mystique* off the old library shelf and start pumping out reprints. The 'get breeding first' message as the *only* so-called 'model' is dangerous stuff. The inevitable limitations of such a path mean some women will curtail their tertiary education and/or postpone entry to the workforce at a sufficiently challenging and satisfactory level. In other words, by the time these women are ready to 'go off and have a career', as Lois put it, it will be too late or too hard to break in and break through. Many of these women will then probably spend years battling against the early breeder's 'handicap' in the competitive world of work. For some of them it won't matter. A secondary job or weaker career position won't bother them. Their family will come first. For others, it will bother them profoundly. Those women may well spend a good part of their thirties and forties frantically trying to carve out a career and make up for lost time in the work force.

American author Sylvia Ann Hewlett is not the first to suggest women find a man, settle down and get breeding before their mid-thirties. Others have said it, and I have no doubt many more will continue to beat the 'breed first' drum as the solution to myriad problems. Hewlett's suggestion that women choose a career 'that will give you the gift of time'—and a company 'that will help you achieve work/life balance'—is a load of poppycock. Please, someone tell her she's dreamin'. If only it were so simple, so straightforward. If only we could join companies, such as those Business Council of Australia members who claim to have 'family-friendly' polices, that really *are* family friendly. The lack of 'family friendliness' and flexible work arrangements, coupled with a growing resentment between parents and non-parents in the workplace, highlight how old-fashioned and terribly unsophisticated the Australian labour market really is. We need to grow up.

Nicola Roxon, the federal shadow attorney-general, starts wringing her hands, literally, when we talk about the inflexibility of the workplace and the lamentable lack of childcare options for working mothers. 'I wish we were further along the track,' she says. 'I wish there was more urgency in it. I wish there was a stronger sense of urgency that we have to fix this.' Ironic, isn't it, that the very place in which Roxon and her colleagues work each day, Australia's federal Parliament House, has no childcare facility at all. It has bars, eateries, a gym and even a meditation room, but no place for kids.

'Some of the young Labor women in parliament are always patching arrangements about kids,' says Labor's Julia Gillard. 'It's just mind-numbingly hard. I don't know how they cope.' Content to be childless, Gillard can only look on in awe and perhaps with a little relief that it's other women and not *her* doing the mummy juggle–struggle. 'I guess I have got the luxury of being able to do the job without those added pressures.' What Gillard sees as a 'luxury'—that state of being unburdened with parenting responsibilities—I seriously doubt would ever cross the minds of most of her male colleagues.

For men, being unencumbered in the workplace, with a wife or partner in the wings looking after the family and kids stuff, is the norm: a given. What man ever talks about being able to do a full day's work without having to attend to children as a 'luxury'? Gillard says that when she looks around at her group of friends the single biggest issue among them is the work and family–life balance:

> Choices and decisions around how to make it work are happening at a very pivotal point in people's careers: their mid-thirties and forties . . . We've moved from the model of the old, but we haven't quite worked out what the model of the new is yet, how it's going to work. And for so many, it doesn't.

There's that word again: 'model'. Perhaps I'm the only one who cringes at the thought that life paths can be based on a model. Nevertheless, Gillard is right in suggesting we need some kind of new model to help parents, in particular women, make it work. What we're doing now, and the so-called work 'model' on which we fashion ourselves, clearly sells women short. As Nicola Roxon so astutely puts it, 'Did we fight, or did the women before us fight, just for us to have a chance to work as men? Or have we fought to have the chance to be able to be ourselves?'

Is it any wonder that many young women today cringe at the juggle–struggle they see women in their thirties and forties doing? Why wouldn't they postpone, delay, put off or avoid child-bearing altogether? As we know, while some are consciously choosing that path, a much bigger number is blithely—some blindly—slipping down it. For the pregnancy procrastinators, it's all just too hard.

Lois Lane's 'breed young' model might work for some, but it fails to acknowledge that the twenty-first century woman will never fit into 1950s-style shoes. There is no going back. The timetable of women's lives has changed dramatically since our mothers and grandmothers were our age. Sure, we have sex at an earlier age, but everything else we do later. We finish our education later, settle down with a partner later, get married later, take out a mortgage later and start wearing sensible shoes and modest clothing later. In essence, we grow up . . . later. Of course, if we have children, we have them later.

The message now seeping out about age-related female infertility and childlessness may encourage some young women to start breeding early, but I do not believe many will heed that call. Women are not going to give up the vast array of opportunities and options open to them. Now that we're here, we are stuck with striving to 'have it all'. The women behind us will stick with it too. Women will not be bullied into lowering their expectations and asking less of the world. Which is why we urgently, desperately, need to talk about it to ensure those expectations are grounded in reality. We need to cut the crap and be honest about the heavy load, the juggle–struggle and the very high price paid for each choice we make in our quest to 'have it all'. While we tell it like it is, we also need to start asking for more.

Yes more!

About a year ago I had a bizarre and somewhat pathetic three-way conversation with a human resources manager at my work and one of my interstate female colleagues, a TV journalist and on-air presenter, who wanted information about the network's maternity leave policy. She wanted the lowdown on what sort of job security was enshrined in law and what her chances were of returning to her current position if she took time off to have a child. I acted as the go-between as my colleague didn't want to be identified. She was terrified that anyone at the network, even the HR manager, would get a whiff of the fact that she was considering pregnancy, as they might start lining up her replacement and her career would begin the ugly and humiliating downward spiral we've all witnessed other women endure.

For a day or two there were whispered conversations down the phone and a rapid exchange of emails as I relayed the HR information. None of it gave her much encouragement. Not because the network doesn't have a half-good scheme of maternity entitlements—it does: we work in the Commonwealth public service—but because my colleague struggled to *believe* the platitudes and promises. Streetwise and savvy, she knew the reality of taking time out from the fast-moving, demanding and competitive industry in which we work, only to return maybe six or twelve months down the track as a new mother, was undoubtedly going to damage her career. After spending her twenties doing the hard slog, she had finally landed a great gig and was clearly reluctant to let it slip from her grasp. It was agonising to watch this emotional struggle. And try as I did to offer positive optimism, she knew, I knew, in fact we all knew, what was at stake.

It is now year or so down the track and my colleague is still steaming ahead in her job, working furiously hard and looking desperately in need of a holiday. There has been no more talk of pregnancy or maternity leave. I guess she's put it in the 'possibles'.

The fact that as women we have won a number of tangible rights, such as maternity leave (albeit unpaid in the vast majority of Australian workplaces), these 'wins' have nevertheless done little to change the way the world is organised. It is still organised and structured to suit men. Women have just had to learn how to 'fit in', as Professor Marilyn Lake puts it.[2] And we do, but at a great cost. In Australia women are participating in the workforce in unprecedented numbers. Unlike in my mother's generation, where plenty of women never held a paid job, it is now unheard of for women of generations X and Y not to spend time in the workforce. Plenty of time. In fact, the current norm is for women to spend only a short period *out* of work while child-bearing and caring for toddlers. The pendulum has swung and the arrow is still pointing in men's favour, just as much as it always did. The workplace still functions according to 'male rhythms', as Lake puts it; a rhythm that assumes the worker is 'masculine—independent, autonomous and free from domestic responsibilities'.[3] While Professor Lake says she finds it 'astonishing that women still accept this',[4] I find it downright depressing.

Until we blow apart the notion that the World is now 'Wonderful for Women', and get serious in our demand to be ourselves—and not just skirt-wearing clones of our male colleagues in a world constructed to meet the needs of men—until we demand a better deal, women will continue the lonely business of pushing that bloody rock up a hill, wondering why the load is so heavy and the damn thing keeps knocking them down, pushing them back. The worst of it is the sense of utter isolation. The sense that the failure to 'do it all', 'be it all' and 'have it all' is our *own* fault. In our isolation we struggle on, believing we have to find answers and solutions to these problems alone. We don't. You don't.

It is time to collectively demand a better deal.

# Notes

Chapter 1

1 Australia, Senate, 8 March 2004, Debates, pp. 20960–964.
2 Sophie Cunningham, quoted in 'And Baby Makes Me', *The Age*, Anne Manne, 1 June 2002.

Chapter 3

1 Betty Friedan, *The Feminine Mystique*, Penguin, 1963, p. 64.
2 *The Feminine Mystique*, p. 267.
3 Simone de Beauvoir, *The Second Sex*, Book Two, Part V, 'The Married Woman', Penguin Modern Classics, 1983 (First published 1949), p. 496.
4 Wendy McCarthy, *Don't Fence Me In*, Random House, 2000, p. 90.
5 Sylvia Ann Hewlett, *Baby Hunger*, Atlantic Books, London, 2002, p. 42.
6 Malcolm Turnbull, 'The crisis is fertility, not aging', *The Age*, 16 July 2002.

Chapter 4

1 Germaine Greer quoted by Jan Moir in 'She's back—and she's angry' (A review of Germaine Greer's *The Whole Woman*, 1999), *Sydney Morning Herald*, 22 February 1999.
2 Germaine Greer quoted by Kira Cochrane in 'Tasting Blood Again', The Insight.co.uk, 2000, <www.nigelberman.co.uk/feature1_27.htm>.
3 op. cit., 'She's back—and she's angry'.
4 Anne Summers, 'Letter to the Next Generation' in *Damned Whores and God's Police*, (first published in 1975), Penguin, 1994, p. 524.
5 An interesting postscript about the woman who brought us 'Superwoman': Shirly Conran now runs an outfit called the 'Work–Life Balance Trust'. Sounds like Superwoman eventually saw the light.
6 Amanda Gome and Emily Ross, 'The rising stars', *BRW*, October 16–22 2003, p. 39.
7 ibid. p. 44.
8 Allison Pearson quoted in Joanne Hawkins, 'Now we know how she does it', *Sunday Life, The Sunday Age*, 6 July 2003.
9 Katrina Heron, 'A Wonderful life', *Vogue*, 2003, pp. 164–7.
10 op. cit., 'She's back—and she's angry'.
11 Germaine Greer, *The Whole Woman*, (Anchor) Recantation, 1999, p. 3.
12 Pamela Bone, 'Why feminism is still relevant', *The Age*, 3 May 2003.
13 Sarah Maddison, 'Look to the echelons of power, not the sisters, to see why women struggle', *Sydney Morning Herald*, 25 April 2003.
14 Natasha Cica, 'Single, childless and proud to be a feminist', *The Age*, 1 May 2003.
15 John Howard quoted by Jennifer Hewett in 'The mother's club', *Sydney Morning Herald*, 7 September 2002, p. 45.
16 op. cit., *The Whole Woman*, p. 5.
17 Peaches quoted by Sophie Best in 'Wild Peaches', *The Sunday Age*, Agenda, 11 January 2004.
18 Peter Jaret, 'The sexiest vampire slayer alive', *USA Weekend*, 23–25 October 1998.
19 Tobsha Learner, 'The economics of intimacy', *Australian Financial Review*, 16 April 2004.
20 *Cosmopolitan*, March 2002; as quoted by Catherine Redfern in online zine 'The F Word: contemporary UK feminism', 16 April 2002.
21 op. cit., *The Feminine Mystique*, p. 13.
22 op. cit., *The Feminine Mystique*, p. 38.
23 op. cit., *The Feminine Mystique*, p. 293.

24 op. cit., *The Feminine Mystique*, p. 293.
25 Germaine Greer, *The Female Eunuch*, Bantam Books, 1972 (First Published 1970), p. 350.
26 op. cit., *The Female Eunuch*, p. 343.
27 Camille Paglia, *Sex, Art, and American Culture*, Viking, 1992, Sexual Personae pp. 101–9. See also Paglia quoted by Penelope Debelle in 'Today's woman?', *The Age*, 6 March 1993.
28 Pamela Bone, 'Gladly paying the price of feminism', *The Sunday Age*, 11 August 2002.
29 op. cit., 'Letter to the Next Generation', p. 525.

Chapter 5

1 Alison Pearson, *I Don't Know How She Does It*, quoted in online magazine *Fast Company*, Gruner + Jahr USA Publishing, February 2003, <http://pf.fastcompany.com/magazine/67/akreamer.html>.
2 Ann Crittenden, *The Price of Motherhood*, Owl Books, 2001, p. 29.
3 ABS, 2001 Census of Population and Housing, unpublished/customised data: Labour Force Status, Female Parents (created 4 February 2005).
4 ABS, 2001 Census of Population and Housing, unpublished/customised data: LFS (FT/PT) of female parent by age (created 28 April 2004).
5 Barbara Pocock, *The Work/Life Collision*, The Federation Press, 2003, p. 73, Table 4.1.

Chapter 6

1 Barbara Pocock, *The Work/Life Collision*, The Federation Press, 2003, p. 90.
2 op. cit., *The Work/Life Collision*, p. 102.
3 ABS, 2001 Census of Population and Housing, unpublished/customised data: Labour Force Status, Female Parents (created 4 February 2005).
4 op. cit., *The Work/Life Collision*, p. 72, Table 4.1.

5   ABS, 2001 Census, Expanded Community Profile (Catalogue 2005.4: X13 Age by Labour Force Status).

6   ABS, 2001 Census of Population and Housing, unpublished/customised data: Labour Force Status, Female Parents (created 4 February 2005). A total of 1 201 863 female parents with at least one dependent under 15 are in the workforce; 764 886 are not.

7   ABS, Australian Social Trends 2003: Work—Paid work: Longer working hours.

8   International Labour Organization, 'Working Time and Workers' Preferences in Industrialized Countries: Finding the Balance', 22 October 2004.

9   The change from 1982 to 2002 was 10 per cent to 19 per cent. op. cit., Australian Social Trends 2003.

10 op. cit., *The Work/Life Collision*, p. 26.

11 op. cit., *The Work/Life Collision*, p. 24.

12 op. cit., *The Work/Life Collision*, p. 6.

13 *Australian Women's Weekly*, 'I just love being a Mother' by Sue Williams, September 2002.

14 *Australian Women's Weekly*, 'Mum on a Mission' by Sue Williams, March 2004.

15 *Australian Women's Weekly*, 'Kate Ceberano's quiet birth' by Sue Williams, April 2004.

16 Susan J. Douglas and Meredith W. Michaels, *The Mommy Myth*, Free Press (Simon & Schuster), 2004, p. 4.

17 ibid, pp. 3–4.

18 Susan J. Douglas in Jennifer Frey, 'Baby, Just Look At You Now', *Washington Post*, 23 March 2004.

19 'The Case for Staying Home: Why More Young Moms are Opting Out of the Rat Race', *Time Magazine*, 22 March 2004.

20 Susan J. Douglas in Karen S. Peterson, 'Has the motherhood bar been raised too high?', *USA Today*, 24 Feb 2004.

21 Susan Shapiro Barash, *The New Wife*, None The Less Press, 2004, p. 212.

22 Susan Shapiro Barashin quoted by Caroline Overington, 'New Wives look at Generation X and ask: Why?', *The Age*, 24 January 2004.

23 op. cit., *The New Wife*, p. 212.

24 Margarette Driscoll, 'Motherhood's new spin', *Australian*, 15 September 2003.

25 op. cit., *The Work/Life Collision*, p. 6.

26 David Uren, 'Working mum policies trail world', *Australian*, 17 May 2004.

27　OECD Economics Department, May 2004, 'Female Labour Force Participation: Past trends and main determinants in OECD countries' (see Jaumotte, 2003), p. 10, Fig. 3.
28　Business Council of Australia (BCA) 2003 Report, 'Costs, Benefits and Challenges'.
29　ibid.
30　ABS, Births, Catalogue 3301.0, 5 May 2004.

Chapter 7

1　Matt Price, 'F-word used in erection year', *Australian*, 12 May 2004.
2　Christine Jackman, 'Single and Childless? You're screwed', *Australian*, 12 May 2004.
3　Prime Minister John Howard quoted in *Australian*, 13 May 2004.
4　Anne Summers, *Drive* program, Radio 666, ABC Canberra, 13 November 2003.
5　John Howard quoted in Jennifer Hewett, 'The mothers' club', *Sydney Morning Herald*, 7–8 September 2002.
6　George Megalogenis, *Faultlines: Race, work and the politics of changing Australia*, Scribe, 2003, p. 89.
7　ABS, 2005 Year Book Australia, Chapter 5, 'Population', p. 141.
8　ABS, Household and Family Projections, Catalogue 3236.0., released 18 June 2004.
9　ABS, Births, Catalogue 3105.0.65.001: Australian Historical Population Statistics, Table 37: Median Age of mothers, all confinements.
10　ABS, Australian Social Trends 2003, Family and Community: National Summary Tables, Family formation. Females ages 35 and over giving birth for the first time: 1991—12.7 per cent; 1999—23.7 per cent.
11　ABS, Year Book Australia, 2003: Population, Births, Catalogue 1301.0-2003. The proportion of women aged forty years and above giving birth has increased from 0.8 per cent in 1980 to 2.6 per cent in 2000.
12　ABS, Births, Australia, 2002, Catalogue 3301.0.
13　OECD, Social, Employment and Migration Working Papers, No. 15, 7 October 2003: 'Low Fertility Rates in OECD countries: Facts and Policy Responses' by Joelle E. Sleebos in Chapter 1, 'Why Fertility Matters'.
14　United Nations, Population Aging 2002: UN Population Division, Department of Economic and Social Affairs: World Population

Prospects: The 2000 Revision, vol. I: Comprehensive Tables. The number of persons aged 60 years or older (est. 629 million) is projected to grow by 2 billion by 2050. The population of children (0–14 years) will be smaller than this.

15 ABS, 2004 Year Book: Population Projections, pp. 85–8. The proportion of the population under fifteen years will fall from 20 per cent (June 2002) to between 12 and 15 per cent (2051). The proportion of the population aged 50 years and over will increase from 29 per cent (June 2002) to between 46 and 50 per cent (2051).

16 op. cit., United Nations: Population Aging 2002, The 'Potential Support Ration' was nine to one in 2002; twelve to one in 1950.

17 op. cit., United Nations: Population Aging 2002, see <http://www.un.org/esa/population/publications/ageing/Graph.pdf>, 12 June 2004.

18 ABS, Australian Demographic Statistics, September Quarter 2003, Catalogue 3101.0, released 18 March 2004.

19 ABS, Births, Table 4.1, Catalogue 3301.0, released 25 November 2004.

20 United Nations projected world average for 2000–05 is 2.69, as quoted ABS Catalogue 1301.0-2004.

21 ABS, 2003 Year Book Australia; Births, Catalogue 3301.0 and Demographic Trends, 3102.0.

22 ABS, 2003 Year Book Australia; Births, Catalogue 3301.0 and Demographic Trends, 3102.0.

23 The Clearinghouse on International Developments in Child, Youth and Family Policies at Columbia University: Table 1, Maternity, Paternity, and Parental Leaves in the OECD Countries 1998–2002, at <http://www.childpolicyintl.org/issuebrief/issuebrief5table1.pdf> 14 June 2004.

24 World Bank 2002 Genderstats: Sweden, TFR (total fertility rate), 1990—2.1, 1995—1.7; 2000—1.6. By 2004, according to CIA World Book data, Sweden's TFR is estimated to have improved marginally to 1.66.

25 Anne Manne, 'How to breed Australians', in the *The Age*, 15 December 2001.

26 Laurie Oakes, 'A baby budget', *The Bulletin*, 21 May 2002.

27 CIA, *The World Fact Book 2004*, updated May 2004; Sweden TFR 2004—1.66 (est.), at <http://www.cia.gov/cia/publications/factbook/index.html>, 19 June 2004. Also, The World Bank Group 2002: Genderstats; Sweden,

1980—1.7, 1990—2.1, 1995—1.7, 2000—1.6, at
<http://devdata.worldbank.org/genderstats/home.asp>, 14 June 2004.

28 Professor Peter McDonald quoted in 'Nappy Families', *The Courier Mail*, 13 May 2004.

29 Combined source for TFRs: United Nations Fertility Report 2003; The World Bank Group 2002: Genderstats; ABS Australian Social Trends 2002, Population Projections: Fertility Futures; and The World Fact Book 2003 <www.bartleby.com/151/fields/30.html>, accessed June 2004.

30 CIA, The World Fact Book 2004, updated May 2004: USA TFR 2.07 (est 2004). Also, The World Bank Group 2002: Genderstats; USA, 1980—1.8, 1990—2.1, 1995—2.0, 2000—2.1 at
<http://devdata.worldbank.org/genderstats/home.asp>, accessed 14 June 2004. Also, United Nations, Fertility Report 2003: USA fertility rate in 1970 was 2.5; by 2000, 2.1.

31 CIA The World Fact Book 2004, updated May 2004: UK 1.66 (2004 est.); United Nations, Fertility Report 2003, UK 2000—1.6. Also, The World Bank Group 2002: Genderstats; UK 2000—1.7. Also, BBC News Online, 'More women staying childless', UK birth rate—1.64, 28 June 2002.

32 ABS, 2005 Year Book: Australian Demographic Statistics (3101.0); Marriages and Divorces, Australia (3310.0). While registered marriages numbered 103 130, the crude rate of marriage (per 1000 population) was the lowest on record at 5.3.

33 ABS, 2005 Year Book: Australian Demographic Trends, Catalogue 3102.0; Births, 3301.0; Marriages and Divorces, 3310.0. The crude birth rate for 2001 was 12.7; for marriage 5.3.

34 ABS, Australian Social Trends 2004. Population, Echoes of the baby boom, Catalogue 4102.0.

35 CSIRO, October 2002, 'Future Dilemmas: Options to 2050 for Australia's population, technology, resources and environment', Report to the Department of Immigration and Multicultural and Indigenous Affairs.

36 ABS, Australian Social Trends, Catalogue 4102, 2004: Population, p. 3.

Chapter 8

1   ABS, Australian Social Trends 2002: Family—Family Formation: Trends in childessness.
2   ABS, Special Article—Lifetime Childlessness, September 1999.
3   op. cit., *Baby Hunger*, pp. 91–2.
4   ibid., p. 26.
5   ibid., p. 13.
6   Janice M. Horowitz, Julie Rawe and Sora Song, 'Making Time for a Baby', *Time Magazine*, 15 April 2002, pp. 48–54.
7   op. cit., pp. 261–2.
8   ibid., p. 256.
9   ibid., pp. 256–7.
10 F. Baum, 'Choosing not to have children' (1994) as quoted by ABS, Population: Special Article—Lifetime Childlessness, September 1999. Baum identified four main reasons given by women for their state of voluntary childlessness: hedonists, emotional, idealistic, practical.
11 Mardy S. Ireland, *Reconceiving Women*, The Guilford Press, 1993, p. 7.
12 Madelyn Cain, *The Childless Revolution: What it means to be childless today*, Persus Publishing, 2001, p. xi.
13 ABS, Australian Social Trends 2002: Family—Family Formation: Trends in childlessness.
14 ibid.
15 ibid.
16 op. cit., 'Making Time for a Baby', *Time Magazine*, pp. 48–54.
17 ABS, op. cit., Special Article—Lifetime Childlessness, September 1999.
18 op. cit., *The Childless Revolution*, p. xii.
19 Dr Nicholas J. Parr, 'Family background, Schooling and Childlessness in Australia', analysis of data from women aged 40–54 years of age in Wave 1 of the HILDA survey, 2004.
20 Associate Professor David Charnock and Kathleen Fisher, 'Partnering and Fertility Patterns: Analysis of the HILDA Survey, Wave 1', presented at the HILDA Conference, Melb University, 13 March 2003, accessed online at <http://www.melbourneinstitute.com/hilda/pdffiles/KFisher.pdf>, June 2004.
21 Rosangela Merlo, 'What Women Want: Antecedent Conditions for the Initiation of Childbearing', paper presented at the annual meeting of the Population Association of America, Boston, MA, April 1–3 2004.

22 Monash IVF, Factsheet: Age and Fertility, accessed July 2004 at
   <http://www.monashivf.edu.au/library/factsheets/age_and_infertility.html>.
23 Dr Rick Porter, 'Missed Conceptions', Channel 9's *Sunday* program, 2
   May 2004.

Chapter 9

1   Quoted in Lee Tulloch, 'Sex and the City: The final curtain', *The
    Australian Women's Weekly*, April 2004.
2   Bob Birrell, Virginia Rapson and Clare Hourigan, 'Men and Women
    Apart: The Decline of Partnering in Australia' (report commissioned by
    the Australian Family Association), Centre for Population and Urban
    Research, Monash University, 2004, p. vii.
3   ibid., p. 3.
4   ibid., p. viii.
5   ibid., p. 3.
6   ibid., p. 12, Table 2.1. Figures quoted are from 2001 Census data;
    comparisons are with 1986 and 1996 Census data.
7   ABS, Marriages and Divorces 2002, Catalogue 3310.0: Chapter 5,
    Table 5.8. 'Never married' men between ages 25 to 44 totals
    1 107 799, whereas, 'never married' women across the same age
    brackets totals 821 220. The total male surplus is 286 579.
8   op. cit., 'Men and Women Apart: The Decline of Partnering in
    Australia', p. 8.
9   op. cit., ABS, Marriages and Divorces 2002, Table 5.3.
10 Miranda Devine, *Sydney Morning Herald*, 25 March 2004.
11 ibid.
12 M.C. Western, and J.H Baxter, 'Who Are The New Two-Earner
    Families?', paper presented to the Australian Social Policy Research
    Conference, Sydney, 9–11 July 2003. The study found 34 per cent of
    women compared to 25 per cent of men in couples without children
    held Bachelor degrees.
13 Mark Western quoted by Christine Jackman, 'Women trading down
    for husbands,' *Australian*, 12–13 July 2003.
14 op. cit., 'Men and Women Apart: The Decline of Partnering in
    Australia', Table 3.3, pp. 27–9.
15 Dr Bob Birrell quoted by Kim Wilson, 'First among equals', *The
    Sunday Age*, 'Agenda', 30 May 2004.
16 Zygmunt Bauman, *Liquid Love*, Polity Press UK, 2003.

17 ibid., Foreword.
18 ABS, Population, Marriages and divorces, Catalogue 1301.0, 2003: Crude rate of marriage in 2001 was 5.3. The number of divorces granted was 55 330, only surpassed once in 1976 when a spike of 63 230 divorces, resulting from changes to the *Family Law Act 1975* (enacted January 1976), which for the first time enabled 'irretrievable breakdown', measured by one year's separation, as sufficient ground for divorce—also known as the 'no fault divorce'.
19 Pamela J. Smock, 'Cohabitation in the United States: An Appraisal of Research Themes, Findings, and Implications', *Review of Sociology*, 26: (200), 1–20, 3: quoted by Barbara Dafoe Whitehead in *Why There Are No Good Men Left*, Broadway Books, 2003, p. 118.
20 Alan Close, 'This bachelor's life', *The Good Weekend*, 7 June 2003.
21 op. cit., *Why There Are No Good Men Left*, p. 123.
22 Angus Fontaine, 'Grabbed by the balls', *The Walkley Magazine*, August/September 2004, p. 5.

Chapter 10

1 George Kokonis, Oak Park, 'Selfish Women', *Herald Sun*, opinion page (19), 6 August 2004.
2 Paul Wicking, Mordialloc, 'IVF Plan Scandalous', *Herald Sun*, opinion, page (20), 4 August 2004.
3 Bernadette Green, Regent, 'So singles pay taxes', *Herald Sun*, opinion, page (20), 4 August 2004.
4 *Herald Sun*, Reader Question: 76 'yes' votes; 1116 'no' votes, 3 August 2004.
5 op. cit., 'IVF Plan Scandalous'.
6 DeAnne Kelly, Australia, House of Representatives 2001, *Debates*, 26296; quoted by Jennifer Lynne Smith, University of Queensland, in 'Suitable mothers': lesbian and single women and the 'unborn' in Australian parliamentary discourse', *Critical Social Policy*, issue 74 p. 83.
7 op. cit., 'Suitable mothers': lesbian and single women and the 'unborn' in Australian parliamentary discourse'.
8 ibid., p. 78.
9 op. cit., DeAnne Kelly, *Debates*, p. 80.

10   Alan Cadman, Australia, Housse of Representatives 2001, *Debates*, 26198, quoted in op. cit., 'Suitable mothers': lesbian and single women and the 'unborn' in Australian parliamentary discourse', p. 80.

Chapter 11

1   Madelyn Cain, *The Childless Revolution*, 2001, Perseus Publishing, 2001, p. 24.
2   E-zine, June 2004, at <http://www.worldchildfree.org/cfmag/childfree2.pdf>.
3   'Lobbying', accessed 1 Sept 2004, <http://www.childfree.com.au/>.

Chapter 12

1   Canberra Fertility Centre, Factsheet, 'IVF vs GIFT', at <http://www.canberrafertilitycenter.com.au/treatment_invitro_fert.htm>, accessed 5 February 2005.

Chapter 13

1   Matt Price, 'Great Expectations', *The Weekend Australian Magazine*, 30–31 August 2003.
2   Kate Legge, 'Kitchen-think drama', *The Australian*, 29 January 2005.
3   Cameron Stewart, 'Woman on the verge', *The Australian*, 25 January 2005.
4   Cathy Pryor, 'Ar flagship at risk of "being eclisped"', *The Australian*, 7 January 2004.
5   Susan Ryan, *7.30 Report*, ABC TV, reporter Heather Ewart, 1 February 2005.
6   Comcare Annual Report 2003–04, Director's Report, p. 3, released November 2004. In its report Comcare forecasts that claims for psychological injury in Australian government agencies will increase by 38 per cent in 2004–05.
7   Anne Summers, *The End of Equality*, Random House, 2003, p. 261.

8   Mardy S. Ireland, *Reconceiving Women*, The Guilford Press, 1993, p. 44.
9   ibid., p. 46.

Chapter 14

1   Paul Austin, '150 Years—A Journey', *The Age*, 16 October, 2004, p. 9.
2   Marilyn Lake, quoted in 'Breaking the Waves', Stephanie Peatling, *Sydney Morning Herald*, 11 November 1999.
3   Marilyn Lake, *Getting Equal*, Allen & Unwin, 1999, p. 265.
4   op. cit, 'Breaking the Waves'.

Acknowledgments

I guess like many births, this book's conception was the easy part. It was the gestation and labour that had me riding a rollercoaster. Throughout the experience I have been blessed by the kindness and good sense of some wonderful people.

My deep thanks to the exceptional Jo Paul from Allen & Unwin. Her faith, gentle wisdom, careful guidance and meticulous attention has helped keep me afloat and this book alive. Thanks also to Alexandra Nahlous whose editing and eye for detail has been a godsend; to Jane Ogilvie for the early encouragement; to Jenny Buerckner for patiently transcribing countless hours of interviews; to my understanding colleagues at the ABC; to the wonderfully helpful staff at the Australian Bureau of Statistics, and to the many others who provided information, data, research and expert advice.

My loudest thanks goes to the women who were interviewed for this book. I will remain forever grateful and utterly humbled by their exceptional courage, generosity and compassion. These women and the many, many other unnamed friends, colleagues, even strangers who have also shared with me their thoughts, stories and experiences, have been my driving force.

My blessings are extensive. Without the support of some dear friends I may never have had the stamina, confidence or courage to continue this project. In particular I thank Carrie Zivetz, who helped me begin this journey; Emma Cliff and Nicole Mitchell for their daily counsel; Kate Shaw and Suzanne Olb. My thanks also to my family for their loving tolerance, support and encouragement throughout: Fiona, Jane, Louise, Tony and Andrew Haussegger, and each of their wonderful partners. And it goes without saying that my parents, Joan and Karl, are my anchor.

Of course none of my story could be told without my dearest and best friend Anne Marie McFadyen. She remains one of the most important parts of my life (even though her heartfelt renditions of 'I am Woman' in my loungeroom did nothing to advance the progress of our interview). Thanks also to David McClune for listening, supporting and keeping up the supply of woodies; and to Lucinda and Emma.

My thanks to Greg, for his generous encouragement in all I do. Although he has had no part in the preparation of this book, his life—for a long while at least—was interwoven with mine, and is therefore part of my story. For that I will always be grateful.

Lastly, and most importantly, I thank Mark. This book has challenged and confronted us both. For very long periods I have been absent. Mark has been exceptional. He has given me jokes, laughter, love, nurture and plenty of space. No wonder I love him as much as I do.